CEYLON COOKERY

CEYLON COOKERY

CHANDRA DISSANAYAKE, M.Sc.
PRINCIPAL, SCHOOL OF HOME ECONOMICS
CEYLON, SRI LANKA

**A Stamford Lake
Publication
2005**

Fifth Edition 2004
Sixth Edition 2005

National Library of Sri Lanka - Cataloguing - in - Publication Data

Dissanayake Chandra
Ceylon Cookery/Chandra Dissanayake
Pannipitiya: Stamford Lake, 2003
607 p.; ill; 21cm.

ISBN 955-8733-06-7 Price : Hard Cover Rs 1450.00

i. 641.5 DDC 21 ii. Title
1. Cookery, Sri Lankan

Computer Typesetting
Stamford Lake

Cover Design and Photographs
Laksiri Wickramarathna

Printed by
Lake House Printers and Publishers
No. 41, W. A. D. Ramanayaka Mw.
Colombo - 02

Published by

STAMFORD LAKE (PVT) LTD
366, High Level Road, Pannipitiya, Sri Lanka.
Tele/Fax : 2846002, 4208134
E-mail : stamford@eureka.lk
Cyber Shopping Mall : www.avakasakade.com

PREFACE

TO THE FOURTH EDITION

Ever since I began teaching cookery, I have felt the need for a book that would give some guidance to those seriously interested in the subject. This book has been written to help the beginner to understand the ingredients used in cooking, why they are used, where substitutes may replace normal ingredients, how they may be substituted and the effect of different methods of food preparation.

This book is confined to Sri Lanka cookery, particularly the making of rice and curry as it is generally done in Sri Lanka. Beginners in this field will find the theory section on rice and curry preparation very useful in understanding the essential elements of this type of cookery before attempting the recipes. A section on recipes of foreign dishes as locally prepared has also been included in this work.

There is a popular myth in Sri Lanka that the consumption of curries is injurious to health because of the variety of pungent spices and condiments used in their preparation. On the contrary, curries are actually good for health if prepared with the ingredients discovered and used by the ancients. Most spices and condiments used in curries are preservatives, some have antiseptic value, others are carminatives, and still others are rich in oils, vitamins and minerals. However, incorrect methods of cleaning and cooking may cause reduction or complete loss of food value in spices and condiments.

In many of Sri Lankan homes today, the daily cooking is still done by the servants, who have no idea of the nutritive value of different foods. There are those who believe that foods should be thoroughly washed before cooking, little realising that, a part of the nutritive value in some foods is washed off down the drain in the process. Take for instance, the cooking of raw rice - with every wash, valuable Vitamin B is lost!

This book has been written to serve the needs of a wide scope of readers. For the young student offering Home Economics as an examination subject, it should prove useful and instructive. For the harrassed housewife, who considers cooking of rice and curry a drudgery, this book may, I hope, make the task easier and pleasanter and help towards, an appreciation of the need to preserve food values in cooking. For the professional cook this book may provide a new and practical approach and present him/her with as wide a variety of recipes as possible so that monotony may be avoided in the process of preparing rice and curry meals.

For interested cooks in other lands, I hope this book will be a happy welcome to Sri Lanka food and the Sri Lankan art of cookery. Above all, I fervently hope that this book will help to make cooking a satisfying art and a real pleasure to the amateur and the professional alike.

My sincere thanks are due to Mrs. Thelma Rungart, Miss Ruth Mac Intosh, Mr Dereck Riches and to the late Mrs Christine Blackler, for their patience in reading the manuscript and offering me valuable suggestions. I also take this opportunity to thank my other numerous friends and students who have helped me in many ways.

I must also express my thanks to the Publicity Officer of the Department of Agriculture for his valuable advice and line drawings included in the book, to the Research Officer of the Fisheries Research Station for readily giving me information about the varieties of cheap edible fish that are easily available and not commonly known to the consumer, and to my cousin Dr. T S U de Zylva for kindly taking the photographs for the illustrations in this edition.

To the members of my teaching staff, Mrs Carmen Gomes, Mrs Kusuma Goonetilleke and Mrs Kanthika Fernando, I am deeply indebted for their assistance particularly in testing the recipes, and to Mrs. Cecilia Cramer, my secretary for typing and retyping the manuscript. To Mrs Daniele Dissanayake Mrs. Regina Pereira for proof reading. Miss Sandhya Pelis for atteding to all the administrative work in connection with this edition.

I owe a special word of thanks to Felix Printers Limited for the promptness and understanding with which they have carried out their task.

Chandra Dissanayake.

No.8, 36th Lane
off Bullers Road
Colombo 8
Sri Lanka.

September 12, 1990

PREFACE

In view of the wide demand for this book on Ceylon Cookery, it has become necessary to publish the Fifth Edition, though sadly it is after the death of its indefatigable author Mrs. Chandra Dissanayake, my beloved wife.

I am very thankful and much obliged to the publishers, Stamford Lake (Private) Limited for the efficient and prompt manner in which they have set about the task of reprinting this book.

It is my son Tilak's help and guidance in several ways, too numerous to mention, that made it possible to get this edition ready for publication. To him it has been a labour of love and I am deeply grateful.

My sincere thanks to Mrs. Carmen Gomez and Mrs. Kusuma Gunetilleke who had been of great assistance to the author in numerous ways even in respect of the original publication of this book when Chandra ventured into the field of culinary literature. Carmen and Kusuma have very willingly continued their support by proof-reading this Fifth Edition. Their voluntary service so readily given is worthy of praise.

To the author's nephew Laksri Wickramarathna, I am much indebted for the excellent photographs taken by him for this edition. The helpful suggestions given to him regarding the photographs by Baboo Wickramaratna, the author's brother, are also much appreciated.

I am very thankful to Attorney-at-Law Miss Ramani Pereira, a long standing and close friend of my family for her helpful suggestions in regard to the contract.

Last but not least a word of special thanks to Mr Walter Lowe for the final proof-reading.

T. B. Dissanayake
January, 2004

CONTENTS

List of Illustrations

Part One

General

1 THE KITCHEN

Cooking of rice and curries is considered to be one of the most time consuming and tedious tasks of the average housewife. What has given rise to this impression so far as Sri Lanka is concerned is the lack of organization in the average kitchen which, in the past, was normally manned by untrained domestic staff so that the housewife need spend as little time as possible there. However, with the greater use of kerosene, electric and gas stoves in urban and some rural areas, and the scarcity of domestic labour, the average kitchen in Sri Lanka need no longer remain a drab hole black with soot. Today even the rural housewife can have a smokeless fire place and pleasanter surrounding than in the past. Nowadays the housewife spends more time in the kitchen than previously and because of this she is keen to make her kitchen a pleasant and labour saving place, vibrant with colour, well organised and with the minimum essential equipment, making the untrained staff conscious of a new desire for better work-habits.

The cooking of rice and curry following well-planned work patterns, will give the housewife the pleasure of turning out a very appetizing and nutritious meal, satisfied with the thought that the least amount of time and cost has been involved. At the same time it will also delight the family to be served a piping hot meal prepared especially to suit their palates. If the following simple rules are followed, with slight variations to suit each kitchen, the housewife need never spend more than 1 ½ hours in the preparation of a rice and curry meal for 6-8 persons and the tidying up of the kitchen afterwards. This plan is worked out on the basis of a household possessing only a two burner cooker or fire place and having no domestic help.

Organisation of Ingredients for Cooking

i. Gather all ingredients and utensils necessary, on one table or work place. It is easier and pleasanter to sit whilst working. Always make provisions for a stool to suit your working height and work table. The average height of a table for the Sri Lankan housewife may be 30″ - 32″

ii. Take all the ingredients that need washing, to the sink. Wash and set aside.

iii. Scrape coconut and squeeze out milk according to the required amount in different strengths. The refuse may be used again for a thinner extract.

iv. Put aside any dhals or pulses to be cooked on fire with milk until cutting of vegetable, etc, is done. Dhals and other pulses may even be washed and soaked over-night so that they give greater volume when cooked.

v. Cut up all vegetable including onions and dress all curries.

vi. Attend to the grinding of any ingredients if required.

vii. Cook vegetables and other curries beginning with curries that take the least amount of time. The normal procedure in a work pattern is to commence with the cooking of dishes that take the longest time. However to make the best use of the facilities available in an average Sri Lankan household, that is, where there is a 2-burner cooker, a reverse procedure is recommended so that dishes taking the shortest cooking time will be prepared first and served into serving dishes. The same pans can then be rinsed and used for cooking the other curries.Thus the number of pots and pans to be washed finally will be reduced.

Meat and rice are dishes that give the best result with prolonged cooking on a low fire and these are therefore put on last. Dishes that have already been cooked and placed in the serving dishes may be placed on the lids of the pans to keep warm.

viii. Finally, cook meat and rice on a low fire. Rice gives greater volume and is lighter and fluffier if cooked slowly.

ix. Whilst rice and meat are simmering, wash and tidy the work place.

Cooking done in this manner gives you two piping hot dishes, meat and rice, and the housewife's time is utilized to full advantage for the shortest possible time from the moment she enters the kitchen. There will be no waiting about for the rice and meat to cook in order to utilise the flame for other cooking, or hastening of the cooking of meat and rice on a hot flame resulting in tough meat and decreased rice volume.

Every member of a Sri Lankan household enjoys rice and curry, at least once a day. But a family will accept other cereal diets with a selection of well prepared curries even if rice is not available.

The Kitchen

A large kitchen is not necessary. A small well planned area with everything at hand is what is needed.

Storage: Curry powders and spices should be stored in small bottles with secure lids and plastic spoons in each bottle. A small bowl with a plastic cover will be useful to store the ground ingredients so that left overs can be put back without much loss of aroma or drying up.

All curry leaves keep better, and loss is reduced if they are placed in plastic bags. Even if the leaves are withered they can be utilized without waste. The habit of putting curry leaves in an open bottle and placing near a sink is wasteful as the withered leaves tend to fall off and get washed away. It is suggested that curry ingredients should be bought whole, washed, sun or even oven dried, powdered and put away in air-tight bottles. What is used weekly should be kept in smaller bottles so that the aroma of the main stock will not be affected by daily opening of bottles.

Making Curry Powders

In the making of curry powders, numerous combinations are possible. With the basic curry powder mixtures a housewife may use her own formula in devising a mixture to suit her family. It is strongly recommended that condiments be kept separate as greater flavours can be developed by using them in different proportions.

The list below gives suggested ingredients for a housewife buying curry ingredients on a monthly basis.

Cardamoms

Chillies

Cinnamon

Cloves

Coriander

Dhal

Fenugreek

Ginger

Goraka

Maduru

Mustard

Peanuts

Pepper

Suduru

Table Salt

Tamarind

Turmeric

Utensils in the Kitchen

The choice of utensils in the kitchen is the biggest problem for most housewives, especially those beginning to set up house. Choice should be based on her needs but it is worth bearing in mind that planning for everyday work is easier where the housewife confines herself to a minimum of equipment. If aluminium pans are used, buy thick gauge aluminium ware rather than thin gauge. It is more durable, and is less vulnerable to dents. When dents appear food tends to stick in these crevices which are difficult to clean and harbour germs which breed infection. Heavy gauge pans maintain an even base, transmit heat better and will thus help to save fuel.

A nest of pans with flat lids is recommended for easy storage and the flat lids have several other uses as well. No pan should be bought without a lid. Avoid pans with rolled rims which harbour bacteria that may lead to numerous digestive troubles. It is better to begin with the minimum basic utensils. For a Sri Lankan family of 6-8 persons the following basic set is suggested.

List of basic Kitchen Equipment for Rice & Curry

1 nest of five pans with flat lids made of heavy aluminium.

16-18 gauge diameter, 5″, 6″, 7″, 8″

1 aluminium stew pan, 16-18 gauge, 6″-8″ diameter.

1 aluminium saucepan 8″-10″ diameter 16-18 gauge.

1 set of three aluminium bowls 6″, 7″, 8″ diameter.

1 aluminium basin 12″-14″ diameter.

1 aluminium pot or kettle for water 6-8 pints.

1 aluminium steamer 7″ in height.

1 aluminium strainer for coconut milk, 6″-8″ diameter.

1 set aluminium measuring cups.

1 set aluminium measuring spoons.

1 coconut scraper or grater on ball bearing, screw-on-type for table top.

1 coconut shell (polished) spoon for milk

2 chopping boards, 5″ x 8″ x 1″ and 10″x 1″

1 dust bin

1 dust pan

12-18 dishcloths.

1 frying pan 5″-7″ diameter 16-18 gauge

1 deep frying pan 9″-10″ diameter, 16-18 gauge with frying basket

1 Iron griddle for roti, thosai etc. made of heavy cast iron,

11″ - 12″ diameter (not aluminium).

1 grinding stone 15″ x 10″ x 1 ½ with rubber mounts on the under side.

1 flat grater with different sized holes.

2 hopper pans with lid cast iron 6″-7″ diameter

1 hopper spoon.

2 knives 3″ and 5″-7″

2-4 knitted swabs for cleaning.

1 mortar and pestle unglazed type used by the chemists 4″-6″ diameter.

1 pan with flat lid 16-18 gauge, 10″-11″ diameter.

1 nambiliya cast iron.

2-3 wooden spoons.

1 slotted frying spoon.

1 string hopper mould, aluminium or wooden.

18 string hopper watties made of good cane and the border rimmed.

1 enamel funnel medium size

1 iron rod 1 ½″ diameter, 15″ length for cracking coconuts

2 scrubbing brushes 3″-4″ and 6″-8″ length.

1 sieve 6″ - 10″

Storage bottles with lids and spoons.

Storage bins

I wire soup strainer 5″ diameter, medium.

It is possible to store and use equipment in a kitchen for which an area of 10′ x 5′ or 12′ x 4′ is adequate. Such an area is easy to clean and saves time and energy. Usually rice is cooked in pots, but the largest size of a nest of pans would give you just as good results and facilitate easy storage and cleaning. It is suggested that you have a tin of ash sieved free of coals and unburnt wood readily available. Then, if your cooker is the type that tends to blacken your pans, prepare a stiff mixture of ash and water and apply a thin layer on the bottom and sides of the pan prior to cooking. The soot formed on ash-water paste applied to the pan, can easily be removed in washing. If the cooker is smoking you should attend to it by replacing the wicks, adjusting the level, and cleaning out your chimney. It is always advisable to do a weekly cleaning of your cooker and drain the oil once a month. A little attention daily to your kerosene oil cooker will not only ensure its continued good service, but save you a good deal of cleaning, for, a clear blue flame will never blacken your pans.

2 COOKING METHODS

In the preparation of dishes the method of cookery involved should be thoroughly understood and appreciated so that the best results can be achieved. The methods of cookery are divided into two sections.

A. Cooking by *moist heat*, commonly used for the preparation of rice and curry.

B. Cooking by *dry heat* not so commonly used for the preparation of rice and curry. This method is usually done in a covered vessel such as a clay pot or tin oven or in a gas or electric oven.

A. COOKING BY MOIST HEAT

I. Boiling

II. Steaming

III. Stewing

IV. Braising

1. Boiling

In boiling, the food is cooked in some liquid such as water coconut milk, fresh cow's milk, sterilised milk, tinned unsweetened milk or stock, or brine etc. The liquid may be either cold or at boiling point. Boiling meat, fish or vegetables softens the fibres thus rendering such food easy to digest. Furthermore, most forms of harmful bacteria may be killed by this process making it safe for consumption. Water boils at 212^0 F (or 100^0 C) at sea level, and the boiling point is lowered 1^0 F for every rise of 500 ft. in altitude.

This temperature need not be maintained right through the process of cooking when the method of boiling is followed in respect of certain foods. Meat and other protein foods, when boiled, should be cooked in fast boiling liquid only for a few minutes at 212^0 F so that the coagulation of the outside protein takes place sealing the nutrients. Cooking continues thereafter at simmer point (180^0-190^{0}F) or just below boiling point, to soften, the food. Excessive heat will cause shrinkage by the hardening of the protein, nor will prolonged very slow cooking help the heat to penetrate into the food to be cooked.

The term "simmering" is used frequently in recipes, and may need explanation. Simmering is a continuation of the boiling process on at a lower temperature to that of boiling i.e. 180^0-190^{0}F. This is above *stewing point* ie. 160^0 -180^{0}F. In simmering occasional bubbles will appear at regular intervals on the surface of the liquid unlike the ebullition (dancing bubbles) noticeable in boiling liquid which has reached 212^{0}F.

POINTS TO BE REMEMBERED

a. Salt is generally added to water *after* it has reached boiling point. The addition of salt tends to lower the temperature of the liquid..

b. The liquid must be kept at boiling point (212^0 F) or at simmer point (180^0 - 190^0) until the food is cooked.

c. Use sufficient liquid so that the food does not burn with the evaporation of the liquid. A lid, if used, should be well fitting to minimise evaporation of liquid.

d. In boiling all types of *yams* special care must be taken. Plenty of water should be used.The yams should be covered with water to well above the level of the yams. Special mention must be made of *Manioc* (tapioca), In certain tapioca yams prussic acid is present. Prussic acid is poisonous, but very volatile. Therefore, when cooking tapioca all yams should be completely submerged in water, and the vessel in which the tapioca is cooked should be kept open. This will help the volatile prussic acid to escape.The liquid in which tapioca or other yams are boiled should never be used for stocks and gravies. Once the water is drained from the boiled yams they may be kept on low heat for a short time to allow excess moisture to evaporate and prevent stickiness.

e. In boiling leafy vegetables, the smallest quantity of water should be used. The pan should be kept *open* topreserve the green colour. Soda bicarbonate should not be added to greens to preserve the colour as vitamin C is destroyed thereby. Liquid left over from boiled leafy vegetables may be used for stocks, gravies or as liquid for soaking grated coconut prior to squeezing to extract milk. The liquid is rich in food nutrients such as mineral salts and water soluble vitamins.

f. All starches such as rice should be boiled for the first half of the cooking with pan *open* to prevent frothing of water due to excessive starch, as this is likely to spill over and spoil the cooker or put out the fire in the case of an open hearth.

g. All pulses should be boiled from the start with plenty of water and the left-over water always utilized for making gravies, soups or stocks or as liquid for extracting coconut milk, as it contains nutrients. If pulses are washed and soaked for sometime ,this tends to shorten the average cooking time. The water used for soaking may be utilized for cocking.

II Steaming

Steaming is cooking by moist heat, vapour or steam given out from boiling water. Steamed foods are lighter than foods cooked by other methods. This method therefore is used frequently in the preparation of foods for invalids and infants. There are two methods of steaming,

(i) direct steaming

(ii) indirect steaming

(i) Direct Steaming

The Steam comes directly in contact with the food to be cooked e.g. pittu, string-hoppers etc. The food to be cooked is placed in a vessel with small perforations so that steam may pass through the perforations directly into the food to be cooked. In this method the pressure of the steam need not be controlled when cooking starchy foods, but better results are obtained if pressure in the steam is low especially in the steaming of meat, fish and preparations rich in egg. e.g. custards, watalappan.

(ii) Indirect Steaming

The food to be cooked is placed in a bowl or other receptacle and this is placed in a vessel half filled with boiling water. The heat from the boiling water as it comes in contact with the vessel in turn cooks the food by conduction or convection currents.

POINTS TO BE REMEMBERED:

a. The water level must be maintained and the pan with the water must never be allowed to get dry. If more water is to be added to maintain the water level, only boiling water should be added.

b. A pan with a well fitting lid should be used when steaming foods to prevent the escape of steam. It is important not to over-steam fish or egg dishes. Over cooking causes shrinkage and toughening of the protein which spoils the appearance of a meat product and makes it tasteless and tough. Egg dishes may be removed from the heat when the sides are set although the centre is still slightly soft. The heat contained in the dish will be sufficient to cook the centre. This method prevents curdling or separation which may take place if the protein is overcooked.

III Stewing

Stewing is cooking by moist heat over a low flame (160^0-180^0F) in a minimum quantity of liquid over a prolonged period of time. The liquid is always served with the cooked food and sufficient liquid for this purpose is added from the start. Preferably the pan should be of a heavy quality to prevent burning of the food during prolonged cooking and should have a tight-fitting lid to minimise evaporation of liquid. This method is usually followed when cooking foods that are fibrous or tough in order to soften them and thus facilitate digestion. It is commonly used in the cooking of meat curries and vegetables that are fibrous. e.g. tender jak fruits, roots of the lotus etc.

POINTS TO BE REMEMBERED

a. Low heat right through the cooking period and the temperature maintained throughout at 160^0- 180^0F.

b. Stewed foods such as fruits, vegetables and meat should never be cooked to the point where the food breaks into minute pieces. Each piece of cooked food must maintain its shape, but should cut or break easily.

c. If the gravy is a little more than the desired amount, the pieces should be removed and the gravy reduced to the required consistency and added to the pieces of cooked food.

IV Frying

Frying is a method of cooking by moist heat, the liquid being always some kind of oil. In this particular method the temperatures reach a fairly high degree. However, temperature instructions should be carefully followed for each type of fried food. There are three ways of frying.

i. Dry Frying

ii. Shallow or Pan Frying

iii. Deep Frying

i. Dry Frying

In this method of cooking no oil is used in the pan, foods are put into a heated pan and tossed around until the food is fried. Only foods very rich in fat are fried according to this method, for during the cooking process the fat in the food melts with the heat in the pan, and the food is fried in its own fat. e.g. bacon and all pork products. In Eastern countries this type of dry frying is quite common with condiments and spices that have a certain amount of volatile oil. One of the most important constituents of a condiment or spice is the volatile oil or essential oil to which its aroma is due. This aroma is generally brought out prior to use by dry frying in a heated pan. These spices also have important flavouring matter in them which is accentuated by dry frying; condiments and spices mostly rich in these essential oils are the following; dry chillie, coriander, cardamom, clove, cinnamon, black cummin, sweet cummin, mace, curry leaves, lemon grass, rampe, fenugreek, garlic. In the dry frying process an oiliness is noticeable and it is this which brings out the aroma. Further cooking will then give the desired colour. The process of dry frying is sometimes referred to as pan roasting, but strictly speaking in Eastern Cookery it should be classified as dry frying.

ii. Shallow Frying or Pan Frying

Shallow frying is cooking in a small quantity of oil where at no stage is the food completely covered in oil. With different shallow fried foods the amount of oil used varies as the following example illustrates:

a. **Pancakes** - The pan is only smeared with a trace of oil to give an oiliness to the pan and thus to prevent sticking:

b. **Omelettes** - One or two dessertspoons of oil for a two egg omelette, depending on the size of the pan;

c. **Potatoes or Beef Cutlets** - If cooked with butter and crumbs, these should have oil half way up the cutlet. However, if a fish or beef fillet is uncoated and dusted only with seasoned flour the depth of oil in the pan should not exceed 1/8″. Thus three variations of shallow frying may be distinguished in Eastern Cookery:

In the third variation mentioned in © above, the quantity of oil prevents the food from sticking to the pan and is also sufficient to partially cook or lightly fry the food. While shallow frying, and in order to prevent burns from spluttering oil, food should be placed away from the cook, in the pan.

Tempering

The term 'temper' is not found in any Western or Eastern Cookery Book but is typical of Sri Lankan curry. Its origin is from the Portugese 'temperadu' which means 'to fry and season'. The culinary association of 'temper' in Sri Lankan cookery is with shallow frying of onions, curry leaves and possibly other condiments, to release the flavour or accentuate it.

Generally the oil is heated to a very high temperature to bring about instant browning and release of the aroma. This aroma helps in the secretion of digestive juices and whets the appetite. In certain cases, the tempered ingredients may even be the curry powder itself or only onions, or both; sometimes food that is completely cooked may be tempered before serving to produce a more oily appearance and increase the flavour; or curry powders and fragrant powders (Suwanda Kudu) specially prepared, are tempered for a few seconds and sprinkled over the curry for appearance and flavour, just prior to serving.

Saute-ing

This method of cooking is quite commonly used in Sri Lankan curry. It is the cooking of foods in a quantity of oil in which the ingredients are tossed until cooked. In saute-ing non-starchy food, the oil is not all absorbed by the food, though the food may be cooked. The extra oil is drained off prior to serving (e.g. Kankun, Mukunuwenna.)

In the case of potatoes and other starchy foods the oil is fully absorbed by the time the food is cooked. This method is sometimes, followed also as a first step to cooking vegetables such as beans, leeks, carrots or beef in order to bring about different flavours with the curry powders, or to retain the green colour of some vegetables. The food is first saut d in a small quantity of oil until it is partially cooked and then the coconut milk is added and the food is allowed to simmer. This definitely improves the flavour of meats and colour of green vegetables. Where the liquid does not completely cover the food to be cooked, a lid must not be placed on the pan if the green colour is to be retained.

iii Deep Frying

In this method of cooking the food is completely covered with oil. Though more oil is used than in other frying methods the results are excellent, as deep fried foods, if properly cooked will never be greasy whilst other methods of frying e.g. dry, shallow, tend to make the cooked food greasier in appearance.

In deep fried foods high temperatures are necessary. Different temperatures are maintained for different foods, but generally the temperatures are above 320^0 F. In deep frying it is important that protective coverings should be used in the frying of meat and fish to prevent shrinkage and the escape of the nutrients into the oil. Vegetables according to use, however, may be deep fried without a protective covering. e.g. brinjals, onions, plantains etc.

The following temperature chart is a guide to the heat required for frying oil in this process.

Temperature Chart

Brinjals for Curry	...	360°F
Onions for seeni sambals	...	360° F
Pappadam	...	370° F
Cutlets or croquettes	...	350° F
Pan Rolls	...	360°F
Fried Fish (with Batter and Crumbs)		350° F
Fritters (Plantain fritters)	365°F	375°F

POINTS TO BE REMEMBERED IN DEEP FRYING:

a. Oil–The importance of the choice of the oil to be used cannot be over stressed. In fact success of deep fried foods depends mainly on the selection of the oil. The following points may be noted: (i) the oil should be odourless (ii) it should be capable of reaching a very high temperature without smoking or burning.

Coconut oil is the general choice for the cooking of rice and curry in Sri Lanka. Two varieties are used: the refined and the unrefined. The refined oil is colourless, odourless and capable of reaching very high temperatures. The unrefined oil has the very haracteristic smell of the coconut and is not always capable of reaching high temperaturs without smoking for on reaching high temperatures the oil tends to impart a burnt flavour into the fried foods. Unrefined oil becomes rancid more readily than the refined oil due to its higher water content.

Other oils are used for frying: gingelly oil (sesame oil) is the most common of these. Except for its characteristic flavour (not acceptable to most people as the flavour of the food is lost by the flavour of the oil) this oil is capable of reaching a very high temperature. Corn oil and mustard oil are other varieties used.

b. Sufficient oil must always be used to cover the food completely and to a depth of approximately 1″above the food.

c. Oil should be heated to the correct temperature according to the type of food to be fried.

d. Only a few pieces at a time should be added to the pan. The pan must never be over-crowded as it lowers the temperature of the oil.

e. The oil must be allowed to reach the correct temperature before the next batch of food for frying is added. If continuous frying is done with crumbed foods the oil should be strained from time to time to prevent burning of crumbs that settle down at the bottom of the pan.

f. Oil must always be strained, clarified, and stored after use. Deep fried oil can be used over and over again if this precaution is taken.

g. Deep frozen food, if added direct from the freezer, the temperature should be raised to a higher degree than the normal temperature required for fried foods and only a few pieces should be added at a time to prevent a sudden lowering of the temperature.

h. When very moist foods are fried, the tendency is for the oil to bubble over the brim of the pan. When frying such foods a frying basket should be used, and a tray kept handy so that the frying basket may be taken off the oil and placed on the tray for a few seconds till the bubbles have subsided. The basket should then be gradually lowered into the oil.

i. If the pan of oil should ever catch fire switch off the flame on which cooking is being done and cover with a heavy *dry* sack or rug. *Never* pour water or use a damp sack or rug to put out the fire as the water will turn to steam and splatter the hot oil.

j. All handles in frying pans and frying baskets should never protrude outwards; accidents resulting from someone knocking against the handle and spilling the heated oil can cause serious injury.

k. If handles are not heat proof a pot holder must always be used and not a kitchen towel; if a duster is used it should be folded into a pad.

Protective coverings for Fried Foods

A. Batters

Egg

Egg & Flour

Flour & Water Flour & Milk Flour, Milk & Egg Gram Flour & Water Seasoning to be added to batters	To be used plain, or foods may be dipped in any one of these batters and coated with dry or fresh crumbs.

B. Pastry

C. Miscellaneous coatings

Chopped cadjunuts

Semolina

Seasoned flour

V. Braising

This is the most complicated method of moist cooking. Very good results are obtained in the prepared food if the process is carried out correctly. Generally in the preparation of rice and curry this method is not used but it is adopted for different types of meat, poultry and game to obtain very delicate flavours.

Braising is cooking of meat that has been allowed to marinade in a mixture of olive or other suitable oil and seasoning. This meat is then browned in a small quantity of oil to seal in the meat juices. The browned meat is placed on a bed of vegetables that has also been browned in a small quantity of oil to bring out their aroma. Vegetables such as onions and carrots are generally used in the following proportions but these proportions may be changed according to taste.

Carrots and onions	-1 oz. each	to a 1lb. of meat.
Bacon Rind	-1 ½ ozs.	
Garlic	-1 clove	

Seasoning pepper, salt, bouquet garni.

Turnips are sometimes added if a stronger flavour is desired in the same proportion as carrots.

These fried vegetables and bacon are placed in the braising pan which should preferably be of heavy metal with a well-fitting lid. The browned meat is then placed on the bed of vegetables, the left-over marinade is poured over it and the food is allowed to slow cook until only a clear liquid oozes from the meat when a skewer is pushed right into the centre of the meat. Any trace of blood means that the meat is not done. Basting should be done from time to time.

It is essential to note that the liquid must cover the vegetables only and should not cover any part of the meat or else the flavour will be similar to boiled meat. This braised meat once done is served with the gravy, strained and thickened with pureed vegetables from the braised meat or flour to make a rich thick sauce. Some chefs may object to the insertion of a skewer or to the breaking up of any part of the meat braised after the sealing in of the meat juices by browning. In such a case pressure of the thumb against the meat is the only test to check if the meat is cooked. The insertion of a meat thermometer at the very start after browning is another very accurate method.

B. COOKING BY DRY HEAT

1. Roasting and Grilling

These two methods do not strictly follow the method of Western countries in which a more sophisticated method of over cooking is performed. In Sri Lankan cookery, baking or grilling is usually done in hot ash or over live coals. The food prepared in this manner develops very delicate flavours and also retains most of its own moisture. This is due to the heat preparations being very gradual and indirect. The banana leaf in which the food is wrapped also imparts a special but subtle flavour to the baked food without marring the flavour of the food.

In Western Countries baking or grilling over coals is becoming quite popular with the use of tinfoil as a protective covering. The tinfoil has no flavour of its own nor any moisture content. Once heated it retains greater heat than the banana leaf and cooking is more rapid and generally considered more hygienic.

The food to be baked is always wrapped in a number of layers of banana leaf. This wrapped food package is embedded in hot ash over which are placed live coals. The heat from the hot ash and live coals bake the food. If the foods baked do not have sufficient fat the banana leaf is very lightly smeared with a coating of oil. It is interesting to note how a small variety of fish 6" - 8" in length 'Kumbalawa' when stuffed with well seasoned raw flesh of its own and baked with a light smearing of seasoned oil on the outside, retains the freshness of th raw fish in appearance on the skin. This manner of baking gives the minimum loss in evaporation and the heat penetration is very even. Even though oil has been used for baking, the baked product gives no appearance of grease. This method also releases very subtle flavours into the baked foods which cannot be produced in any other manner. (This is partly due to the use of the banana leaf as a wrapper for the baked food.)

Coconut, ash plantain skins, and brinjal, baked in hot ash and coals, then ground and made into sambols make excellent accompaniments to a simple rich and curry meal.

In Sri Lanka, baking in the oven is becoming quite common. In rural areas kerosene oil, electric or gas ovens are not freely available. However, ovens made of clay (a type of clay oven used) consist of a large mouthed clay pot filled with half to one third coarse sea or river sand. The mouth of the clay pot is covered with a flat clay vessel filled with live coals. Heat is only applied to the pot to heat the sand. This makes quite a satisfactory oven.

A tin with a well fitting lid filled with ½" - 1" coarse river sand. This is another improvised oven for baking purposes. the tin is heated with live coal as in the pot.

II. Pot-Roasting

This is quite a common method of roasting followed in the absence of an oven. It used to be done only in a clay pot but now aluminium pans are used. (Better results are obtained in using the clay pots as the heat is better controlled). Types of food, generally to be pot-roasted are big cuts of meats, and poultry uncut. The meat to be pot-roasted is well seasoned, and browned evenly on all sides in a small quantity of oil to seal in the meat juices. Care must be taken to keep turning the meat to ensure even browning. After browning, a small quantity of hot liquid is added to the pan to prevent burning. The pot is closed and the flame reduced to low heat until the meat is done. (Test meat as for braising). The roast should be turned from time to time and basting done with the liquid in the pan.

Basting

Basting is the pouring of liquid every 15-20 Minutes over meat that is roasted or baked. The liquid may be pure oil, or one-third water or stock with two thirds oil. Generally meat and poultry are basted during roasting and baking to prevent drying. In order to avoid basting and also to keep a baked product moist the food can be wrapped in tin foil or double thickness of grease proof paper and opened during the last 15-20 minutes of baking for browning of baked product (if done in an oven).

III Grilling

Grilling is a method of cooking that is commonly used amongst certain fishing folk and in the Veddah community (Veddah: aborigines of Sri Lanka). They cook fish and game directly over the flame. Foods are grilled over live coals in the primitive method, even today, where the open hearth is used, as the flavours developed in this manner cannot be obtained in any other way. The charcoal burnt appearance of the food is desired by some. This method has become very popular with a few adaptations in the West where barbecuing is the fashion in outdoor cooking. A charcoal broiled steak can also be produced in a modern oven.

In ancient times, amongst the Veddah community the fire kept off the wild animals and also helped them to cook their food. These fires serve a dual purpose amongst the fishing community. It gives them a certain amount of warmth and also acts as a beacon for the other fisher folk at sea. They can also cook a quick meal using fish washed with sea water, held over the flames of the fire with a stick or rod; or very often, the fish is placed directly over the live coals for a few minutes and turned from side to side. The ash, if any, is brushed off and the fish eaten hot. However this practice is no longer popular.

Amongst the Veddahs, the aborigines of Sri Lanka, monkey flesh is also grilled in this manner after the skin is removed. Salt is the only seasoning that is added to the flesh. This preparation is considered a delicacy and the fire to grill the flesh is always made on a stone or rock so that the heat from the stone is also made use of. The wood is lit and only after the fire has died down and the ash has been blown off, is the monkey flesh grilled directly on the live coals until done.

Certain foods such as the kernel of the coconut, Bombay duck, smoked herrings, dry fish are placed directly over dying embers and turned from time to time with a pair of improvised tongs until the food is done. The ash is brushed off and the food used as required.

These grilled foods are generally ground into sambols or broken up into bits and added into onion chillie sambol e.g. burnt coconut sambol, Bombay duck or herring onion sambol. These methods are generally not followed nowadays since the open hearth is going out of use and the labour and time involved in preparation is considerable.

POINTS TO BE REMEMBERED

In certain ovens the grilling element or unit is placed in the upper part of the oven and heats only when the temperature is switched on beyond 550^0 F. In other ovens the grilling element is placed above or directly under the surface of cooking units. Irrespective of the placement of the grilling element the food to be grilled is always cooked by the radiation of heat directly on the food.

a. Grilling

i. The grilling element must always be preheated before the food is placed under the grill.

ii. If the element is in an oven, the oven door must always be kept open to allow the fumes from the oil to escape. The spluttering of oil sometimes can ignite and damage the oven and the fumes spoil the flavour of food. The free circulation of air is desirable.

iii. The distance from the heat must be adjusted according to the food to be grilled.

iv. Only suitable cuts of meat and tender poultry should be used for grilling.

v. The food should be allowed to marinade or sufficient oil should be applied prior to grilling to retain the moisture of the grilled food.

vi. The thickness of the food to be grilled should not be more than 1 ½″ - 2″

vii. The grilling times for each type of food should be observed as far as possible according to the type of grilled food required.

'Rare'	...	5 mins.
'Medium'	...	6-7 mins.
'Well Done'	...	9-10 mins.

b. Baking

i. The oven must always be preheated.

ii. The oven door should, as a rule, be gently closed but never banged.

iii When baking is done the oven door should not be opened until a specified period of time has passed. The time will depend on the type of food.

iv. The oven should never be over-crowded as this would prevent free circulation of heated air.

v. The pans of the baked products should not touch one another or the sides of the oven. If possible placing one pan directly over another should be avoided. 1″- 2″ clear space should be allowed away from the walls of the oven.

3 RICE COOKERY

1. Washing

Rice should be cleaned of sand, stone or other foreign matter prior to cooking.Cleaning can be done by hand, winnowed or washed in a special vessel used for washing rice, namely the "nambiliya"... The nambiliya is a concave grooved vessel that holds the sand or grit in its grooves.

For certain types of rice, the washing operation should be quick and as little water as possible should be used. This applies especially to country raw rice, as this is rich in vitamin B which is water soluble. With each wash more vitamin B is washed away. In washing raw country rice, only the first water should be thrown away as it may contain dust. The rice can be cooked in the water used for the subsequent washings, as it will contain some of the vitamin B washed out of the rice.

On the other hand, in the case of white imported rice known as "American rice" or white raw ration rice, where the starch content is very high repeated washing helps to wash away some of the starch. In cooking this type of rice, if a grainy boiled rice is desired the rice must either be steamed prior to cooking or boiled for sometime and the water drained to remove excess starch, and fresh cold water can be added with a few drops of oil or a pat of butter to prevent lumps. The rice is then cooked on low heat till all excess moisture has been absorbed.

In the case of all parboiled varieties of rice whether it be polished or unpolished, a certain amount of vitamin B is absorbed in the starch when the paddy is boiled with the husk. Therefore the percentage of vitamin B lost by washing in water is negligible.

2. Proportion of Water to Rice

Normally to every cup of rice two cups of water are added. This leaves the rice grainy when boiled and not lumpy. However, this is not a hard and fast rule for all types of rice. In the case of parboiled country rice the older the paddy, the more is the amount of water required. Here the quantity of water required can vary up to as much as four or five cups of water to one cup of rice. The Sududuru Samba types of rice require the least amount of water: 1 ½ or 1 ¾ cups of water to one cup of rice. Thus every type of rice must be treated differently although one cup of rice to two cups of water is a good general rule with more cold or hot water on hand to add if necessary.

3. Boiling of Rice

The proportion of ingredients at this stage is:

1 level teaspoon of salt (per cup of rice)

2 cups of water

1 cup of rice or 8 oz. of Rice

When rice is put on the fire with the required amount of water, the lid should be left off the pan. The fire should generally be hot so that the rice can boil fast until the water level and the rice level are the same. From that stage onwards the lid should be put on the pan and the fire reduced to very low heat so that the absorption of water takes place slowly making the rice fluffier, keeping the grains separate and permitting the rice to come to its volume. This operation may be carried out in an oven, if baking is being done, at a temperature between 300°-350°F. Should rice become mushy or lumpy sprinkle a little oil on top and place it in an uncovered pan in the oven on a low temperature between 250°- 275°F; this will help to separate the grains; or an alternative method is to place the pan on hot ash and deposit live coals on the lid of the pan. (This is one of the advantage of a flat lid as suggested in Chapter 1.)

4. Parboiled Rice

Parboiled rice consists of paddy which has been boiled for 40 - 45 minutes or until the husk begins to crack. The boiled paddy is allowed to dry well in the sun and then hand - pounded or milled to remove the husk. Different methods of husking or milling can either retain the brown colour or make the rice white. Although it is polished this rice contains a high percentage of vitamin B, due to its absorption into the starch from the bran, the outer covering of the grain adhering to the inside of the husk, in the boiling process. The darker the colour of the parboiled rice the greater the vitamin B content.* This type of rice is consumed mainly by people in the rural areas who thus get the necessary daily vitamin B requirement from rice.

The volume of cooked rice will also vary according to the type of rice and the procedure adopted; but if the correct procedure disclosed in this section is followed it will give the maximum yield in volume for any type of parboiled rice, as against other varieties of raw rice.

5. White Raw Rice (imported variety)

White rice is usually raw, highly-milled rice and may be cooked in the same way as country parboiled rice; but it has a very high starch content which makes it sticky. It is suggested that this rice be steamed prior to cooking, or cooked in plenty of water until the water reaches boiling point. Then all water should be drained off to remove excess starch. This will not cause any loss in the nutritive

* *The drained water may be used for starching clothes*

value as there is no vitamin B in this type of rice; only the starch is washed away. This rice is ideal for breakfast preparations such as string-hoppers, hoppers etc.

6. Raw Rice (Country or local variety)

Local raw rice is obtained by milling or pounding the paddy to remove only the husk. This rice may be the polished raw rice in which the bran has been removed or it may be the dark variety where most of the bran is retained. As has been mentioned earlier it is this type of rice from which the vitamin B content is removed by repeated washing. In cooking, the tendency is for this rice to become lumpy due to the presence of uncooked starch, contrary to the tendencies of parboiled rice. The lumpiness or stickiness can be avoided by quickly boiling the rice and letting it simmer after the water level has reached the rice level. Occasionally, while cooking is in progress stir with the handle of a wooden spoon or with a fork to avoid lumps and at the same time sprinkle additional water. Water may be either hot or cold. The water that is sprinkled will be in excess of what would generally be used for boiling the rice and the amount cannot be specified accurately. The water should never be drained away in this variety of rice as the vitamin B would also be thrown away.

7. Milchard, Samba, Sududuru Samba

Milchard, Samba and Sududuru samba all fall into the same category where cooking is concerned. All are varieties of parboiled rice and may be cooked in the same manner subject to the following variations:-

Milchard requires 2 to 2 ½ cups of water to 1 cup of rice. Generally a fairly strong odour is given out in the cooking of this type of rice, and this may remain even after cooking. To prevent this odour, add two to three pieces of "rampe" or lemon grass or a combination of both, or bay leaves which give a fragrant smell as this will help to remove this offensive odour.

Sududuru Samba requires 1 ½ to 1 ¾ cups of water depending on the age of the rice. If more water is necessary, hot or cold water may be added later. The method of cooking is the same as that given for parboiled rice. Careful watching is necessary as this rice cooks fairly fast.

Samba is the same as sududuru samba, but the grains are bigger. The proportion of water is usually 1 ¾ or 2 cups to 1 cup of rice; in certain cases even a higher rate of water to rice may be required.

8. Volume in Rice after Boiling

It has been found that country parboiled rice from very old paddy gives the best volume in rice thus giving more portions per equal weight than any other type of rice. The Milchard variety gives the poorest volume. The rest of the varieties gives more or less similar volume as has been said earlier. The volume of rice can be affected by the methods used in cooking; fast boiling at the start with very slow cooking after water level and rice level are equal and until the water has dried up, gives the best results in respect of volume.

If the rice is cooked on high heat right through the operation irrespective of the type of rice used, the volume obtained is less as a rice grain takes some time to absorb moisture to its maximum capacity even though the rice itself is cooked through.

4 INGREDIENTS USED IN CURRIES

1. **Chillies.** *Bot*: Capsicum; *Sinh*: Miris; *Tami*: Kochikai

Chillies play an important part in the preparation of curries. There are many different varieties, mainly in shape and size. The chillie when unripe is generally green but some unripe chillies are known to have a cream, green, yellow, orange, purple or blackish colour. The ripe chillie is generally red but some types of chillie may be yellow or orange. Chillies that are comparatively thin with a smooth pericarp have the highest piquancy or pungency (hotness on the tongue) and are used as condiments for curry.

The pungency of the chillie may be judged from the thickness of its pericarp for the thicker the pericarp the less the pungency. The high or low pungency of the chillie is determined by the percentage of capsain present on the inner side of the pericarp. Dry medium-size red chillies with a thin pericarp and few seeds are supposed to have the highest pungency and also fetch the highest market value. There are some 60 known varieties of chillies but in Sri Lanka only a few varieties are commonly used.

(a) **Kochchi.** *Bot*: Capsicum; *Sinh*: Kochchi

This is the smallest variety of chillie, It is generally used in a fresh or dried form for pickles and jardi (salted fish) preparations. It is very rarely used in the making of curries except in rural areas, due to its high pungency and lack of colour. When finely ground with coconut it serves as a very pungent coconut sambol or as Lunu Miris (a type of sambol without coconut); it is usually eaten with boiled jack and breadfruit. In the chutneys and pickles for which kochchi is normally used no red chillie or peppercorns are used as the kochchi supplies the necessary pungency. Lime Pickle is generally cured with Kochchi or dry kochchi is added to cured lime pickle before storage. It is the experience of the writer that in place of pepper, one or two dried kochchi chillies finely powdered and rubbed into beef before roasting gives a very fine flavour for those who desire a pungent spicy flavour in roast beef.

(b) **Dried Red Chillies**. *Bot*: Capsicum;

Sinh: Velichcha Miris

This is commonly used in the making of curries. It is a variety of green chillies that is allowed to ripen on the tree. It is later dried and used either ground or powdered with the seeds. The brighter the chillie the more attractive the appearance when used in curries. It is commonly accepted in Sri Lanka that all curries should have some form of chillie, but the excessive use of chillie is not advisable. This type of chillie can also be broken up into small pieces and fried to "temper" dhal and other curries where the accent on the fried ingredients is desired. Special sambols are also made with whole dried chillies fried and mixed with fried onions and other appetisers, such as salted prawns, dried fish and sprats. The proportion of chillie to be used is often dependent on personal taste. Ripened red chillie ground fresh and used as a base makes an excellent hot sauce for savoury rice preparations.

© **Green Curry Chillies**. *Bot*: Capsicum; *Sinh*:Amu Miris

This is really the green chillie before it has ripened. A wide variety of this is to be found and the thinner the darker and the greener the chillie, the greater the pungency. These are used for all "white" curries without red dried chillies. Green chillies are also used in combination with chillie powder in certain curries. In all fresh sambols and mallums that require a pungent flavour this type of chillie is used. Dipped in an acid and brine solution and sun dried it can be stored in bottles. These chillies make good appetisers if deep fried, served plain or with other appetisers such as prawns and sprats. They can be ground fine with coconut for fresh sambols and eaten with various breakfast prepartions, such as Thosai and Iddlie.

(d) **Capsicum Chillies**. *Bot*: Capsicum Fruteacens; *Sinh*:Malu Miris

This type is generally not used as a condiment in curry-making for two reasons: first, it is costly and secondly it is not sufficiently pungent for the average Sri Lankan palate. These chillies may be used in salads that do not require a pungent flavour and for all white curries prepared for invalids and children. This chillie is very popular as a curry, either plain or stuffed with meat, fish or vegetable filling. It can also be stuffed with a savoury filling as a short eat, deep fried with a protective covering, or blanched or scalded before stuffing and served unfried.

(e) **Peppers**. *Bot*: Capsicum grossum;

Sinh: Takkali Miris

This type of chillie has a very thick pericarp and it rarely used as an ingredient in the making of curries, but the pericarp itself is used as a vegetable due to its lack of pungency. It is also in popular demand for salads to add variety in colour and texture and is used in certain other forms such as cayenne pepper (paprika) for which the pericarp is dried and powdered, and pimento puree, in the preparation of non-Sri Lankan dishes.

2. Coriander Seeds. *Bot*: Coriandrum Sativum;

Sinh: Kottamalli

All parts of the coriander plant can be used in the preparation of curries; for instance, in certain eastern countries the young plant is used for sauces and chutneys while the seeds are used to flavour curries and soups. Normally in Sri Lanka only the seeds are used. They are extensively used as a condiment for curry powders and as a preservative spice, for instance, in sausages. In certain Western countries coriander is used for flavouring liqueurs, particularly gin. The seeds are supposed to have a carminative, diuretic, stomachic and antibilious effect on the digestive system.

The aromatic odour and taste of the coriander seed is due to an essential oil and coriander seeds from the tropics have a better aroma than those from colder countries. There are two well-known varieties of coriander seeds in the market: one small, the other large. As in the case of chillies, the smaller the coriander seed the stronger is its flavour. Both varieties are used extensively for cooking purposes.

Coriander is always used finely powdered or finely ground and never in the seed form for the making of curries. Generally coriander is used in the preparation of almost all meat, fish and vegetable curries. In the preparation of fish curries the use of coriander depends on the type of curry to be cooked. The average amount set for a pound of meat fish or vegetables would vary according to the flavour required in the curry from about two to four teaspoons to the pound.

Coriander leaves may be deep fried or used fresh for garnishing dishes.

3. Cummin. *Bot:* Cuminum Cyminum; *Sinh*: Sududuru

This seed is referred to by different names in different parts of the world by culinary experts e.g. small cummin, black cummin or cummin. Like coriander there is the very fine and the less fine variety. The cummin has an aromatic odour and a spicy somewhat bitter taste; therefore its use in a curry must be moderate, so as not to override the flavour of the food to which it is added.

In Sri Lanka it is generally added either powdered or ground and not generally used as a whole seed, but in certain other countries the whole seeds are fried with a little butter or oil and rarely used in powdered form. A simple but effective rule in the use of cummin is to limit it to exactly half of whatever portion of coriander is used. However, it may be used alone without the combination of coriander.

It is very similar to the caraway seed, and, indeed, in Europe it has been replaced by caraway seeds in the preparation of pickles and cheese and seasoning for breads and cakes.

Cummin seeds are said to have a stimulant and carminative effect. They are stomachic and useful in diarrhoea. The volatile oil in the cummin seed is also used in the preparation of perfume, liqueur and cordials.

4. Sweet Cummin. *Bot*: Foeniculum Vulgare;

*Sin*h: Maduru

This is usually referred to as sweet cummin, big cummin or white cummin. It is used in combination with coriander and black cummin for the making of curries, pickles, chutneys and sauces but very often in Sri Lanka sweet cummin us used more in the preparation of sweetmeats; whereas in certain parts of India it is popularly used in the preparation of curries due to its sweetish pleasant aroma.

In Sri Lanka it is generally combined with black cummin in equal proportions (but never more of the former). Equal portions of coriander and sweet cummin are not used in Sri Lanka as it gives a very sweetish flavour which is not as favoured as it is in certain parts of India. A sambol could be made out of the fresh cummin leaves or they may be ground and added as a thickening agent to fish curries or used as a garnish, fresh or deep fried.

5. Turmeric. *Bot:* Curcuma Longa; *Sinh:* Kaha

This is erroneously referred to as saffron. It is a rhizome that is cured, sun-dried, powdered and used in curries. It is indispensable in all white curries to give colour to a curry but in the case of meat and dark curries it may be omitted. It is generally accepted that if the strong odour of fish is to be removed, tumeric, lime or goraka should be used or they may be used together.

Tumeric as such does not give very much of a flavour but it is used in every curry, as it is considered to have stomachic and carminative effects. Its general effect on a curry is neutral except that it adds colour to food. No special flavour as such is derived, but it is added for its medicinal value.

It is interesting to note that turmeric is considered a purifying substance. Hindu places of worship and business places are sprinkled with turmeric water every morning as soon as the premises are swept. In the case of infectious diseases like chicken-pox and measles turmeric water is sprinkled in the house because it is traditionally believed to be a disinfectant.

6. Fenugreek. *Bot:* Trigonella Foenum-graecum:

Sinh: Uluhal

This is a small brown, square-shaped seed generally used with all meat and fish curries and some vegetable curries. It is also added to white gravy that requires body or thickening.

The seed becomes coated with mucilage when soaked in water, and this gives the necessary body. It is fairly strong in odour when roasted and has a slightly bitter flavour. It is best used unroasted to avoid too strong a flavour. The fenugreek must be boiled sufficiently so that a slimy texture is noticed in the gravy, before the first extract of coconut milk is added.

A little of fenugreek is all that is required in meat or fish curries but a large proportion must be used in a gravy and kiri hodhi (white gravy with coconut milk) to give the necessary binding or thickening effect. Besides its culinary value, it is used extensively in hair oils prepared for little children by Muslim and Tamil families and as a beauty treatment for the skin. It is soaked overnight and boiled with sliced lime for the washing of the hair and skin. This preparation is rather slimy but it is supposed to rid the hair of any dandruff and gives the hair added lustre.

7. Cinnamon. *Bot*: Cinnamomum Zeylanicum;

Sinh: Kurundu

Cinnamon is the outer bark of the cinnamon tree. The peelings off the bark are rolled to form quills. It is said that the quality of Sri Lanka cinnamon ranks the highest in the world. The finer the bark, the more superior is the quality of the cinnamon. It has a pleasing fragrant odour and a sweet aromatic taste. Since it is available freely and has a pleasant flavour it is used in larger proportions than are necessary in fish, meat and vegetable curry.

Generally it is not used in leafy mallums (cooked shredded leaves) and fresh sambols. An inch-long slice would be all that is required for any curry where the ingredients weigh approximately one pound. A little excess of cinnamon is not unpalatable in any dish unlike other condiments such as cloves, fenugreek, etc. Cinnamon is used extensively in sweets due to its pleasant flavour. It is sometimes used in medicinal drinks made with coriander and sometimes also in tea.

8. Cloves. *Bot*: Eugenia Caryophyllate; *Sinh:* Karabu

The cloves are the unopened flower buds, picked when they turn red at the base. The flower stalks are the clove stems of commerce that are used for culinary purposes. The dried cloves are used for their very strong aromatic odour and hot pungent aromatic taste. It should, however, be used in moderation for the flavour is sharp and not as palatable as cinnamon and cardamom and it must be used with caution so that it does not dominate over other flavours. Cloves should be bruised to give the desired effect and one to two cloves per half pound of rice or per one pound of meat or fish may be used. For medicinal purposes the clove oil is used.

9. Cardamoms. *Bot*:Elettaria Cardamomum; *Sinh*: Enasal

Cardamoms are the pods of an aromatic reed grown extensively in Sri Lanka. It is harvested when it is green, and sun-dried. The pod contains several seeds with a pleasant aroma and an aromatic taste that is very characteristic of the spice which is slightly pungent. Cardamoms are used widely in the preparation of all meat, fish sambols and some vegetable curries. Cardamom powder is used widely in the making of sweetmeats. Among the rural folk they are also served to guests as a mark of cordiality and greeting. It is further used as an ingredient of a chew of betel.

10. Mustard. *Bot:* Brassica Juncea; *Sinh*: Aba

Mustard seeds are of two varieties, the white or yellow mustard and the black mustard. The white or yellow variety is not freely available in Sri Lanka, and has a mild pungent taste. The black mustard seed has a very sharp piercing, irritating and pungent taste. It is used extensively in the preparation of pickles, chutneys, certain meat, fish and vegetable curries. Usually for the preparation of pickles, etc. it is used in finely ground or powdered form using vinegar for grinding. The seeds, however arc somctimes used in-curries when onions and curry leaves are "tempered". Mustard seeds if allowed to over-fry or over-roast give a very pronounced bitter irritating flavour to the curry.

11. Aromatic Ginger. *Sinh*: Ingurupiyali

This type of spice is used in special preparations only. It is a rhizome that is cured, sliced and dried like ginger. It is used in meat preparations and certain rice preparations for its fine aromatic flavour. It has a very mild pungent taste. Aromatic ginger lightly roasted and powdered makes a very good addition to a pork curry.

It is sometimes used along with cinnamon, cardamom and cloves in spiced tea. It is used as an ingredient in a chew of betel.

12. Garlic. *Bot*: Allium Sativum; *Sinh*: Sudulunu

Garlic is a bulb belonging to the family of onions, but is far more pungent with a very piercing flavour. Three to four cloves of garlic are generally used for about a pound of fish or meat in a curry and in sambols.

The use of garlic in vegetable curries is restricted according to the type of vegetable. It must be pointed out that when garlic is ground or crushed and rubbed into meat or fish, small quantities should be used. If, however, it is used chopped and fried it gives a more pronounced flavour. It is generally used in all meat and fish curries and seeni sambols. A little extra use of garlic in a curry will not mar the flavour unlike certain other condiments..

Garlic has a diuretic effect and is a preventive against flatulence. It is also administered to relieve rheumatic pain. It makes excellent eating mixed with jaggery after being roasted over hot ash wrapped in a banana leaf. Garlic cooked as a curry is excellent and makes a very popular curry.

13. Ginger. *Bot*:Zingiber Officinale; *Sinh*: Inguru

Ginger is a rhizome and there are two varieties found in Sri Lanka. One is a very pungent, thin finger-like variety which is very fibrous and is used in two forms;- as fresh, finely chopped, sliced or ground ginger in curries; and as a powder, after it has been cured and sun dried. The latter form is usually used more for sweets than for curries and occasionally also for drinks.

The second variety of ginger which is known as Chinese or Canton ginger is fibreless when it is tender, and the diameter of the rhizome can vary between 1″ to 2″. The pungency is very mild and it is generally used in the preparation of preserves such as Ginger in Syrup or Candied Ginger.

The pungent Ginger is a "must" for curries, chutneys, pickles and certain types of sambols due to its pungency. Care should be taken to use only small quantities. In certain parts of India, however, it is sliced and used very generously in curries, pickles and other appetisers.

14. Curry Leaves. *Bot*:Murraya koenigil *Sinh:* Karapincha

There are many varieties of curry leaves and some that are typical of Sri Lanka and these are found in plenty in the forest. They are generally used fresh in meat, fish or vegetable curry and in sambols. They may, However, be sun-dried and used in this form but this is very rarely done in Sri Lanka due to its ready availability and low cost.

Curry leaves give a very distinctive flavour and the aroma it produces during frying has the effect of whetting the appetite. Curry leaves are generally fried in oil until crisp and then added to the curry which makes the aroma more pronounced. It is after frying curry leaved that the other ingredients are added to the oil.

Curry leaves can also be finely shredded before being added to curries. This helps to make the flavour more pronounced and four to five leaves would be the usual amount to add per pound of meat, fish or per cup of rice. More can be used without any harmful effects.

15. Rampe. *Bot*:Pandanus latifolia; *Sinh*: Rampe

Rampe is a thin long leaf with a certain percentage of volatile oils that gives out strong aromatic flavour when fried in oil or even when heated in a pan. Generally rampe is not used in vegetable preparations but it is a "must" when boiling any type of rice e.g. Milchard, which has a strong unpleasant odour, since it helps to eliminate or reduce the odour due to the strong fragrance of its leaves. Like curry leaves they may be cut up, sun-dried and stored for use.

16. Lemon Grass. *Bot*: Cymbopogon citrates; *Sinh*: Sera

It is a type of grass with a strong flavour. The fleshy, lower part of the plant in a dry or fresh form is used in small pieces which are added to all meat curries and some fish curries. It is generally avoidedin vegetable curries because of its dominating flavour, but it is an essential ingredient in seeni sambols.

Lemon grass is sometimes dried and put into rice when stored as the strong flavour of the lemon grass keeps weevils and other pests from growing or living in the rice. Like rampe and curry leaves, it may also be dried and stored for use. In certain parts of Indian and other Asian countries this is boiled and taken in place of tea.

17. Onions. *Bot*: Allium Cepa; *Sinh*: Loonu

In Sri Lanka there is a wide range of onions for different uses. As in the case of chillies the smaller the onion the more pronounced is its flavour and very little is required for curry. Nevertheless it is an essential ingredient in every curry whether it be meat, fish, vegetable, sambol or mallum.

In the absence of onions the white part of the leek, shredded may be substituted to give a similar flavour.

(i) Red Onions *Bot*: Allium Rebrum; *Sinh*: Ratuloonu

This small reddish onion is generally used for all types of pickles, mojus, and for types of seeni sambols that are intended to be kept for a period of time, as its water contents is easily dried up, unlike the fleshy Bombay onion. Red onions, sliced and put into meat or fish curries in smaller proportions give a more pronounced and richer flavour than the Bombay onion, though many prefer to use Bombay onion as it is easier to clean chop and is cheaper.

(ii) Madras Onion. *Sinh:* Madarasi Loonu

These onions are the size of small limes, very strong in flavour and of a deep magenta colour. They may be used in pickles and in fresh salads and in all types of curries for flavour in lesser quantities than the Bombay onion.

(iii) Bombay Onion. *Sinh*: Bombaie Loonu

There are, in fact, two varieties known as the Bombay onion; the yellowish one called the Spanish onion and the pink one known as the Bombay onion. The Spanish onion is mild in flavour and suitable only for fresh onion salads or ground and used as a thickening agent.

The pink Bombay onion is a variety that has a sharper flavour than the Spanish onion. As onions are a necessary ingredient in curries these varieties may be used with advantage.

18. Nutmeg. *Bot:* Myristica Fragrans;
Sinh: Sadikka

Nutmeg is the seed from the fruit of the nutmeg tree. The seed is enclosed in a brittle shell, which is grated and is used in Sri Lanka more to give flavour to sweetmeats than in the making of curries.

It can be used with great advantage for the preparation of other meat dishes, moreover, though not commonly used in Sri Lanka a little grated nutmeg in a meat or fish curry improves its flavour. Once the shell is removed the seed should be stored in an air-tight tin to prevent mildew. They may be kept indefinitely if they are well sun-dried and stored with the shell intact. The outer fleshy part, or pericarp, resembles the apricot and makes an excellent jam which is very rich in pectin.

19. Mace *Sinh*: Wasa-vasi

Mace is the red-coloured lacy structure that adheres to the outer side of the brittle shell of the nutmeg. In Sri Lanka it is used more for medicinal than for culinary purposes. However, a small amount of crushed dried mace in certain meat or fish curries, or sweetmeats, definitely improves the flavour. If may be powdered and used for puddings.

20. Mint. *Bot*: Mentha Viridis; *Sinh*: Meenchi

Mint is used more in the preparation of sambols and meat dishes than in vegetable and fish curries. It is very rarely used in any vegetable preparation but is sometimes used in meat and fish preparations. A mint sambol is a necessary accompaniment to buriyani rice.

21. Parsley. *Bot*: Petroselinum Sativum; *Sinh*: Parsley

Parsley is not extensively used in the making of curries. It may sometimes be finely chopped and added to a meat or fish curry in place of coriander or fennel leaves. It may be used deep fried, or fresh as a garnish for a savoury rice preparation.

22. Celery. *Bot*: Apium graveolens; *Sinh*: Seldry

It is not used extensively in the making of curries but is put to the same uses as parsley.

23. Fennel. *Bot*: Foeniculum vulgare;

Sinh: Enduru, Dividuru, Mahaduru, Bata-enduru

A hair like leaf, similar to the Dill leaf. The seeds are used extensively for flavouring liqueurs and in confectionery. In curries,

it is used for fish curries or for ground sambols. It has a very mild but subtle flavour.

24. Pepper. *Bot*: Piper nigrum; *Sinh*: Gammiris

Black and white pepper are the berries of a climbing vine that is cultivated in certain parts of Sri Lanka and other countries. The berries grow in clusters, green in colour when immature, and turning yellow and red when ripe. Black pepper is produced from pepper-corns which are usually sun-dried after harvesting, and in this process they become black. The white pepper-corns are the berries that are allowed to soak in stagnant water for about 2-3 days to allow the outer pericarp to rot. The berries are then taken out, washed to remove the outer pericarp, again washed well to make them white, and sun-dried.

Black pepper has a characteristic, penetrating aromatic odour but the white pepper is not so pungent. It is sometimes used in place of chillies or as a combination with the chillie to give the necessary pungency to a curry.

White pepper is very rarely used for cooking due to its high cost and it's not available freely in the Sri Lanka market. However it may be substituted for chillies in certain recipes if desired. Pepper tastes best when freshly ground or crushed immediately prior to use.

It is interesting to note that in some dishes practically all the ingredients listed above are used in such a manner that one flavour does not supersede another. The blending should be such that one flavour enriches the other, thus improving the food to which it is added. In a well-blended curry all the ingredients should be added in such proportion that the flavour of the meat, fish or vegetable is not killed by the use of the condiments and spices. They should be added only to enrich or bring out the flavour of the main ingredient.

Because of the variation in blending ingredients, curries and rice preparations may vary from country to country and even from person to person and therefore may not have the same taste though they may be known by the same name, e.g. Khorma, Buriyani, Meat or Fish curries.

A knowledge of the different uses of ingredients used in curries is helpful to one who desires to try out various combinations to produce flavours. The following ingredients are essential for all meat curries, but the flavour of each meat curry would vary according to the manner in which the ingredients are introduced, (see chapter 5. Methods of Introducing Ingredients into Curries) and the proportions used:

chillie,	turmeric,	garlic,
coriander,	cloves,	ginger,
cummin,	cardamoms,	curry leaves,
sweet cummin,	cinnamon,	rampe
lemon grass,	onions,	nutmeg,

together with the necessary thickening agents and acids.

With these ingredients hundreds of different flavoured curries may be made and it will be a fascinating experience for those who venture into this field of cookery, if they try out their own proportions for different curries.

5 METHODS OF INTRODUCING INGREDIENTS INTO CURRIES

It must be remembered that more or less the same basic ingredients are used for all curries. Different flavours are obtained by combining them in different proportions and also by introducing them to the main ingredients in different ways e.g. (a) all the ingredients are pan roasted together and powdered; (b) commercial powdered ingredients are lightly pan roasted prior to use or, (c) powdered ingredients are tempered in oil, or (d) ingredients are added plain to a curry or mixed with the meat, fish or vegetable to be cooked and tempered, with the result that different flavours are obtained.

In the past when whole ingredients were prepared daily for use by the housewife (unlike the present when powdered curry stuffs are used) these ingredients were roasted or sun-dried prior to grinding or powdering. They were roasted in a pan to the desired colour, light, dark, or very dark so that flavours were mild or pronounced. This operation was usually done by heating an earthenware pan and stirring each ingredient in the pan until the different flavours were brought out and the desired colour was obtained. Usually each ingredient was roasted separately so that the finer ingredients such as fenugreek, cummin etc., were not burnt whilst the coriander, chillie cardamoms and cinnamon reached the desired colour.

This method, of course, is very time consuming and very rarely tried out or practised to-day in the urban household. It is still followed in some of the rural areas when the older folk cook. When the roasting of the whole ingredients is completed, they are either powdered together and sieved, or ground on the grinding stone with the addition of salt water to facilitate grinding. The salt also acts as a preservative. These ground or powdered ingredients are usually kept for a few days, or roasted daily according to the practice followed in different households.

This method requires less curry stuffs as flavour of fresh condiments is more potent than powders that have been exposed. Thus it gives a more pronounced and fresh flavour to curries.

Powdered curry stuffs available in polythene bags have their advantage in the sense that it is labour saving but due to prolonged shelf life and also due to use of packing material that permits the escape of the flavour of the curry ingredients, it is necessary sometimes to use more curry powders to obtain the desired flavours.

It is advisable always when purchasing packets of powdered ingredients to put them into air tight bottles or tins immediately after purchase and to buy in small quantities.

The following are some of the methods of adding these ingredients to a curry to obtain different flavours:

i. Cold Method

In this process the condiments used are all mixed with the raw vegetable, meat or fish. The thin milk, or second and third extract of the coconut, is added first or sometimes thick and thin milk are added at once, and the curry brought to the boil and allowed to simmer until done.

This is one of the commonest methods used in every household but it involves the use of a fairly large quantity of milk. Curries cooked in this manner are sometimes "tempered". This gives it an oily appearance. Fried onions impart a flavour which is more pronounced when added just before serving or after cooking than when added uncooked initially.

ii. Mix with Curry Ingredients

The second method of introducing curry ingredients or condiments begins as in (1) above by mixing all the condiments, spices and seasoning to the meat, fish or vegetables to be cooked. This mixture is then tempered in a very small quantity of oil to bring out a more pronounced flavour of the condiments. In the case of vegetable curries this method of introducing the vegetables into the hot pan with a little oil preserves the colour and makes them brighter.

Cooking is continued in this small quantity of oil for a few minutes (5-7 mins) till a slight aroma is given out from the condiment. Then the necessary amount of coconut milk is added and allowed to simmer until done. In the case of green vegetables they should be cooked with the lid off to retain the colour.

iii. Curry Powders Roasted in Oil

In this method the condiments and spices are added to a very small quantity of oil and allowed to fry until a very pronounced flavour is obtained. Thereafter the meat, fish or vegetable is added and allowed to fry for a few minutes. The coconut milk, water or stock is then added and cooking continued until the food is done.

iv. Roasted Curry Powder

In the fourth method the condiment powder is roasted in a heated pan for a few minutes prior to being added to the meat, fish or vegetable. Thereafter the cooking is continued following either the first or second method as mentioned above.

v. Roasted Whole Ingredients

In the fifth method whole condiments and spices are roasted and powdered or ground prior to immediate use. This gives the food the most pronounced flavour in the use of condiments.

DIFFERENT CURRY POWDER MIXTURES, WHERE ONLY ONIONS, LIQUIDS AND ACIDS HAVE TO BE ADDED

INGREDIENTS	MEAT				MEAT Sun dried and Powdered	VEGETABLE Sun dried and Powdered
	*(1)	*(2)	*(3)	*(4)	†(5)	‡(6)
Chillie	4 oz.	1 oz.	-	-	2 oz.	-
Coriander	3 oz.	3 oz.	3oz.	4oz.	2 oz.	2 zs.
S. Cummin	1/4 oz.	1/4 oz.	1/4 oz.	2 oz.	1 oz.	1 oz.
Cummin	1 oz.	1 oz.	1 oz.	2 oz.	1 oz.	1 1/2 oz.
Cadju	1 oz.	1 oz.	1 oz.	-	1/2 oz.	-
Fenugreek	1 oz.	1 oz.	1 oz.	-	1/2 oz.	1 oz.
Cloves	6	6	6	6	6	-
Cardamoms	6	6	6	4	4	-
Cinnamon	1/4”	1/4”	1/4”	1”	1”	-
Rampe	3”	3”	3”	1”	3”	-
Sera	2”	2”	2”	-	2”	-
Curry Leaves	6 sprigs	6 sprigs	6 sprigs	2 sprigs	4 sprigs	3 sprigs
Coconut	1 1/2 oz.	1 1/2 oz.	1 1/2 oz.	-	1 oz.	1 oz.
Rice	1 1/2 oz.	1 1/2 oz.	1 1/2 oz.	-	1 oz.	1/2 oz.
Aromatic Ginger	2 pieces	2 pieces	2 pieces	-	2 pieces	-
Pepper	1/2 oz.	-	1/2 oz.	-	1/2 oz.	-
Mustard	2 tsp.	2 tsp.	2 tsp.	-	-	-
Turmeric	1/2 tsp.	1/2 tsp.	1/2 tsp.	-	-	1/4 tsp.

* 1,2,3 & 4 to be roasted until golden brown for meats.

† 5 to be sun dried & powdered for meats.

‡ 6 to be sun dried & powdered for vegetables.

FRAGRANT POWDER (SUWANDA KUDU)

Well roasted until coffee colour to sprinkle on Vegetable and other white curries prior to serving

INGREDIENTS			VEGETABLE (1)	VEGETABLE (2)	POL KIRI BADUM (Red Curry) (3)
Cummin	...	...	4 oz.	1 oz.	2 oz.
Sweet Cimmin	...	...	-	1 oz.	2 oz.
Cinnamon	...	...	1”	-	-
Cardamoms	...	...	5	6	-
Cloves	...	...	6	1	-
Cariander	...	...	-	4	4 oz.
Fenugreek	...	...	-	1	-

6 ACIDS USED IN CURRIES

It is surprising how one may use a wide combination of acids without the flavour of any one acid being predominant and obtain very desirable and fascinating flavours in their combination. One acid may be substituted for another in the case of curries with the exception of Goraka in Ambul Thial, a special fish preparation.

(a) **Vinegar** *Sinh:* Vinakiri

Two types of Vinegar are used in Sri Lanka. They are made from the sap of flowers; from the coconut palm-coconut vinegar and from the kitul palm-kitul vinegar.The coconut vinegar is a variety that is freely available. The sap is stored in wooden barrels to mature with the addition of certain acids; it is later strained, distilled and sold as vinegar. The chief acid in vinegar is acetic acid which helps as a tenderiser in meat preparations. Vinegar is used with meat and some fish preparations and in all pickles, sauces, chutneys and mojus. The average strength of vinegar should be of a concentration of 4 per cent acetic acid. It is not used very freely in vegetable preparations except salads in the absence of lime juice.

(b) **Lime** *Bot*: Citrus Acida; *Sinh*: Dehi

Lime is the most commonly used type of acid in all types of

meat, fish, vegetable curries and sambols. It is therefore, used by itself or in combination with other acids. Lime is essential and only lime must be used in a coconut sambol, where the lime flavour must be predominant. In onion sambol, the lime juice is usually added first to the sliced onion with salt and set aside before the addition of chillie and other ingredients. This gives the onion sambol a sharp flavour and a pinkish tint which makes it attractive.

When lime juice is added to a curry where thick coconut milk is used, it is usually added just before the curry is taken off the fire. The curry must be stirred from time to time to prevent the curdling of the coconut milk. Citric acid is found in lime juice.

Lemon has become very popular as an acid in recent times. It is used in curries rather than in sambols due to its mild flavour. Lemmonine is slightly stronger in flavour than the lemon and may even replace lime in time to come due to its easy cultivation, quick bearing period and profusion of fruits.

Preparation of Lime Pickle: Cut limes half way into four from stem and downwards. Pack with salt. Stack in earthenware pots or jars beginning with a layer of lime. Cover with crushed kitchen salt and end with a salt layer. Set aside for 5-7 days. Sun-dry daily dipping limes in brine solution until limes are well encrusted with salt. To balance brine add equal quantity of vinegar. Prepare sufficient brine, a handful of kochchi also sun-dried in brine solution. Pack limes in jars so that liquid completely covers the lime.

© **Tamarind** *Bot:* Tamarindus Indica

Sinh: Siyambala

Mallic acid is the acid found in tamarind. Tamarind is a pod of the tamarind tree–a tree well known for its beautiful grained wood which is very expensive and used for furniture.

When the pod is mature the seed with its fleshy covering can easily be separated from the pod. The mature pod becomes brittle and brown and the softer fleshy covering of the seed becomes a chestnut brown in colour. The seed itself is hard and dark brown and is not used for any culinary purpose. It is the fleshy acidic covering of the seed which is used for cooking.

This acid is fairly strong and can eat into aluminium if kept in aluminium vessels. Tamarind is usually used by dissolving the fleshy part with salt water or thin coconut milk, depending on the purpose for which the acid is used. The remaining extract is the acid. This extract if fairly thick can act also as a thickening agent. Tamarind is rather widely used in the making of curries by the Tamils in Sri Lanka and in Southern India. It is almost indispensable for seeni sambols and certain fish and meat preparations.

The tamarind is preserved by adding kitchen salt to the ripe tamarind after removing the seeds and storing it in earthenware pots or jars. The tamarind flowers which are quite small and of yellow range hue also make an excellent curry with a sharp acid flavour.

(d) Tomatoes *Bot:* Lycopersicum esculentum

Sinh: Takkali

Tomatoes are added to certain curries for a threefold purpose: (a) for its flavour (b) acid content and (c) as a thickening agent. Tomatoes are used in white fish curries, in meat preparations and certain vegetable curries, to give a mild acid flavour. The raw tamato is used as a curry with onions, or to give an acid flavour to vegetable curries in the absence of lime juice.

(e) Goraka *Bot*: Garcinia Cambogia

Sing: Goraka

Goraka as found in the market is black in colour and kidney shaped but in its natural state it is a beautiful orange (segmented) fruit. The kidney shaped piece is one segment of the whole fruit. When the fruit is ripe, it is sun-dried and stored. Sun-drying turns the orange colour to black.

The older the goraka, the stronger the acid, which is used extensssively in fish preparations. With a little soaking the old goraka can be crushed into pulp. In the preparation of Ambul Thial only goraka is used for the acid.

It is interesting to note that in rural homes the goraka is stored away above the open hearth with the result that it becomes quite soft and the acid improves with keeping. In the maritime provinces of Sri Lanka goraka is seldom ground but is soaked in salt water, crushed and added to curries. In modern homes where the open hearth is not available the tendency is to use the ground goraka, as freshly dried goraka cannot be crushed.

Goraka is also a thickening agent and as an acid can be used in the preparation of some meat curries. It is also used in the washing of fish to remove the strong fish odour.

For its storage salt is added and it is kept in earthenware pots or jars. Never use aluminium for the storage of goraka..

(f) Billing *Bot:* Averrhoa Bilimbi

Sing: Billing

This is a very acidic fruit with a high concentration of water and is used in combination with other acids or in their place. It has a tenderising effect on meats and is often used in a combination with other acids for meat curries where acidity is required.

The fruit may be dried and stored for use during the off season when the fresh fruit is not available.

The fresh fruit makes an excellent curry or a sambol and the acidity is removed completely or slightly by the addition of certain quantities of calcium chloride (the "chunam" used for chewing betel)

The dried billing fruit makes excellent pickles and mojus and the ripe fruit may be made into a preserve or jam. The two common methods of drying billing are as follows:-

a. Remove sepals and stems from fruit, immerse in boiling water for 1-2 minutes, drain, slice, and sprinkle with crushed kitchen salt. Arrange in an earthenware pot finishing with a layer of salt on top. Let it remain in the pot for 2-5 days. Thereafter take the fruits out of the pot and sun-dry daily putting them back into the pot each day and repeating this process till the fruits are well dried and encrusted with salt. The pot with the brine is also kept in the sun until the billing fruits are well dried and encrusted with salt. Store, in polythene bags or bottles. It may be kept indefinitely with a little sunning occasionally.

b. Remove sepals and stems. Prick with a fork. Arrange in an earthenware pot in alternate layers of billing and rushed kitchen salt ending with a layer of salt. Sun-dry after 4-5 days in the same manner as in method (a) above.

(g) Mango *Bot*: Magnifera Indica

Sinh: Amba

Dried or fresh mango is a good acid used widely for fish, meat and vegetable curries, in place of more generally used acids such as lime juice, goraka, tamarind etc. A little thickening effect can also be obtained by using mango as an acid in curries due to the presence of starch in mango. Further, it has a tenderising effect.

Immature mangoes that are often allowed to go waste may be treated in the following manner, stored and used for chutneys etc.

(a) Half mature mangoes that fall from the tree may be preserved and stored for use as these are usually not eaten. Wash and wipe mangoes, cut them into four, right through the seed. Bruise slightly, stack in an earthenware pot with kitchen salt in between with a final layer of salt on top and leave for seven days. At the end of the seventh day, sun-dry daily dipping the mango pieces in the brine solution contained in the pot, till the brine solution is used up and mango pieces are encrusted with salt.

(b) Blanch pieces of mango after slicing them fine, drain well, arrange pieces of mango in earthenware pot with alternate layers of salt. Store for three days, sun-dry daily and put back into liquid brine in pot at the end of each day until pieces are dry and encrusted with salt. Store, use when required. The dried mango makes excellent chutney. Soak in vinegar 24 hours before use.

Other Acid Fruits

All fruits with a high content of acid, like amberella, kambaranga, lovi, num num etc., may be used finely sliced in vegetables, fish and meat curries. They must be added initially to the curry and cooked until pulpy. This will act as an acid and a thickening agent.

(h) Lovi *Bot:* Flaccourtia inermis *Sinh*: Lovi

These fruits may be dried and stored using any of the methods employed for mango and biling. This is a fruit generally not used though found in plenty, and makes an excellent acid when added to meat, fish and vegetable curries. Once again the fruit must be cut into small pieces and added. It not only acts as an acid but also has a slight thickening effect. Another method for preparation and use of lovi is given below:

a. Prepare a liquid brine solution using the following proportions:-

BRINE SOLUTION FOR BRINING FRUITS

(Salt to be added for 1 gallon of water)

1st	day	add	2 oz.	of	salt	to	1	gallon of	water
2nd	”	”	2 ”	”	”	”		”	”
5th	”	”	3 ”	”	”	”		”	”
7th	”	”	3 ”	”	”	”		”	”
9th	”	”	4 ”	”	”	”		”	”
11th	”	”	10”	”	”	”		”	”
12th	”	”	8 ”	”	”	”		”	”
13th	“	”	10”	”	”	”		”	“

3-5 grams or a pinch of Potassium Metabisulphite may be added to the water to prevent any kind of mould growth.

b. Place well-ripened lovi fruits in the brine solution. Increase the strength of brine solution by adding salt every alternate day. At the end of the period, sun-dry fruits until encrusted with salt. Brine solution may have to be sprinkled on the fruits occasionally during sun drying. Store and use when required. Excellent for pickles, mojus and chutneys.

7 THICKENING AGENTS

A thickening agent is a comparatively new term in Sri Lankan cookery. In the past, ingredients were added to obtain a particular flavour without the cook being conscious of their thickening effect on the gravy of a curry. Most spices and condiments used in the preparation of curries have a binding effect on the liquid used especially when added in a ground paste-like state. Powders have the same effect to a slightly less degree.

Compared with Western practice, Eastern cookery has a very wide variety of thickening agents used in the thickening of the gravy of a curry.

In Sri Lanka, coconut milk has been the traditional thickening agent in a curry which is boiled down until the gravy is thick. This is being gradually replaced by the use of condiments and spices and other thickening agents on account of the cost of the coconut the ill-effect of its excessive use on* health and the labour involved.

A combination of thickening agents, apart from the spices and condiments used, gives a much better and richer flavour to a curry than a thickening agent used individually. It has been the writer's experience that rice, cadjunuts or peanuts, coconut roasted or plain onion and green chillie used as a combination give a very fine flavour and richness to meat and vegetable curries. Fresh grated coconut,

---

* *Excessive use of coconut milk is said to be one of the many causes of Thrombosis. Coconut milk has an excessive amount of Cholesterol.*

rice and onions act as good thickening agents for curries that are cooked without the addition of the condiments and spices which add a brownish colour to the curry. White curries are only coloured with the addition of a pinch of turmeric for eye appeal, and as a rule are not so pungent in flavour as darker curries. For vegetable curries other than white curries the addition of a few grains of rice, roasted coconut, onion and a little bit of dhal gives the necessary body and flavour. The combination of thickening agents may be done according to individual tastes.

1. Coconut *Bot*: Cocos Nucifera: *Sinh*: Pol

In Sri Lanka the cooking of rice and curry is very closely associated with the use of the coconut in some form or another. Generally coconuts are sold in the market and one has no choice selection except in respect of the size and price. Care must be taken to choose coconuts that are quite mature but not dry.

To an inexperienced person the only guide for choosing a coconut is its weight more than its size; if a coconut is heavy and the water in it produces the minimum sound when the coconut is shaken it can be taken as a well matured coconut which is still not dry. If, on the other hand, a coconut is light in weight and little sound is produced then the nut is not so mature (known as "kalati" or tender). On the other hand if a coconut is light in weight and a fairly noticeable sound is produced when shaken, then it is a mature dry nut.

Fresh but not fully mature coconuts (kalati) are best suited for use in the preparation of roti, pittu and sambol. Fresh, mature coconuts give the best extract of coconut milk and are generally suitable for the preparation of curry. Dry mature coconuts are best suited for the preparation of coconut oil and sweetmeats such as kaludodol and Muscat where a certain amount of oil is required in cooking the sweetmeat, but not the addition of oil.

When coconut milk is used as thickening agent the quantity of milk added should be 1 ½ to 1 ¾ times the amount actually required in the finished product and this liquid must be simmered to the required quantity to give the necessary body to the curry. This involves a great deal of waste in fuel as well as in the use of the coconut milk itself. The present day tendency is to use the minimum of coconut milk in the cooking of curries. The excessive use of coconut milk involves more labour and time as a greater quantity of coconut has to be scraped and squeezed.

(i) How to Extract Coconut Milk

In some western countries the water in the coconut is referred to as coconut milk. The coconut milk is really the extract taken from the grated, or scraped kernel of the coconut. If three quarters the weight of the scraped coconut is added to water a fairly rich milk is obtained (8 oz. coconut scrapings to 6 oz. water). This, of course, would depend on the maturity of the coconut; fresh mature coconuts and not dry mature nuts, give the best quantity and quality of milk. Tender coconuts do not yield much milk.

After the first extract of milk is taken, the second and third extracts are obtained by adding half the weight of the coconut scraping to water with each extract (e.g. 4 oz of coconut scraping to 2 oz of water). Usually the second and third extracts are put together though extracted separately. If a fourth extract is desired from the coconut refuse, it should either be ground or pounded before the extract is taken. In a modern household where a food blender is available the required quantity of water is added to coconut scrapings and into the blender and worked for two to three minutes. This gives a fairly rich milk, even in the fourth extract.

How to roast Coconut

(a) Add the grated or scraped coconut to a heavy bottomed pan or a clay pan and when well heated stir all the while until the desired colour is obtained.

(b) The scraped coconut may be place on a baking sheet and put in the oven at 250^0-300^0F until the desired colour is obtained. The coconut has to be stirred from the edges of the baking sheet from time to time to prevent uneven browning.

(c) The scraped coconut may be spread evenly on a baking sheet and placed under a grill or salamander to brown to desired colour. The coconut will have to be stirred occasionally to ensure even browning.

(d) The kernel cut into pieces, wrapped in plantain leaf and placed in hot ash or on hot coals until dark brown or black or it may be roasted over a heated clay pot or pan. This method is used for special types of sambols only.

(ii) Grated Coconut

Fresh grated coconut is sometimes finely ground and is used for the thickening of white curries, especially the vegetables belonging to the gourd and pumpkin families, (e.g. snake gourd, pumpkin and cucumber). These vegetables contain a very high content of water and a thickening agent is essential. The grated and ground coconut is added after the vegetable is partially cooked. Fresh grated coconut which is ground is used for sambols (thosai sambol) or served plain as an accompaniment to rice and curry.

(iii) Slightly Roasted Coconut

Coconut is roasted to a light brown colour, finely ground and utilised in the preparation of meat, fish and some vegetable curries. The roasting of coconut gives it a special aroma and this improves the flavour when added to curries. Roasted coconut ground with garlic, pepper etc., makes an excellent sambol.

(iv) Coconut Roasted Till It Is Almost Black

This is usually used only in the preparation of certain dark curries such as ash pumpkin curry and sambol. Though roasted till almost black in colour, no burnt flavour is noticeable when used in curries.

Coconut Sliced

The kernel is finely sliced and added to vegetable curries but the thickening effect is only very mild as the pieces are kept whole even after prolonged cooking. It is used in a type of curry with tender jack and coconut.

Tender Coconut (Kurumba)

This is immature coconut with soft and opaque kernel. The kernel cannot be scraped because this type of coconut has a soft and non-brittle shell and soft kernel. The water inside is usually used as a refreshing drink and the soft tender kernel may be scooped and used as a curry prepared in the same manner, with the same ingredients, as a meat curry.

2. Nuts

Cadjunuts, peanuts, country almonds (Kottan) are all used finely ground in the proportion of roughly one to two dessert spoonful per pound of meat or fish in the preparation of meat and fish curries. A combination of these nuts may be used or each used separately. The oil content in a curry is thus increased but not noticeably.

3. Raw Rice or Parboiled Rice

This is usually ground or roasted until light brown and used as a thickening agent. This gives body as it is a form of starch. Certain varieties of samba and par-boiled rice are used, where a lesser thickening effect is desired. The raw varieties give a greater thickening effect. Rice is ground unroasted for all white curries.

4. Gingelly Seeds *Bot*: Sesamum Indicum

Sinh: Tala

Gingelly seeds washed, soaked and ground also give the necessary thickening effect and increase the oil content in a curry. It must be noted that the grinding of gingelly seeds is not very easy. Prior soaking of the seeds makes grinding or pounding easier.

5. Tomatoes *Bot*: Lycopersicum escutentum

Sinh: Takkali

Tomatoes are a thickening agent apart from their use as an acid in curries. To serve as a thickening agent they must be scalded, then cut into small pieces and added to curry from the very start. It must be remembered, however, that if tomatoes are used without scalding they must not be cut and kept for sometime as enzyme action sets in separating the liquid from the solids which will not produce the desired thickening effect. Tomato puree is essential in the preparation of

Eastern dishes for international meals, as this gives the necessary bright red colour with the minimum use of chillie powder and also gives body to a curry.

6. Onions *Bot*: Allium Cepa; *Sinh*: Lunu

Onion ground to a paste also gives the necessary thickening effect in meat, fish and vegetable curries. In a sambol this is the base for binding the other ingredients e.g. maldive fish, chillies etc.

7. Green Chillies or Capsicum Chillies *Bot*: Capsicum
Sinh: Malu Miris

Green chillies or capsicum chillies ground give a medium thickening effect in the preparation of curries. The use of ground chillie and onion is not so common in Sri Lanka as in India and other Eastern countries.

8. Ground Leaves

Coriander leaves, fenugreek leaves, mustard leaves, mint leaves, fennel leaves, parsley leaves or a combination of these leaves or any one of them may be ground and used as a thickening agent. They impart flavour as well as body to a curry. They may be used in meat, fish and some vegetable curries.

9. Dhals and other Pulses

Various types of dhals, and pulses, Mysore gram or Bengal gram, and Moong gram, may be ground and added with advantage to meat, fish or vegetable curries. Once again this is a very common thickening agent in Indian and other Eastern countries, but not so common in Sri Lanka. Gram flour may be added sometimes to curries but a combination of different types of dhal and pulses give better results.

10. Maldive Fish *Sinh*: Umbalakada

Maldive fish is usually a variety of tuna fish processed in a special manner and the entire moisture content removed through smoking and drying. Maldive fish finely ground or powdered not only acts as a thickening agent but improves the flavour of a curry. Care should be taken, however, not to allow the maldive fish flavour to predominate over other flavours. As a rule maldive fish is not generally added to a meat or fish curry, though it may be used. All curry condiments have some thickening effect to a greater or lesser degree depending on the starch and mucilage content in each condiment.

11. Fruits

Most types of fruits have some pectin present in them. The pectin in mature or semi-ripe fruits may be used in a curry with advantage to give the desired binding or thickening effect. The flavour of the fruit would also add flavour to the curry. This is not generally done, but may be tried out by enterprising amateurs willing to experiment with new flavours and textures. Fruits most suitable are papaw, guava with seeds removed, lovi, amberella and kabaranga. The proportion would be 2-3 dessertspoons chopped fruit which should be well matured or about to ripen or ripe but not over-ripe, added to the curry with the main ingredient.

12. Jak Seeds

Dried and powdered jak seeds may be added to any curry 1- 1 ½ dessertspoons per pound of ingredient with very good results.

13. Poppy Seeds *Bot*: Kus-kus

These seeds are generally added to special meat curries such as Khorma, but in Sri Lanka these seeds are very rarely used due to their high cost. However they give a meat curry a very rich flavour.

14. Curd - see Tenderising Agents. *Sinh*: Mudavapu Kiri

15. Prawn Shells and Heads

The heads and shells of fresh prawns may be used powdered. The heads and shells are washed free of sand and dirt, oven dried and powdered. This powder is added to a curry 1-2 dessertspoons per 1 lb. of fish, meat, or vegetable. This also enriches the flavour of a curry.

8 TENDERISING AGENTS

In the cooking of meats some form of tenderiser is very necessary due to the type of meat available in Sri Lanka. In general, only meat of freshly slaughtered animals is available with the result that even the rigor mortis stage is not complete by the time the meat reaches the consumer. Secondly, the cooking time is also short due to the habit of the housewife of purchasing her requirements of such meat daily. Animals in Eastern countries are not especially bred with a view to making their meat tender for food. The animals are generally used for labour as a result of which their muscles are toughened and then later sold in the market for flesh. Some form of meat tenderiser, therefore, is absolutely necessary to soften the meat and this also shortens the average cooking time. Commercial tenderisers which are used in Western countries are not freely available but local tenderisers are easily obtainable at very little cost. They not only soften the meat but add special flavour to a curry.

1. (a) Bark of Papaw Tree

2 to 3 pieces of the papaw tree bark are crushed and added to a meat curry and removed on serving. The papain in the bark acts as a tenderiser without imparting any flavour.

(b) Raw Papaw Slices

Slices of the raw papaw fruit are added to the raw meat prior to cooking and allowed to stay for sometime and then removed before cooking or else finely chopped slices of raw papaw are added to the meat and cooked. The milk or papain in the fruit acts as the tenderiser and in addition if the fruit is chopped and cooked with the curry, it helps as a thickening agent.

© Papaw Leaves

The leaf of the papaw tree is washed, dried and crushed between the palms to bring out the papain from the leaf. This leaf is used for tenderising meat to be grilled in the following manner. The meat to be grilled is seasoned and coated with some liquid fat. It is then wrapped in the crushed papaw leaf and set aside for a few hours prior to grilling. If the meat is kept too long in the leaf, it breaks up into small pieces when cooked and irritation of the palate can take place due to the excess papain.

(d) Papain

A pinch of dried papain is crushed and rubbed into the meat along with the seasoning. In certain Western countries papain is injected into animals prior to slaughtering as this has a general tenderising effect on the meat fibre.

2. Asafoetida (Perunkayan)

This is added in a very small quantity to most meat or dhal curries. In certain cases when people dislike the flavour a small piece- the size of a small-size marble - is stuck to the inner side of the lid so that the steam melts a very small portion into the curry. This piece of asafoetida can be used over and over again. This is a very well known tenderiser and is used in India extensively. It is also said to aid digestion.

3. Curd - Yoghurt - Lactic-Acid

Curd or Yoghurt or soured milk is used as a tenderiser. The curd is applied to meat and allowed to remain for some time. The lactic acid in milk helps to soften the meat fibres. The use of curd helps to increase the nutritive value of the food and also gives a thickening effect.

4. Acid - Vinegar - Acetic Acid

The acetic acid in vinegar helps to soften meat. Vinegar is mixed with the meat and allowed to remain for ½ - ¾ hour prior to cooking.

5. Lime Juice - Citric Acid

Lime is the mildest of acids used for tenderising meats (see under Acids)

6. Tamarind - Mallic Acid (see under Acids)

7. Goraka (see under Acids)

8. Mango (see under Acids)

9. Other acids used in curries (Chapter 6).

10. See Other Acid Fruits (Chapter 6).

9 HOW TO CHOOSE AND PREPARE MEAT FOR COOKING

In Sri Lanka unlike in Western countries a variety of cuts of meat is not readily obtainable. All beef is sold by the pound at a fixed price irrespective of the cuts. One is at the mercy of the butcher and it is necessary to know how to make the best use of the meat that is available. In buying meat it is best always to buy a week's supply, if storage facilities are available, or to buy a few day's supply. Where refrigerator facilities are not available, it can be cooked using methods which do not require cold storage. Purchasing a large cut of beef is more economical than buying small amounts daily.

Hints on Buying Beef

Buy preferably beef that is of a reddish colour. Coarse fibred meat with a deep maroon colour is usually buffalo beef and should be avoided. Even if the beef becomes softer in cooking the fibres remain very coarse. Beef that is oozing or sweating with water should not be bought as it has been iced and partial decomposition has set in and keeping qualities are poor. Dry surfaced beef is the best. Fresh beef which is also moist with bright red blood should be avoided, if it is to be used within a few hours as this makes the curry very tough but is best for purchasing if it is not for immediate use, as keeping qualities are good. Beef that has an offensive smell and is bluish in colour should be avoided at all costs. Beef marbled with streaks of fat is preferable to beef with a thick layer of fat for general purposes of curry making.

How to Prepare beef

Wash and dry the beef with a clean cloth before cutting. Remove the fat and sinews and set it aside for the preparation of fat or stock. Always cut beef against the grain. If a week's supply of beef has been purchased at once, cut and set aside beef for various preparations such as steaks, fillets etc. Use the remaining pieces for curry. If there are still more odd bits of beef, set aside for beef loaf, bolle curry, cutlets etc. In this manner all beef that has been bought may be utilised to the maximum without waste. If bones are available it may be added to stock and gravies or soups. Generally, it must be pointed out that the average housewife first cuts beef and then washes the cut pieces. It must be stressed that this tends to reduce the flavour and the nutrients of the beef and should never be done.

Liver

Liver should always be washed and the membrane removed along with all noticeable blood vessels and pieces cut according to use but not too thick. When liver is cooked it is important that the cooking should be done only up to the point where the red colour of the liver disappears. The liver when cooked, must be soft and tender. Liver must never be over cooked to the point of making it hard and leathery. This makes it very unpalatable.

Kidney

If full kidney is used, it must first be washed, the outer thin membrane removed and separated into two; fat and other white parts removed and the kidney placed in salt water for about 1 ½ -2 hours to draw out any impurities that might be present. This is something that is very essential and it must be remembered that the kidney is an organ that excretes waste matter from the body and these impurities if any must be removed before cooking.

Brain

After the fine transparent membrane is removed, the brain should also be well washed, several times to remove all traces of blood. It may also be placed in salt water for sometime, if time permits, before use.

Tripe

This is very commonly used as it is quite cheap and freely available. Very special care must be taken to see that the cleaning is thoroughly done even though the butcher has it partially cleaned. The casing should be turned inside out and washed in several changes of water and to each change of water a little salt may be added. Very often it is easier to wash the tripe after cutting it into shorter lengths. It may also be soaked in salt water for sometime before it is used. Salt helps to draw out many of the impurities and the cleaning is more thorough.

Heart

If the heart is used for curry-making it may be cut and washed taking care to cut out all the blood vessels that could otherwise make the general texture of the curry very tough. In cooking the heart, it must be remembered never to over-cook as the meat tends to be very tough and leathery. Slow cooking is the best method recommended.

Poultry

Dressed poultry is very popular and freely available and it is therefore not necessary here to discuss how to dress poultry. However, it is necessary to know how to cut poultry for a curry so that portions may be of a suitable size without it being chopped into pieces which are too small.

a. Cut off wings from body.

b. Cut legs off main body and separate drumsticks from thigh: 4 portions.

c. Remove neck, and cut breast into two vertically: 2 portions. If chicken is over 2 ½ pounds cut each section of the breast into two: 4 portions from breast and only the two segments of the wings are cut off for stock or soups. The two wings, gizzard and liver may be counted as one portion if necessary.

In using he broiler chicken for curry the following suggestions are recommended:

(i) Cut and wash the chicken and wipe dry.

(ii) Rub in the condiments and seasoning and set aside for sometime as the cooking time is very short and the flesh sometimes tends to be insipid. (Complete thawing should be allowed, if not already done during this stage. Frozen or partially frozen meat makes a very insipid curry).

(iii) Do not use the cold method of cooking curries. but use some method recommended where the meat is first tempered in oil with or without curry ingredients. Cooking in a small quantity of oil should be done for at least five minutes.

(iv) The quantity of liquid added should only be the quantity required in the finished curry. Cooking from the point at which liquid is added should always be at simmer to help the flavour of the condiments to penetrate into the flesh.

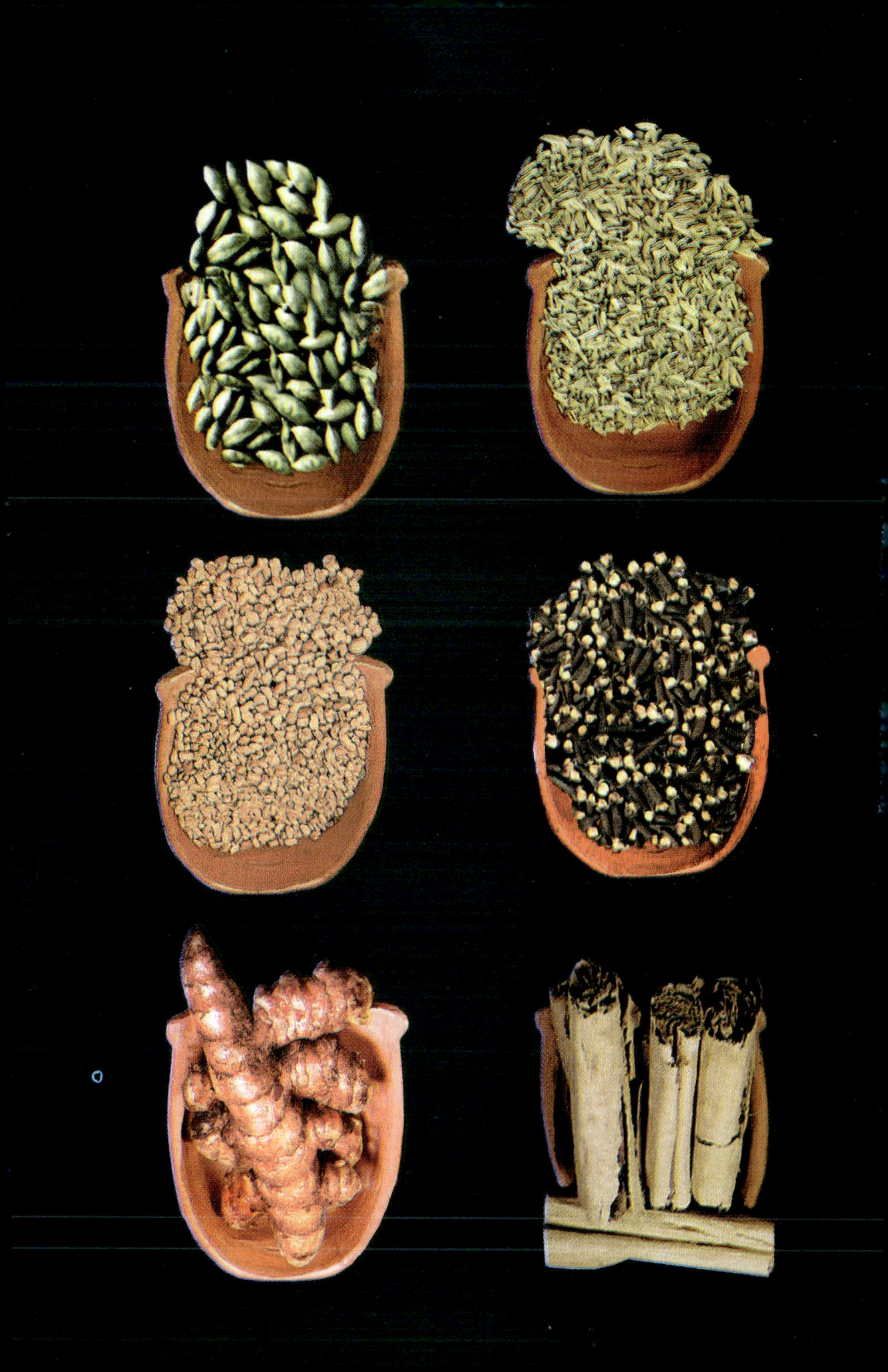

(v) The procedure as in (i) to (iv) above is recommended as the full cooking time of a broiler chicken to make it tender will not be more than 10-12 minutes after the liquid is added. Broiler chicken should not be overcooked.

Pork

Any of the meat, mutton or poultry recipes may be followed in the preparation of pork but the following points must be observed:-

(a) The fat used in any recipe is omitted. Instead, the pork fat is chopped and melted for frying.

(b) Coconut milk if used is reduced and the 2nd and 3rd extracts are preferred as this reduces the fat content in the cooked curry.

(c) Prolonged cooking of pork is very essential to kill any tape worm cysts that may be present in pigs that are not reared under hygienic conditions.

(d) All excess fat is drained off after cooking prior to serving. This fat may be rendered and used in place of other fats for preparing curries.

Note: Beef or Mutton may be used in all the meat recipes.

10 PREPARATION OF SEA FOOD FOR CURRIES

Fish

When choosing fish, look out for the following good points -

(i) Bright bulging eyes.

(ii) Shining skin with a slimy texture.

(iii) Firm flesh, if the fish is cut, test for firmness near the middle bone.

(iv) Gills bright red or reddish colour, not purple, blue or black.

(v) No offensive smell.

How to Wash and Clean Fish

If fish is being used for curries, cut the head off, remove the intestines and cut into pieces of the required size. Fish is generally washed with goraka, turmeric powder or any type of acid such as lime juice or vinegar to remove the strong smell found in certain varieties. If there is any suspicion of the fish not being fresh, place in strong salt solution with some acid added for about half an hour. The fish should be washed, unlike meat, in several changes of water to remove the strong fish odour although this strong odour may not be found in all types of fish.

If scales are found on the fish, they must be first removed before the fish is cut into pieces.

Generally the skin is not removed when cooking fish curries except in shark and certain other varieties of fish that have a leathery skin. Generally the skin of the fish is very thin and can be consumed. In small fish the gills and the intestines only are removed and the fish is cooked or deep fried whole e.g. sprats, sudayas and salayas. This increases the nutritive value as the bones contain calcium. Small fish may be cooked in a pressure cooker for 10-15 minutes, with all condiments used for a curry or such fish even may be used, mashed up, complete with bones that become pulpy, for sandwiches as paste; the nutritive value in this form is very high. It makes not only a nutritive product, but also cheap one as small fish are generally cheaper than the larger varieties and are available in plenty.

How to choose Prawns

Prawns must always be fresh and to the touch they should be firm with no odour. In no circumstances should prawns be bought that have developed an orangish or bluish colour, as this is the first sign of spoilage. The same treatment as for fish may be given to prawns if there is the slightest suspicion that they are not quite fresh e.g. *before* they develop an orange colour.

Washing Prawns

Wash prawns and remove all sand, remove the head and shells and leave the tail, if required for attractive presentation. The middle black line or intestine must always be removed either by slitting it right down or slitting it at tail point and drawing it our from head point. Once this preparation is finished, wash prawns in several changes of water. Drain and use as required.

When prawns are available and cheap they may be bought, head and shell removed, deveined, deep frozen in packets according to portions required for the household or heads may be removed, the prawns deveined without removing the shell and washed and deep frozen. In deep freezing fish and prawns, it must be remembered that a certain percentage of water is required to prevent dehydration. In fact after they are partially frozen they may be sprinkled with water to preserve the fish in a fresh state when thawed. Prawn heads, skin and tails may be washed in several changes of water and deep frozen for future use, or used minced or ground or pounded in a motor and pestle. This is mixed with thin coconut milk or water and the extract added to prawn curry or used in any vegetable curry such as potatoes, brinjals etc, in place of some of the coconut milk. It also gives the curry added flavour.

The heads, skins etc, can also be washed very well, drained and oven baked at 275^0-300^0 F until very crisp. The shells etc., should be powdered and may be used as a substitute for Maldive fish. They also make an excellent substitute for seeni sambols.

Crabs

When choosing crabs buy heavy crabs that are alive and not according to their size. Each crab may be tested for weight by holding the crab in the hand. Sometimes the crabs may be large but hollow and light. The most humane way to kill a crab is to drive a sharp skewer into the brain which lies on the under side of the body or live crabs may be plunged into fast boiling water which kills it instantaneously. Sometimes the crabs are put into tepid salted water with vinegar but this only makes the crab stupefied and does not kill it at once. The live crab may even be quick frozen. The first two methods are recommended as against the third and fourth.

To dress crabs for curry, remove the big claws and set aside.

Remove and throw away: (i) the under-shell or body of the crab; (ii) or lungs that lie around the top of the big shell; (iii) the spongy fingers or lungs that lie around the shell; (iv) any green matter in the big shell. Cut the crab right through the centre leaving the small claws intact with the body so that the number of portions would be two per crab: half the main body and a claw per person.

However if the crab is large and heavy the main body may be cut vertically with claws on either side and then diagonally again, into four portions. Crabs may be boiled and deep frozen but there is then a tendency for the crab meat to be watery when the meat thaws. Only sea crabs are recommended to be bought even though dead.

Lobsters

Lobsters, like crabs, should be bought alive and killed using one of the methods used for crabs. The head is removed from the main body carefully along with the intestine or black vein that runs along the body. The shell is cracked and removed from the meat that is used for cooking or the shell is cut into segments. Wash well in several changes of water specially if shell us used. The legs are broken at each segment and cooked with the main curry. The recipe used for fish, meat or prawn may be used for lobsters. It is traditional to add the leaves of the drumstick tree to the curry in its final stages when cooking all types of shell fish.

Cuttle Fish

Remove flat bone-like structure and pouch with blackish blue fluid and contents of cavity. Remove the fine membrane covering the outside. Wash the inside of the fish very well by turning the pouch inside out. Remove hard ball-like structure near head., If cooked whole (small variety) the cuttle fish is not cut. Otherwise it is cut into rings (see Fish recipe No.7). The very large variety is cut into small 1″ squares or strips. Cook according to recipe.

11 FROZEN FOODS

In Sri Lanka the use of deep frozen food is becoming quite popular. Hence a few hints on how to use frozen products successfully is included here.

1. Fish

Fish is the most common frozen food used in Sri Lanka homes. It is recommended that the fish be allowed to partially thaw in the polythene bag, as this facilitates cutting. Complete thawing before cutting sometimes tends to break up the fish if it has not been deep frozen quickly and whilst quite fresh. The washing of the fish will help in the complete thawing. Fish, if cooked in a frozen or semi-frozen state for a curry, tends to be insipid as the cooking time of fish is very short and there is hardly any time for the condiments and seasoning to add any flavour.

In the case of seasoned frozen fish fillets coated with batter and crumbed, better results are obtained when the fish is taken in a deep frozen state, and plunged straight into deep fat for frying, provided the piece of fish fried is not more than1 ½" and the number of pieces fried at one time is a few (see note on deep Frying)

2. Meat

Meat should be completely thawed before using for curries. The meat may be washed in a frozen state, cut whilst partially thawed as cutting is easier and allowed to thaw completely before cooking. The condiments and seasonings may be mixed with the partially thawed and cut pieces of meat and set aside for complete thawing before the preparation of the curry.

If frozen meat is cooked the pieces in the curry tend to be tough and tasteless. Sometimes prolonged slow cooking helps to soften the texture of tough meat fibres, but the flavour of the meat is poor unless fully thawed before cooking.

3. Vegetables

All frozen vegetables must be plunged into boiling water using the minimum amount of water. Thawing of frozen vegetables tends to make the cooked product soggy.

4. Baked Products

All frozen baked products should be placed in an oven 275^{0}-300^{0} F immediately on removal from freezer. Thawing tends to make baked products soggy and heavy in texture.

5. Fruits

Cooked frozen fruits may be allowed to thaw and used heated or cold after thawing.

6. Frozen Curries

Frozen curries should be allowed to thaw in their own container placed in warm water over low heat. Heating a frozen curry placed directly on heat tends to dry the moisture and leave the centre of the frozen product very icy, unless cooked for a long time. The frozen curry may even be placed in a warm oven covered and allowed to heat. Frozen rice should be steamed over slow boiling water.

FREEZING

Freezing of curries or even rice is labour saving. Sometimes double portions of curries may be made and deep frozen for another meal. Quite a few curries freeze well. All meats and fish curries freeze well, as well as any type of plain or savoury rice preparations. Vegetables which belong to a group with a very high content of water, cucumber, bottle-gourd, ash pumpkin etc., do not freeze very well. All leaves freeze fairly well but tend to loose their colour on thawing, if thawing is done under heat. If allowed to thaw on its own the collection of a little moisture is evident especially in leafy curries with a high water content in the leaves; e.g. Thampala. This water can be removed by heating the thawed curry on a quick flame.

It cannot be over-stressed how important it is to follow the correct procedure in freezing. The need to use some protective covering to prevent dehydration of frozen products can never be overemphasized, if you wish to have a first rate frozen product. In this section a note is added on frozen broiler chicken as it is commonly used for curries.

The chicken should be cut whilst partially thawed, washed and dried well. All ingredients with seasoning should be well rubbed into the pieces of chicken and set aside for a minimum period of half an hour or until completely thawed. The meat should then be fried with or without onions in a very small quantity of oil for at least 5-10 minutes, and only the required quantity of liquid or even a little less added, brought to boil and simmered until tender only for another 10-15 minutes. The cooking of broiler chicken does not take more than 15-20 minutes. All broilers must be completely thawed before cooking.

12 CLEANING OF VEGETABLES

Root Vegetable

First wash the mud and dirt away, using either a brush or coconut husk. Most root vegetables are prepared for curry making by scraping off the skin. This may be done by using a knife or potato peeler. In the case of the smaller yams like innala and kiriala it is easier to clean by adopting any of the following methods.

i. Put the yams into a small jute bag, rub the bag on the floor to cause friction.

ii. Knock the yams in an up and down movement on the floor in a jute bag.

iii. Rub the yams in the koraha or nambiliya (grooved vessel used for washing rice).

iv. They may also be boiled and peeled off (innala).

Care must be taken to cut off or throw away completely any part of the yam that may be discoloured (bluish green). Yams thus affected may cause violent digestive reaction due to the presence of various poisonous acid e.g. prussic acid in the manioc.

Leafy Vegetables

All mature parts of stems and withered leaves should be discarded and the leaves washed several times under running water to remove all traces of sand that may adhere to the leaves and the hairy stems in some plants. As a general rule the cutting or chopping of the leafy vegetable should be done, only after the washing has been completed and water allowed to drain. This is done in order to retain the maximum amount of water-soluble vitamins and minerals in the food to be cooked. Do not allow leafy vegetables to soak in water for long. The only exception is in preparing anguna leaves that are very bitter. These leaves are washed, shredded very fine, almost hair-like, and allowed to soak in salt water to reduce the bitterness. It is always preferable to break leafy vegetables than to cut them with a knife.

Other Vegetables

Each type of vegetable needs special treatment.

Thalanabatu, elabatu, and thumba karawila are usually crushed to remove the seeds. A quick method of cleaning is to place the fruits between two chopping boards and crush them. This is quicker than cutting the fruits or placing the fruits in a jute bag and knocking it with a coconut or any heavy object to crush the fruits. Thereafter the seeds are separated and the fruits washed before cooking. In the case of thibbatu the fruits are first washed, crushed lightly and cooked with the seeds.

Vegetables that Discolour - Plantains, breadfruits, potatoes, etc. After peeling, these vegetables should be put into plain water with some acid. The rubbing of coconut refuse also helps to prevent discolouration. The oil in the coconut helps to give the vegetable a thin coating of oil which prevents discolouration due to enzyme action.

Beans

All varieties of beans should have their strings removed and if very mature only the seeds should be used and not the whole pod.

Jak fruit

Before removing the pericarps of the fruit, the knife used for cutting the fruit and the hands must be smeared with oil to prevent the koholla or gum sticking to the knife or hands.

Kohila

Kohila strings are also removed with a little oil or by rubbing a little grated coconut on the cut pieces of Kohila.

Removal of Bitterness in Vegetables

Usually the fruits such as bitter gourd are boiled whole if used for stuffed vegetable, or sliced and few pieces of goraka or some acid added to remove the bitterness when boiling.

Slimy Vegetables - Ladies Fingers etc. All slimy vegetables must be first washed and then cut for curry just before it is required.

Skins of Vegetables

Very valuable nutrients are thrown away with the disposal of vegetable skins which are very often edible and could form an extra curry, providing variety with no extra cost e.g.

1. Plantain skins	-	sambol, fried, tempered, mallum or curry
2. Watakolu	-	curry, tempered or mallum
3. Diyalabu skins	-	mallum, curry or tempered
4. Ash pumpkin	-	black curry

13 MENU PLANNING

It must be remembered that when a menu is planned in rice and curry, the normal principle of general menu planning must be applied. It is advisable, however, to have variety in the texture of the vegetables and variety in colour and in flavour. Normally for a plain and simple rice and curry meal for daily consumption there should always be some form of meat or fish, or, in their absence, a variety of dhal or lentil.

In addition a fresh salad and two different vegetables, one of which should be a non-leafy vegetable, such as carrot, beetroot, beans, jak seeds, breadfruit etc., should be provided. It is wise to have them cooked differently to have variety. One may be pungent and dark in colour, another white, another with a sharp acid flavour and still another tempered in oil. Chutneys, pickles, fried papadam, prawns and sprats may be served as accompaniments to the main meal, if so desired.

The number of curries will depend on the time and money available. As a labour-saving device a number of vegetables and meat or fish may be cooked as one curry. The resulting combination gives better flavour and also brings down the cost and saves labour and money. However, it must be remembered that in planning combinations, it must be on the basis of at least 2-3 oz. of meat, 8-10 oz. of vegetable, and 3-4 oz. of rice per person per meal. This proportion will normally provide a balanced meal and the necessary calories.

The following points may be observed in menu planning:-

(1) Plan a full day's meal with particular attention to a balanced diet.

(2) Consider foods in season as these foods would be cheaper, (see table)

(3) Wherever possible it is easier to plan a week's menu 3 or 4 days ahead and purchase stocks at once. This is not only economical but also monotony in food could be avoided.

(4) Certain foods may be cooked in bulk and stored in portions to save time e.g. meat curry. The monotony of the meat curry can be changed if on reheating a slight variation is made to the curry.

(5) Include fresh fruits that are available in plenty at low cost at least once a day, as a desert. These should as far as possible be served in their fresh form eg. plantains, pineapples, mangoes, etc. (see list)

(6) Take the correct portions to avoid wastage.

SUGGESTED MENUS

1. Yellow Rice

   Brinjal Pahie or other Fried Brinjal preparations

   Seeni Sambol

   Hard Boiled Fried Egg Curry white or dark

   Liver, Beef or Chicken curry

   Accompaniments : *Chutney, Sweet Date and Lime, mixed pickle, Papadam.*

2. Lampries - Ghee Rice

Lampry Curry

Fricadells

Fried Plantain Curry plain or

Brinjal Pahie

Cucumber Sambol (optional)

} to be packed in Banana Leaves

Fried Hard Boild Egg

Blachan

Accompaniments: *Mango Chutney, Fried Prawns or Chicken Curry plus extra* servings of fricadells.

3. Buriyani - Chicken, Mutton or Egg

Malay Pickle

Mint Sambol

Chicken Khroma

Hard Boiled Egg

Bombay onion Sambol

4. Nasigorenge

Sathe Curry

Prawn Papadam

Liver Curry or Mixed Vegetable Liver Curry (Liver, Capsicum chillie and plantain fried)

Accompaniments: Lunumiris, Mango Chutney, Fricadells.

5. Ghee Rice

   Brinjal Curry or Pahie Preparation

   Pork, Mutton, Prawns or Chicken curry

   Fricadells

   Seeni Sambol

   Tomato onion Sambol

6. Chinese Fried Rice

   Mutton, Chicken, Pork or Prawn Curry

   Fried Prawns

   Chutney or Tomato onion Sambol

   Shanghai Omelettes

7. Vegetable Rice

   Cadju Curry or Paneer Curry

   Tempered Potatoes

   Vegetable Cutlets

   Papadam

8. Savoury Rice

   Liver Peas and Cadju Curry

   Mixed or Malay Pickle

   Fricadells.

Accompaniments: for Menus 6, 7 and 8 may be the same as for those used in 1,2 and 4

9. Plain Rice and Curry

   Meat, Fish, Prawn or Egg Curry

   Cadju Curry

   Tender Jak Curry

   Bean Curry

   Stuffed Chillie Curry

10. Plain Rice

   Dhal Curry

   Pol Sambol

   Tempered Dry Fish Curry or Moju

   Breadfruit White Curry

11. String-hoppers

   Mullagathany

   Pol Mallum

   Chicken Curry or Prawn Badum or any type of Miris Malu

   Fricadells

   Egg Ruloung

12. String-hoppers

   Kiri Hodhi

   Seeni Sambol

   Fried Prawns

Meat, Pork, Egg or Chicken Curry

Cooked Cadju Curry

Suggested garnishings for rice preparation:

(1) Fried kathurumurunga, parsley or murunga leaves.

(2) Slices of fried streaky bacon.

(3) Shoe String Potato deep fried.

(4) Hard boiled Egg chopped or Fried Omelette shredded.

(5) Fried Cadju nuts and sultanas.

(6) Boiled Peas.

(7) Chopped parsley.

(8) Deep Fried onion rings or slices.

(9) Fried Prawns

(10) Cubed Meat or Salami or Ham

(11) Sauted chopped red and green capsicum chillies.

(12) Shredded Gotukola leaves, spring onion leaves or Lettuce.

Dessert for the above menus may be, Fruit Salad, Wattalappan, sweet meats or any of the fruits given below:

A list of popular fruits inclusive of the less popular varieties is given below. When in season they are available in plenty at low cost.

These fresh fruits may be used when ripe as dessert. They may also be canned for off season use, or made into preserves, jams, jellies, sweet sauces or candied.

1. Avocado or Alligator-pear:

    Botany: Persea gratissima;

    Sinhala: Et-pera;

2. Beli Fruit:

    Botany: Aegle Marmelos;

    Sinhala: Beli

3. Banana or Plantain:

    Botany: Musa sapientum;

    Sinhala: Kehel;

Various varieties of Plantains

Anamalu,

Bin-kehel or Dwarf plantain

Embul-hondarawala or Sour plantain

Koli-kuttu

Puwalu

Ranel or Red-plantain;

Rath-kehel;

Suwandel

Alu-kehel or Ash plantain (may be cooked in an unripe state)

4. Brazil Cherry:

Botany: Eugenia Michelli;

Sinhala: Goraka-jambu;

5. Breadfruit:

Botany: Artocarpus incisa;

Sinhala: Rata-del;

6. Camias or Cucumber-tree:

Botany: Averrhoa Bilimbi;

Sinhala: Bilin

7. Carambolo:

Botany: Averrhoa Carambola;

Sinhala: Kamaranga;

8. Cashew-nut:

Botany: Anacardium occidentale;

Sinhala: Cadju;

9. Ceylon Gooseberry:

Botany: Aberia Gardneri;

10. Ceylon Olive:

Botany: Elaeocarpus serratus;

Sinhala: Veralu;

11. Cherimoya or Cherimoyer:

Botany: Anona Cherimolia;

12. Country Almond:

    Botany: Terminalia Catappa;

    Sinhala: Kotamba (Nuts);

13. Custard-apple:

    Botany: Anoma squamesa;

    Sinhala: Anoda;

14. Date-plum:

    Botany: Chrysophyllum monopyrenum;

    Sinhala: Kos-eta-lawaulu;

15. Dwarf or Chinese Banana:

    Botany: Musa Cavendishii;

    Sinhala: Nan-kehel;

16. Durian:

    Botany: Durio Zibethinus;

17. Egg Tree:

    Botany: Garcinia Zanthochymus;

    Sinhala: Cochin-goraka or Rata-goraka;

18. Embal:

    Botany: Phyllanthus Emblica;

    Sinhala: Nellie;

19. Grape-fruit:

    Botany: Citrus grandis;

20. Gauva:

Botany: Psidium Gauva;

Sinhala: Pera;

21. Jak Fruit (to be eaten when ripe)

Botany: Artocarpus integrifolia;

Sinhala: Kos;

22. Jamaica or Red Sorell: Rozelle;

Botany: Hibscus Sabdariffa;

Sinhala: Rata-Bilincha;

23. Java Plum:

Botany: Eugenia Jambolana;

Sinhala: Mahadan;

24. Jujube:

Botany: Zizyphus Jujuba;

Sinhala: Masan;

25. Kana-gona:

Botany: Artocarpus Lakoocha;

Sinhala: Kanagona;

26. Lemon:

Botany: Citrus Limonia;

Sinhala: Narran;

27. Lime:

    Botany: Citrus acida;

    Sinhala: Dehi;

28. Longan:

    Botany: Hephelium (Euphoria) Longanna

    Sinhala: Mora or Rasa-mora;

29. Lovi-lovi:

    Botany: Flacouritia inermis;

    Sinhala: Lovi;

30. Malay Apple:

    Botany: Eugenia malaccensis;

    Sinhala: Jambu;

31. Mango:

    Botany: Mangifera indica;

    Sinhala: Amba;

Various varieties of mangoes:

Rupee or pol-amba;

Jaffna mango similar to the Alphonso mango

Parrot-mango or gira-amba;

Bombay mango or mi-amba;

Maha-mudaliyar or puhu-amba;

32. Mangosteen:

    Botany: Garcinia Mangostana;

    Sinhala: Mangus;

33. Musk Melon:

    Botany: Cucumis Melo;

    Sinhala:Pitikekiri or Cantaloupe;

34. Nam-nam:

    Botany: Cynometra cauliflora;

    Sinhala: Nan-nan;

35. Otaheite-apple or hog plum:

    Botany: Spndias mangifera

    Sinhala: Amberella

36. Papaw:

    Botany: Carica Papaya;

    Sinhala: Pepol

37. Promegranate:

    Botany: Punica granatum:

    Sinhala: Delum

38. Passion Fruit:

    Botany: Passiflora edulis;

39. Pineapple; Ananas sativus:

    Botany: Bromeliaceae;

    Sinhala: Annasi;

40. Rambutan:

    Botany: Nephelium Lappaceum;

    Sinhala: Rambutan;

41. Ramputchi or Governor Plum:

    Botany: Flacourtia Ramontchi;

    Sinhala: Uguressa

42. Rose-apple:

    Botany: Eugenia Jambos;

    Sinhala; Veli Jambu

43. Sapodilla-plum:

    Botany: Achras Sapota;

    Sinhala: Rata-mi

44. Shaddock: Pomelo; Forbidden Fruit:

    Botany: Citrus decumana;

    Sinhala: Jambola

45. Soursop:

    Botany: Anona muricata:

    Sinhala: Katu-anoda

46. Star Apple: Caimito:

    Botany: Chrysophyllum Cainito;

    Sinhala: Rata-lawaulu

47. Star-gooseberry:

Botany: Phyllanthus distichus;

Sinhala: Rata-nelli or Siri-nelli

48. Sugar apple or Bullock's heart:

Botany: Anona reticulata;

Sinhala: Anoda

49. Sweet Orange:

Botany: Citrus Aurantium

Sinhala: Peni-dodan

Various Orange varieties:

Mandarin: Sinhala: Jama-naran

King Orange: a large variety of the mandarin type:

Grape-fruit;

*Wild orange: (used for medicine) and for marmalade and candying

Tangerine or Nasnaran

*Kaffir-lime or Kudala-dehi (used for medicine)

Limes;

50. Tree Tomato:

Botany: Cyhomandra betacea

Sinhala: Gas Takkali

---

* *Suitable for marmalade and candying.*

51. Velvet Tamarind:

Botany: Dialium ovoideum;

Sinhala: Gal siyambala

52. Water Melon:

Botany: Citrullus vulgaris;

Sinhala: Komadu or Peni-komadu.

53. Wax Jambu:

Botany: Eugenia Javanica;

Sinhala: Pini Jambu

54. Wild Breadfruit:

Botany: Artocarpus nobilis;

Sinhala: Bedi or Wal-del

55. Wood-apple or Elephant-apple:

Botany: Feronia elephantum;

Sinhala: Diwul

14 CHUTNEY, MOJU, PICKLE

The use of Chutney, Moju and Pickles as accompaniments form an integral part of a well presented rice and curry meal. They add the necessary "pep" or relish to an Eastern menu. They are the counterparts of "sauces" used in a Western meal. The number of these items to be presented at each meal will depend on the occasion and the other accompaniments to the rice.

In the preparation of the above items the importance of using good quality ingredients such as vinegar, dry fish, fruits, can never be overstressed. These dishes are made and stored for months, sometimes years. Keeping improves the flavour and texture of the product. The fact that a poor ingredient can never give a good finished product must always be kept in mind.

Onions

Always choose good quality dry onions either for pickles or mojus. Never let onions soak for too long in water to facilitate cleaning. The washed onions must be well drained and wiped with a clean dry cloth, if possible, before use. In the preparation of mojus, pickles etc., it is far better to clean the onions without soaking them in water even though cleaning is tedious. It is interesting to note that loss of weight as a result of cleaning onions would be roughly 15-20% and by deep frying 25-30%.

Deep Fried Products

Deep fried products should be well fried until crisp or hard. The oil should never be smoking as this will brown the product quickly and leave the inside raw. Oil should be between the temperatures of 325^0-350^0 F, and fried right into the centre. e.g. dry fish, fried prawns.

Vinegar

A good brand of vinegar should be used. If ever in doubt about the quality of vinegar reduce the quantity to almost half by boiling, whereby the strength is increased. Normally commercial vinegar should have 4% acetic acid. As mentioned earlier the type of vinegar that is available in Sri Lanka is usually Coconut Vinegar from the Coconut palm and sometimes Kitul vinegar which is made from the sap of the Kitul tree.

Salt

Kitchen salt is recommended for brining ingredients for use in Pickles, Mojus etc, but before use it should be washed free of dust etc. A good brand of table salt that is free of grit should be used for seasoning.

Oil

Only good quality oil that is refined should be used. Unrefined oils should be avoided as rancidity sets in quickly in the finished product.

Vessels used for Storing

The importance of well sterilized jars, bottles, and lids cannot be overemphasized in regard to the storage of pickles etc. If possible all storage bottles should be boiled or rinsed in boiling water, oven-dried or wiped with a clean cloth until all traces of moisture disappear.

Food when still hot should be put into containers and allowed to cool. If a vacuum sealing machine is not available, a thin coating of heated refined oil should be poured on top to prevent mould growth. Metal vessels of any form should be avoided for the storing of chutney, pickles, mojus etc. as a high acid content in them can cause chemical reaction that may be poisonous.

Part Two

Recipes

1. Handy Measures

2. Recipes

Breakfast

Rice

Fish

Shell Fish

Meat

Liver

Egg

Gravies

Vegetables

Mallums

Sambols

Chutneys

Mojus

Pickles

Sweetmeats

Miscellaneous

Beverages

Western

Sri Lankan with substitutes

HANDY MEASURES

Aluminium measuring cups available in Sri Lanka correspond to the American standard cups. All cup measurers included here are "level" and not "heaped".

1 cup - 7 oz. barley seeds

1 cup - 5 ½ oz. cadjunuts (65-70 cadjunuts)

1 cup - 5 oz. cadjunuts chopped

1 cup - 4 oz. coconut

1 cup - 8 oz. coconut (packed tightly)

1 cup - 3 oz. coriander seeds

1 cup - 5 ½ oz. coffee seeds

1 cup - 3 oz. cummin seeds

1 cup - 6 ¼ oz. dhal gram

1 cup - 7 oz. dhal-mysore

1 cup - 4 oz. flour (white wheat)

1 cup - 4 oz. icing sugar

1 cup - 10 oz. kitchen salt

1 cup - 6 oz. mustard seeds

1 cup - 4 ½ oz. pepper corns

1 cup - 8 oz. raw rice

1 cup - 4 oz. raw rice flour

1 cup - 6 ½ oz. raw rice flour (packed to hold shape)

1 cup - 8 oz. rice

1 cup - 5 ½ oz. roasted rice flour

1 cup - 4 oz. sago

1 cup - 5 ½ oz. semolina-rulang

1 cup - 8 oz. sugar

1 cup - 3 oz. sweet cummin seeds

Liquid Measures (English)

1 teaspoon	= 1 fluid drachms or drams
1 tablespoon=	¼ fluid oz.= 4 fluid drachms or drams
4 gills	= 20 fluid oz.=1 pint
2 pints	= 1 quart
4 quarts	= 160 fluid oz.= 1 gallon

Liquid Measures (American)

1 pint	= 16 fluid oz.	= 2 cups
8 pints	= 128 fluid oz.	= 1 gallon

British Measures and Metric Equivalents

Weight

1 ounce - 28.4 grammes (gm.)

1 pound - 453.6 grammes (gm.)

Volume

1 fluid oz. - 29.6 millilitres (ml.)

20 fluid oz. - 1 pint - 0.59 litres (l.)

OVEN TEMPERATURE CHART

Fahrenheit in centre of oven		*Degrees Fahrenheit*	*Gas Markings*
Very Slow	... ...	below 250°	1-2
Slow	... ...	250-300	
Moderate	... ...	300-350	3-5
Moderately Hot	... ...	350-400	5-7
Hot	... ...	400-450	7-8
Very Hot	... ...	450-550	9

ACCOMPANIMENTS FOR BREAKFAST PREPARATIONS

1. **Hoppers**

   Accompaniments,

   i. Meat, Fish or Prawn dry curry.

   ii. Lunu Miris

   iii. Treacle or Jaggery

   iv. Seeni sambol

2. **Kiribath**

   Accompaniments,

   i. Meat, Fish or Prawn curry with a little gravy,

   ii. Lunu Miris or Seeni sambol

   iii. Jaggery.

3. **Roti**

   Accompaniments,

   i. Meat, Fish or Prawn curry with a little gravy.

   ii. Lunu Miris or Seni sambol.

   iii.. Jaggery or Treacle.

4. String-hoppers

Accompaniments,

i. Kiri hodi or thick coconut milk seasoned with salt,

ii. Pol Sambol, Seeni Sambol, Plain coconut or Pol Mallum.

iii. Meat, Fish or Prawn curry with gravy, (Usually miris malu is used).

5. Pittu

Accompaniments,

i. Thick coconut milk seasoned with salt

ii. Meat, Fish or Prawn curry with gravy

iii. Jaggery or Treacle.

6. Thosai

Accompaniments,

a. Ground coconut sambol

b. Tempered Potatoes

BREAKFAST PREPARATIONS

1. HOPPERS WITH TODDY AND RICE FLOUR

Ingredients for 20-25 *hoppers*

1 lb. rice flour	extract of 1 large coconut 16-24 oz
2 dessertspoons toddy*	salt to taste
1 dessertspoon sugar	water from coconut 6-8 oz.

Method

1. Sieve the flour into a bowl, add salt, sugar and toddy and enough coconut water to make a stiff dough and leave overnight or about 6-8 hours to rise.
2. Then gradually mix with coconut milk, add a pinch of bicarbonate of soda.
3. Grease a hopper pan, heat it over a moderate flame.Pour a spoonful of batter and tilt pan to form a flare round pan. Cover with a sauce-pan lid, or place a pan with live coals on top of hopper pan. Bake till golden brown and ease out with a hopper spoon.

2. HOPPERS WITH TODDY OR YEAST AND WHITE WHEAT FLOUR

Ingredients for 2-25 *hoppers.*

1 lb. white wheat flour (well roasted and sieved)

---

* *When ever toddy is not available use yeast 2 teaspoons per 1-2 lb. of flour depending on time allowed for fermentation.*

1 teaspoon yeast dissolved in 2 oz. water or 2 dessertspoons toddy.

20-24 oz. coconut milk.

salt

water from coconut.

Method

1. Sieve the flour into a bowl, add salt and toddy or yeast and enough coconut water to make a stiff dough and leave overnight or about 12 hours to rise.
2. Gradually mix in coconut milk and add a pinch of bicarbonate of soda.
3. Use as in recipe No.1
4. Remaining batter may be left in the refrigerator for another day and used after allowing to thaw for an hour or so. Add a pinch of soda and sugar before use.

3. HOPPERS WITH TODDY AND RICE AND WHITE WHEAT FLOUR

Ingredients for *20-25 hoppers*

½ lb. rice flour	½ lb. white wheat flour
extract of 1 large coconut	2 dessertspoons of toddy
1 teaspoon sugar	salt
	coconut water from coconut

Method

1. Sieve the flour into a bowl, add salt and toddy and enough coconut water to make a stiff dough and leave overnight or about 12 hours to rise.

2. Then gradually mix coconut milk and a pinch of bicarbonate of soda, sugar and use as in recipe No.1.

4. HOPPERS WITH YEAST AND WHITE WHEAT FLOUR

Ingredients for 20-25 *hoppers.*

1 lb. flour	1 teaspoon yeast dissolved in
16-24 oz. coconut milk	2 oz. water
salt to taste	a pinch of sugar

Method

1. Sieve the flour into a bowl, add salt, yeast and sugar and mix in enough water to make s stiff dough.
2. Leave to rise for 2 or 3 hours. Then gradually mix in the milk and leave for one hour or more to rise. Add a pinch of bicarbonate of soda and sugar and use as in recipe No.1.

5. HOPPERS WITH YEAST AND RICE FLOUR

Ingredients for 20-25 *hoppers.*

1 lb.of raw rice made into flour

1 large coconut (4 cups milk) 32 oz.

1 teaspoon yeast dissolved in 2 oz. water

salt to taste a pinch of sugar

Method

1. Sieve the flour into a bowl, add salt and a portion of the

coconut milk. Gradually mix till the mixture is quite smooth.

2. Add yeast mixture and the rest of the milk to make the batter. Cover and set aside to rise for about 2 hours. Use as in recipe No.1. If any batter remains keep in refrigerator and use the following day.

6. JAGGERY HOPPERS

Ingredients for 30-40 *hoppers.*

1 ½ lb. flour, (rice or wheat*)	milk of one coconut, 16-20 oz
1/2 teaspoon bicarbonate of soda	1 teaspoon powdered cardamoms
1-3 bundles of Kitul jaggery (scraped) (1-11/2lb)	water from 2 coconuts or 1 teaspoon of yeast dissolved in 2 oz. water
salt to taste	
4 eggs	1/4 cup boiling water

Method

1. Put the flour into a pot and add coconut water or yeast dissolved in water and add boiling water and knead it into a dough. Cover it and let it stand overnight.

2. Next morning, add the coconut milk, the scraped jaggery, the eggs previously beaten up, the cardamom powder, salt and the bicarbonate of soda. The mixture should be rather thick. Keep the batter for sometime to rise.

---

* *When using wheat flour for hoppers, pittu or roti lightly toss in a heated pan to slightly change colour from white to off white or ecru.*

3. Apply oil to a pan and cook as for ordinary hoppers.

Coconuts

Large nut weighs approx. 1 1/2kg give 500-600 gm. scraped.

Medium nut weighs 800- 1kg-scraped 400 gm.

Small nut weighs 500-600 gm - scraped 350 gm.

Very small nut weighs 250-300 gm - scraped 250 gm.

7. HOPPERS WITH COCONUT MILK

Ingredients

Same as any hopper recipe, but have an extra quantity of thick coconut milk to pour into hopper.

Method

1. When batter is ready pour a spoonful of the hopper batter on the heated pan and tilt the pan as in the previous recipes. Pour a dessertspoon of thick coconut milk into centre of the hopper instead of the egg and cook till hopper is done.

8. EGG HOPPERS

Ingredients

Same as any hopper recipe.

1 egg per person

Method

1. When hopper batter is ready, pour a spoonful on the heated pan and tilt the pan as in previous hopper recipes.

2. Immediately break an egg direct into the centre of the tilted hopper. Cook till egg is done.

9. BATU KANDA (THALANABATU)

Ingredients for 1-1 ½ *cups*

1 cup heenati or any raw country rice.

4-6 oz. batu leaves (pounded)

1 cup coconut milk or coconut scraped

salt to taste

1 ½ cups water

Method

1. Wash rice well. Put just enough water to cook rice and place it on fire. Pound and squeeze a handful of leaves, squeeze out the juice. Mix the coconut milk and batu juice together or pound the leaves with scraped coconut and squeeze out the juice. Extract to be 1 ½ - 2 cups.
2. When rice is done add the coconut milk or batu juice mixture. Add salt to taste. Bring to boil to get the coconut milk cooked. Serve hot with or without jaggery.

10. GOTU KOLA KANDA

Ingredients for 2-4 *cups.*

½ lb. rice 1 cup of 1st extract of coconut milk

2 cups of 2nd and 3rd extracts of coconut milk mixed with the gotu kola juice from 4 oz. or 1 bundle gotu kola leaves crushed in a mortar or blender.

2 cups of water

Method

1. Wash rice. Add salt and boil with water.
2. When rice is cooked and "mushy" add 2nd and 3rd extracts of coconut milk, mixed with the gotu kola juice, and the 1st extract of coconut milk. Bring to boil.
3. Serve plain or with jaggery.

11. POL KIRI KANDA

Ingredients for 2-4 *cups*

½ lb. rice,	3 cups 1st extract of coconut milk
3-4 teaspoons mustard	2 cups water.
roasted and powdered	1 cup 2nd and 3rd extracts of
2 teaspoons salt	coconut milk
	3-4 cloves garlic.

Method

1. Wash rice, add 2nd and 3rd extracts of coconut milk, water, salt, garlic and cook until the rice is all mushy.
2. Add 1st extract of coconut milk. Bring to boil and just before serving add roasted, powdered mustard.

12. POL PALA KANDA - 2

Ingredients for 2-4 *cups*

½ lb. rice 1 cup 1st extract of coconut milk

2 cups of 2nd and 3rd extracts of coconut milk mixed with the pol pala juice from 4-6 oz. or 1 bundle pol pala, crushed in a mortar.

2 cups water.

Method

1. Wash rice. Add salt and bring water to boil.
2. When rice is cooked and mushy add 2nd and 3rd extracts of coconut milk, mixed with the pol pala juice and the 1st extract of coconut milk. Bring to boil.
3. Serve plain or with jaggery.

13. KIRI BATH (Milk Rice)

Ingredients for 6-8 *portions*

1 lb. raw rice	milk of 1 large coconut or
3 teaspoons salt	1 small coconut 32-40 oz.
3-4 cardamoms crushed	

Method

1. Wash and drain rice. Add the 2nd and 3rd extracts of coconut milk with salt, crushed cardamoms and allow to cook.
2. When coconut milk level is the same as that of the rice add the 1st extract of coconut milk. Stir well and cook until all the grains are well boiled and the mixture is one thick mass.
3. There should be no gravy left. Spread milk rice on a dish, smoothen the top with a piece of grease-proof paper or plantain leaf. Cut into diamond shaped pieces.

14. IMBUL KIRIBATH

Ingredients for 6-8 *portions.*

1 cup pani pol (see mung guli recipe) or

12-16 1″ pieces of jaggery

1 lb. raw rice (see kiribath recipe)

¼ - ½ cup 1st extract of coconut milk.

Method

1. Add 1-2 teaspoons of 1st extract of coconut milk on to a heated piece of plantain leaf.
2. Add 3-4 dessertspoons of milk rice and flatten out into an oval shape. Place jaggery or pani pol in centre and fold over breadthwise.
3. If this is prepared for a harvesting or transplanting ceremony the milk rice used should be double the quantity as it is used for feeding the farmers.

15. *ROTI PLAIN

Ingredients for 4 *portions.*

8 oz. wheat flour or roasted rice flour

10-12 oz. grated coconut, salt to taste.

Method

1. Mix the flour and coconut together in a bowl. Add the salt, and enough water to make a stiff dough.

**Rotis are always circular in shape ranging from 3″-6″ in diameter and 1/4″-3/4″ in thickness.*

2. Knead it well, spread mixture and cut rounds or make balls and flatten out on slightly greased plantain leaf or grease-proof paper.

3. Bake or cook on roti pan or griddle.

16. ROTI WITH SAMBOL

Ingredients for 4 *portions.*

2 oz. onions chopped | 2-3 green chillies

1 dessertspoon maldive fish or dried prawns

Method

1. Chop the onions and green chillies and add to mixture No.1 after tempering or raw.

2. Prepare roties as in recipe No.1.

17. MEAT OR FISH STUFFED ROTI

Ingredients for 4 *portions.*

2-3 dessertspoons minced meat or flaked boiled fish,

1 oz. onion chopped | 2 green chillies chopped

1 dessertspoon oil | pepper and salt to taste

1 portion plain roti mixture

Method

1. Temper chopped onions and green chillies in oil, add fish or minced beef and season.

2. Flatten out roti mixture on a grease paper then cut a round. Spread 2-3 dessertspoons fish or meat mixture,

place on it another round of roti mixture, flattened out on grease proof paper. Roll and press well.

3. Bake at 350^0 F. Glaze with egg and milk mixture when half done or cook on roti pan till half done before putting into oven.

18. PITTU WITH RAW RICE FLOUR*

Ingredients for 8 *portions.*

1 lb. rice flour	1 lb. scraped coconut 16-20 oz.
salt	water to mix,

2 oz. 1st extract of coconut milk.

Method

1. Put the flour, coconut and salt into a pan and mix so that the flour forms into little grains. If necessary add water while the grains are being formed.
2. Place in pittu bamboo or other pittu mould loosely.
3. Steam, pour 1st extract of coconut milk while still hot.
4. Unmould, cut into pieces.

19. PITTU WITH ROASTED WHITE WHEAT FLOUR

Ingredients for 4 *portions.*

4 oz. well roasted flour	2 oz. 1st extract of coconut milk
4 oz. grated coconut	
salt	water to mix

* *If you wish to reduce the intake of coconut in pittu, extract milk from the coconut first, then mix with flour. Use milk to pour over prepared pittu.*

Method

1. Put the flour, coconut and salt into a pan and mix so that the flour forms into little grains. If necessary add water while the grains are being formed.
2. Fill mixture into a pittu bamboo and steam till done.
3. Push the pittu through using a stick.
4. Pour 1st extract of coconut milk while still hot.

20. MANI PITTU

Ingredients for 4 *portions*

1 plain string-hopper mixture, (raw rice flour)

thick coconut milk

extra roasted flour

Method

1. Put some flour on a sieve and press string-hopper mixture on to sieve, through a murukku mould. Sprinkle more flour and shake the sieve till all the pieces are coated and separated and excess flour is removed.
2. Leave a pittu bamboo on a pot of boiling water. Put the pieces inside the bamboo and steam well. When done push the pittu through using a stick, on to plate. Carefully moisten with 1st extract of coconut milk.

21. SAVOURY PITTU

Ingredients for 8 *portions.*

2 oz, onions	2 oz. carrots
2 oz. leeks	2 dessertspoons (cook's joy oil)
2 oz. cabbage	1 lb. prepared steamed pittu mixture
2 oz. prawns	salt to taste

Method

1. Cut the vegetables finely. Break up the pittu free from lumps.
2. Heat the oil in a pan and fry the onions, then add the vegetables, prawn and fry for a few minutes.
3. Add the pittu and salt to taste.

22. KURAKKAN PITTU

Ingredients for 8 *portions*

½ lb. rice flour	½ lb. kurakkan flour
coconut scraped	salt

Method

1. Mix the two kinds of flour and the coconut and salt and make pittu mixture. Steam as for other pittu recipes.
2. This can be served with salted coconut milk, scraped coconut and jaggery.

23. STRING-HOPPERS WITH RICE FLOUR

Ingredients for 8 *portions*

1 lb. rice flour
boiling water
salt to taste

Method

1. Roast the flour well and sieve it into a bowl. Add enough boiling water to make a soft but not sticky consistency.
2. Fill string-hopper mould with dough and squeeze on to very lightly greased string-hopper mats or watties.
3. Steam until beads of water begin to drop from sides of string-hopper cover.
4. Remove from mats. Continue until mixture is used up.

24. STRING-HOPPERS WITH MILLED RAW RICE FLOUR

Ingredients for 8 *portions.*

1 lb. rice flour
boiling water
salt to taste

Method

1. Sieve flour into a bowl, add salt and mix enough boiling water to make a soft mixture.
2. Squeeze through mould on to string-hopper mats and steam. If flour is not sufficiently roasted, roast well before use for a few minutes in a heated pan.

25. STRING-HOPPERS WITH STEAMED FLOUR

Ingredients for 8 *portions*

1 lb. white wheat flour

boiling water

salt to taste

Method

1. Sieve and steam flour well for about 1 hour.
2. Sieve again while it is hot, into a bowl add salt.
3. Pour the boiling water into a bowl and allow the steam to pass off and add enough water to flour, to make a soft but not too sticky a mixture.
4. Squeeze through mould on to string-hopper mats, and steam.

26. STRING-HOPPERS WITH ROASTED WHITE WHEAT FLOUR

Ingredients for 8 *portions.*

½ lb. roasted flour

14 oz. coconut milk, heated

salt to taste

Method

1. Roast the flour well and sieve it into a bowl. Add enough coconut milk and salt to taste to make a soft but not sticky consistency.
2. Squeeze through a mould on to mats, and steam.

27. STRING-HOPPERS WITH KURAKKAN FLOUR

Ingredients for 8 *portions.*

1 lb. well sieved kurakkan flour

1 lb. steamed rice flour

boiling water

salt

Method

1. Mix the flour and kurakkan flour together, add salt and mix with boiling water to form dough.
2. Squeeze through string-hopper mould on to mats, and steam.

28. QUICK METHOD OF MAKING THOSAI

Ingredients for 8 *portions.*

8 oz. undu flour

1 ½ teaspoons yeast

water from 1 ½ coconuts

8 oz. white wheat flour

1 teaspoon sugar

1-1 ½ cups 1st extract of coconut milk

Method

1. Soak yeast in coconut water with sugar and allow to ferment 5 minutes
2. Mix undu flour and white wheat flour with yeast mixture. When double in size add sufficient 1st extract of coconut milk to be of a pouring consistency.
3. Add the following mixture fried well. 1 sprig curry leaves, 3-4 dry chillies, broken up or green chillie finely

chopped, ½ teaspoon fenugreek and ½ teaspoon mustard (optional), 10-15 red onions or 1 medium Bombay onion chopped. Fry until golden brown in 2-3 tablespoons oil and add to batter.

4. Heat thosai pan, smear with a little oil as for pancakes. Pour 1/3 cup of batter. Spread out to form a thin pancake. When little holes appear on thosai, turn over the other side and cook for a minute or two.

29. THOSAI - 2

Ingredients for 8 *portions*

6 oz. undu	15 oz. parboiled rice
20 oz. water	

Method

1. Soak undu, and parboiled rice separately. Grind both on the thosai grinding stone finely, grinding undu first.
2. Add the salt and mix in the water. Gradually make a thick batter. Leave to rise overnight.
3. Follow steps 3 and 4 as in recipe No.28.

30. THOSAI - 3

Ingredients for 8 *portions*

½ lb. undu	½ lb. raw rice
¼ lb. parboiled rice	¼ teaspoon fenugreek
salt to taste	a pinch of turmeric powder
curry leaves	1 oz. sliced onions

a piece of rampe
a few dried or ripe chillies
1 teaspoon cummin seed gingelly oil or cook's joy

Method

1. Soak separately previous morning undu, raw rice, parboiled rice, and uluhal and grind in the evening (to be used the following morning).
2. Mix all soaked and ground ingredients together and make into a thick batter. Add salt to taste and turmeric powder.
3. Heat oil, and fry onions, curry leaves, rampe, red chillies or ripe chillies and cummin seeds.
4. Add the fried ingredients to the batter.
5. Follow step 4 as stated in recipe No.28.

31. THOSAI - 4

Ingredients for 4 *portions.*

4 oz. flour (undu)
2 oz. rice flour
1 teaspoon salt
16-24 oz. water
2-4 oz. parboiled rice flour
1 teaspoon yeast dissolved in 2 oz. water
keep for 5-10 miunutes

Method

1. Sieve the flour into a bowl, add the risen yeast andsalt.
2. Add the water gradually to make a thick batter, leave to rise for about 2 hours.
3. Follow steps 3 and 4 as stated in recipe No.28.

32. THOSAI - IDDILI - 5

Ingredients for 8 *portions.*

Method

1. Pour 2 dessertspoons of any thosai mixture into each iddili pan and steam instead of cooking or griddle.

RICE PREPARATIONS

33. BURIYANI -CHICKEN OR MUTTON - 1

Ingredients for 8 *portions.*

1 ½ lb. rice	1 lb. mutton or chicken
1 ½ teaspoons salt	4 oz. red or Bombay onions
3 oz. curd	4-6 cloves garlic
16-24 oz. water	1″ piece green ginger
3 teaspoons cummin seeds	6-8 cardamoms
8 cloves	3-4 oz. oil
2″ piece cinnamon	1 teaspoon kum kum dissolved in 1 oz. water

Method

1. Wash and soak rice for about 15 minutes. Cut meat into 1-1 ½ cubes and soak in curd for about 20 minutes.

2. Slice onions and grind all the ingredients except the cloves, cardamoms and cinnamon.

3. Heat oil and add the sliced onions and fry until golden brown. Add the meat and the rest of the spices and fry until the meat is brown. Add the rice well drained. Fry for just a short time add the water and cook until almost done.

4. When the rice is three fourths cooked add the kum kum into the centre of the rice and continue cooking till done on a very low fire.

34. BURIYANI - CHICKEN - 2

Ingredients for 8 *portions.*

2 ½ lb. chihcken to be cut into 8 or 16 pieces
3 dessertspoons curd
3-4 cloves garlic, 2 slices ginger, 5-8 cardamoms } finely ground
2 oz. red onions sliced
2″ rampe
2" cinnamon
1 teaspoon curry powder
¾ teaspoon salt per lb. of meat
3 dessertspoons ghee or refined oil
¼ lb. Bombay onions chopped
a sprig of curry leaves
6-8 crushed cardamoms
2 cloves
½ cup tomato blanched and chopped
¼ cup water (if necessary)

Method

1. Cut and wash chicken, drain well, mix with all ground ingredients, curry powder, curd, salt and set aside for 15-20 minutes,

2. Heat oil, add curry leaves, chopped onions, cardamoms, cloves and fry until onions are light golden brown.

3. Add chicken with the ingredients. Fry for a few minutes. Add blanched chopped tomatoes and water if necessary. Cook in a covered vessel, bring to boil, and simmer until chicken is tender.

Rice

Ingredients

2 lb. rice	4 oz. ghee oil	
1 cup of sliced red or Bombay onions	10-15 cardamoms	may be crushed and tied up loosely in a bundle
	2″ cinnamon	
a spring of curry leaves	¼ teaspoon Spanish saffron or	
2″ rampe	1 teaspoon kum kum dissolved in	
1″ sera	1 oz. water	

Method

1. Wash rice and steam if necessary. Heat ghee until very hot, add sliced onions, curry leaves, rampe, sera and fry until light golden brown. Add washed rice. Fry for 5-6 minutes.
2. Add water 8 cups or 5-6 cups if rice is steamed. Add spice bundle and cook until rice is almost done. Add the prepared chicken to the rice, mix a pinch of Spanish saffron or kum kum with water. Mix part of this until a part of the rice is coloured.
3. Seal pan with a thick flour dough and place on coals or place in the oven for about 30-45 minutes.
4. Garnish with hard boiled eggs and peas.

Flour-water paste

½ cup flour ½ cup water

Mix until very stiff add a little more water if necessary and use this to seal the pan.

Garnish

Hard boiled eggs.

Should be at the rate of 1 or ½ egg per portion.

35. BURIYANI - PRAWN - 3

Ingredients for 8 *portions.*

1 lb. prawns
3 dessertspoons curd
3 teaspoons chillie powder
¼ teaspoon turmeric
1 ½ teaspoons curry powder
3-4 cloves garlic
2 slices ginger
10-12 cadjunuts
2 dessertspoons oil
3 large Bombay onions chopped
6 red onions chopped
a sprig curry leaves
2 pieces rampe
10 cardamoms
2" piece cinnamon
3 small tomatoes
1 teaspoon salt

Method

1. Soak the prawns in the curd for 10 minutes with chillie powder, turmeric, curry powder, salt and the garlic,ginger and cadjunuts ground.

2. Heat oil in a pan and fry onions, curry leaves and spices. When the onions are brown add the prawn mixture and the tomato cut into small pieces. Cook until lightly fried and set aside.

Rice-Ingredients

1 lb. rice	1 sprig curry leaves
4 dessertspoons oil	2″ cinnamon
4 oz. red onions sliced	5 cloves
5 cardamoms	2″ piece rampe

Method

1. Heat the oil in a pan. Add the onions, curry leaves and spices and fry until onions are light brown.
2. Add the rice well washed and drained. Cook for a few minutes. Add the water at the rate of 2 cups water for 1 lb. of rice, depending on the type of rice used.
3. When rice is half cooked. add the prawns. Seal the edges of the pan with a flour water paste and bake in over at 300^{0} F for 30-45 minutes. Garnish with fried prawns.

36. BURIYANI- LOBSTER - 4

Ingredients for 8 *portions.*

3 large lobsters boiled	3 sprigs curry leaves
(1 ½ - 2 lb.)	4 cardamoms
½ lb. tomatoes	1 bundle coriander leaves
2 teaspoons coriander powder	4 cloves
2″ cinnamon	½ juice of lime
2 oz. ghee	8 oz. curd
6-8 cloves garlic ground	2 teaspoons chillie powder
2 oz. onions chopped	2 teaspoons salt

Method

1. Shell lobster, cut meat into 1 ½ pieces. Soak in curd with powdered ingredients.
2. Heat fat. Add onions spices and fry until onions are golden brown.
3. Add lobster and all other ingredients and simmer until gravy is thick.

Rice

1 ½ lb. rice	4 oz. onions sliced
2″ cinnamon	4-5 pints light chicken
4″ rampe	stock or lobster stock
2 sprigs curry leaves	6-10 cardamoms
4 cloves	3 oz. ghee

Method

1. Wash and drain rice.
2. Heat fat, fry sliced onions until golden brown and remove from fat.
3. Add balance ingredients except stock and cook for 5-7 minutes.
4. Add sufficient stock and cook until rice is almost done, but with very little water left.
5. Cover lobster meat with partially cooked rice, mixed with ½ fried onions. Slow cook until rice is fluffy and grainy.
6. Serve rice from top and pile lobster mixture in centre. Sprinkle balance onions on rice.

37. DHAL RICE - 1

Ingredients for 8 *portions.*

1 lb. rice	1 lb. dhal
4 oz. chopped onions	a sprig of curry leaves
1 dessertspoon ghee or fat	1-2 chillie
2 dessertspoons salt	2-4 cardamoms

Method

1. Soak the dhal for about 20 minutes, after washing. Clean and wash rice.
2. Heat fat and fry all ingredients except the rice and dhal. When onions are slightly brown add the rice and fry for a few minutes.
3. Add water and bring rice to boil.
4. When the water level of the rice is just below that of the rice, add the dhal and stir and cook until done.
5. Garnish and serve hot. If mixed dhal is used it may be tempered with the rice at the start.

38. DHAL - RICE -2

Ingredients for 8 *portions.*

1 lb. rice	4 oz. mysore dhal
3 teaspoons salt	4 oz. gram dhal
2 oz. onions chopped	3 oz. mochcha cochcha
2 sprigs curry leaves	(large yellow seeds)
6 dry chillies broken	2 oz. moong
into bits	2 cloves

2 cardamoms

1″ cinnamon

3 oz. oil.

rampe

Method

1. Wash and soak dhal and rice separately for 10-15minutes.
2. Heat oil. Add curry leaves, onions, dry chillies, fry until light golden brown.
3. Add all the dhals, fry for a few minutes. Add rice and cook for a further 3-4 minutes.
4. Add salt. Add 10 cups water and more if necessary.
5. Cook until dhal is cooked and rice grainy.

Accompaniments

Paneer curry

Malay pickle

Tempered potatoes

Vegetable cutlets

Papadam

39. DHAL RICE - 3

Ingredients for 8 *portions.*

1 lb. rice

4 oz. onion chopped

a sprig of curry leaves

1-2 dry chillies

2-4 cardamoms

1 ½ chundus mixed dhal or only one type

1 oz. ghee or oil

3 dessertspoons salt

Method

1. Soak the dhal for about 20 minutes, after washing. Clean and wash rice.

2. Heat oil and fry all ingredients except the rice and dhal. When onions are slightly brown add the rice and fry for just a few minutes.

3. Add water and bring rice to boil. When water level of the rice is just below that of the rice add the dhal and stir and cook until done.

4. Garnish and serve hot. If mixed dhal is used they may be tempered with the rice at the start.

40. EGG RICE - 1

Ingredients for 8 *portions.*

No.1	**No.2**
1 ½ lb. rice	4 eggs made into omelettes and shredded fine
3 oz. ghee	
4 oz. chopped onions	4 eggs beaten up raw
3-3 ¾ pints stock	2 oz. cadjunuts
8 cloves, cardamoms	1 oz. fat
10 pepper corns	2 oz. chopped onions
2 cinnamon bruised well and tied in a bundle	2 oz. sultanas

Method

1. Heat oil. Fry onions, curry leaves until golden brown.

2. Add rice, spices and stock and cook until grainy.

3. Heat fat in list No. 2. Add chopped onions, sultanas fry until onions are light golden brown. Add cadjunuts fry till light brown.

4. Stir in beaten eggs off the fire.

5. Add the rice and shredded omelette and mix well.

41. EGG RICE - 2

Ingredients for 8 *portions*

2 lb. rice	6 eggs
3 oz. ghee	3 oz. onions sliced
cloves, cardamoms	3 ¾ pints stock or water
cinnamon, curry leaves	2 oz. cadjunuts
Rampe, sera	2 oz, sultanas

Method

1. Cook rice in stock until grainy.

2. Heat oil, add sliced onions, curry leaves, and all the other ingredients except egg.

3. Take off the fire. Add the beaten eggs into the onion mixture stir for a minute or two, toss in the rice.

42. EGG FRIED RICE - 3

Ingredients for 8 portions.

3 chundus well cooked	6 dessertspoons soya beansauce
grainy rice	4-6 oz. each of finely shredded

5-6 teaspoons salt
thin omelettes made with 6-8 eggs (shredded)
6-7 dessertspoons cook's joy.
lecks, carrots
cabbage, celery, onion, sprouted
moong gram if available

Methods

1. Cook rice until fluffy and grainy.
2. Heat oil until almost smoking. Add vegetable, cook for a few minutes.
3. Add rice and soy bean sauce.
4. Mix well. Mix in half finely shredded omelette and garnish with the other half.

43. FRIED RICE SPECIAL - 1

Ingredients for 8 *portions.*

1 ½ lb. well boiled grainy rice
2-4 oz. chopped bacon
4 oz. boiled shredded chicken
2 eggs
4 oz. boiled chopped prawn or crab
4 oz. each, finely shredded cabbage, leeks, celery stalks, carrots, Bombay onion and tomatoes
3 dessertspoons tomato sauce (optional)
2 dessertspoons soya bean sauce
6 dessertspoons cook's joy
salt and pepper

Method

1. Beat the eggs, add salt and pepper and prepare very thin omelettes, shred, set aside.
2. Heat pan with 1 dessertspoon oil, add bacon and when bacon is fried add all the other meats and fry for a few minutes. Set aside.
3. Add soya bean sauce and tomato sauce to the rice and mix well. Season with pepper and salt.
4. Heat pan and add 5 dessertspoons of cook's joy. When the oil is smoking hot add shredded vegetables and fry for 1 or 2 minutes. Add meats and rice. Toss well and take off. Add half the shredded omelette and garnish with the other half.

44. FRIED RICE SPECIAL - 2

Ingredients for 8 *portions*

1 ½ lb. rice	3 oz. coarsely shredded carrot
3 oz. onions sliced	3 teaspoons salt
2 oz. finely shredded leeks	2 oz. finely shredded cabbage
4 oz. boiled flaked chicken	2 oz. Sultanas
4 oz. boiled chopped Prawns	2 oz. oil
2 oz. Cadjunuts, deep fried	2 oz. coarsely powdered chillie with seeds
3 3/4 -4 Pints stock or water	

Method

1. Wash rice. Heat half oil, add half onions and fry until light brown.

2. Add rice, salt and cook for a few minutes.

3. Add stock or water and cook until rice is fluffy and grainy.

4. Heat balance oil. add prawns, chicken, sultanas and chillies and toss for a few minutes. Add vegetables toss for a few minutes. Add rice, Mix well. Mix in fried cadjunuts.

45. FRIED PRAWN RICE

Ingredients for 8 *portions.*

1 ½ lb. rice
4 oz. each of finely
shredded cabbage, carrots
leeks, (green portion)
celery

1 ½ lb. prawns boiled
3 dessertspoons soya bean sauce
2 dessertspoons soya bean paste
1 oz. oil
2 oz, oil
3 teaspoons salt.

Method

1. Cook rice until fluffy and grainy, with salt.

2. Heat 1 oz. oil. Add shelled and deveined prawns.Mix in soya bean paste. Cook for a few minutes. Add the cooked rice.

3. Heat 2 oz. oil until almost smoking. Add vegetables,cook for a minute or two. Add to rice with soya bean sauce.

4. Mix well before serving.

46. FRIED VEGETABLE RICE - 1

Ingredients for 8 *portions.*

1 ½ lb. rice	2 oz. each of shredded
3-4 cardamoms and cloves	carrots, leeks, cabbage
½″ cinnamon	onions, peas if available
a sprig of curry leave	and tomatoes
or celery	2 ½ teaspoons salt
vegetable stock or water	2 oz. oil.

Method

1. Heat oil and add onions and brown slightly. Add rice and lastly the vegetables and fry for a short time .
2. Add the rest of th spices and cook for a minute or two. Add stock or water and bring to boil. Cook over a slow fire once it has reached boiling point.
3. Garnish with fried shoe string patato.

47. FRIED VEGETABLE RICE - 2

Ingredients for 8 *portions.*

1 ½ lb, rice	½ lb, butter beans, broken
¼ lb. capsicum ripe chillies	into 1″ pieces
¼ lb. peas	¼ lb. onions coarsely chopped
¼ lb. white part of leeks	¼ lb. carrots grated
cut into 1″ lengths	3 oz. oil
2 ½- 3 pints vegetable stock	2 ½ teaspoons salt
2 sprigs curry leaves	4 cardamoms crushed
1″ piece cinnamon	

Method

1. Heat oil add vegetable and cook, do not brown. Drain and set aside.
2. Add curry leaves, spices and brown. Add rice cook 4-5 minutes.
3. Add stock, salt and cook until water level of rice is less than half of rice.
4. Add vegetables, cook on low heat until rice is grainy and well done. Garnish with fried sultanas and nuts.

48. GHEE RICE - 1

Ingredients for 8 *portions*

2 lb rice
4 oz. good ghee
20 pepper corns
2 pieces rampe
2 sprigs of curry leaves
3-3 ¾ pints meat stock or water
2 oz. chopped Bombay or red onions
4 teaspoons salt

Method

1. Heat fat and fry the onions till light golden brown in colour.
2. Add the rice and the spices. Toss for a few minutes.
3. Add the meat stock and bring to boil and cook on very high heat for 5-7 minutes.Then reduce heat lower until the rice is done.

49. GHEE RICE - 2

Ingredients for 8 *portions.*

1 ½ lb. rice
3-3 ¾ pints stock
2 sprigs curry leaves
½ lb. sultanas
¼ lb. broken cadjunuts

4 oz. ghee
4 oz. onions, chopped
8 cloves, 8 cardamoms
10 pepper corns, 2" cinnamon
bruised well and tied
in a bundle.

Method

1. Heat 2 oz. fat, fry onions until light golden brown with curry leaves.
2. Add rice, toss for a few minutes.
3. Add stock, spice, bring to boil. Reduce heat, cook until rice is light and fluffy.
4. Heat balance 2 oz. of fat. Add cadjunuts and sultanas.Fry until nuts are crisp and sultanas are puffed.
5. Add rice and stir well.

50. ITALIAN RICE - 1

Ingredients for 8 *portions.*

1 lb. rice
2 oz. salad oil or
other fat
16-24 oz. water
6 oz. grated cheese

1 ½ teaspoons salt
2 cups tomato juice
¼ lb. minced meat
4 oz. chopped onions
1 clove garlic finely cut
¼ teaspoon pepper

Method

1. Heat oil and brown rice for about 10 minutes. Then add meat, onions, garlic, salt, pepper and cook for about 10 minutes. Stir frequently.
2. Add tomato juice and water, simmer on low heat for about 20 minutes or until rice is tender. Add more water if required.
3. Just before serving add grated cheese and stir over low heat until just melting.Garnish with hard boiled egg and peas.

51. ITALIAN RICE - 2

Ingredients for 8 *portions.*

1 ½ lb. rice	16 oz. tomato purce
16-24 oz. stock or water	8 oz. tomato paste
2 oz. salad oil	4 cloves garlic chopped
2 capsicum chillies chopped	1 lb. spiced sausages cut into 1 - 1 ½ lengths
2 teaspoons salt	

Method

1. Wash and drain rice. Heat oil. Add garlic, sausages and fry for a few minutes.
2. Add rice and chillies. Cook for a further 5 minutes.
3. Add tomato paste, purce, water, salt and stock.
4. Cook. Bring to boil, reduce heat and cook until light and fluffy. Garnish with hard boiled eggs, deep fried potatoes.

52. MEXICAN RICE

Ingredients for 8 *portions.*

1 ½ lb. rice
½ lb bacon
¼ lb. sliced onions
32 oz. tomato juice
2 teaspoons salt
2 oz. oil
1 ¾ - 2 pints water

Method

1. Fry bacon in a pan and add the rice washed and drained and cook until rice starts to colour slightly.
2. Add onions and cook for about 10 minutes.
3. Add tomato juice and stock and cook until soft and grainy.
4. Serve with peas, chopped hard boiled eggs and slices of bacon fried.

53. NASIGORENG

Ingredients for 8 *portions.*

1 lb. rice
1-2 dessertspoons dry chillies
1 ½ -2 pints water
¾ cup peanuts or cadjunuts broken up
2 teaspoons salt
½ - ¾ lb. boiled seasoned meat cut into small cubes
4 oz. margarine or cook's joy
½ lb. boiled prawns

Method

1. Cook rice with salt and water but make sure that it is grainy.

2. Chop the onions and clean and break the nuts into big pieces. Chop the prawns.

3. Heat oil and when hot add the onions, chillie and peanuts. Fry for about 8-10 minutes. Add the cooked meat and prawns. Toss for a few minutes, add the rice and prawns. Toss for a few minutes, add the rice and cook so that all the ingredients are well mixed. Set aside for about 10 minutes before use. Add more salt if necessary.

54. SPANISH RICE - 1

Ingredients for 8 portions

1 lb. rice
4 oz. chopped onions
a pinch of Spanish saffron
pepper
1 teaspoon salt
4 slices bacon and ham
2-4 oz. cooked peas
3 dessertspoons bacon fat
salad oil
4 oz. chopped capsicum
chillies
16 oz. tomato juice (or a mixture of it and water)
1 clove garlic finely chopped

Method

1. Wash and dry rice.

2. Chop bacon and fry. Add bacon fat heated and then the chopped onions, garlic and chillie.

3. Next add the rice and cook for about 10 minutes.

4. Season with pepper and salt and add tomato juice and cook until soft and tender but grainy.

5. Just before serving add the peas. (saffron threads may be added with the tomato juice).

55. SPANISH RICE - 2

Ingredients for 8 *portions*

1 lb. rice	2 lb. chicken (or 1 lb. meat)
4 slices bacon	2-4 oz. oil
24-32 oz. tomato juice	4 oz. chopped onions
	3 oz. cooked peas
2 oz. chopped capsicum chillies	1 teaspoon salt

Method

1. Heat oil and fry chicken cut into pieces or meat cubed 2″, until tender on low fire.
2. Then remove, add bacon slices, chopped onions, chillies and fry till onions are light golden brown. Remove.
3. Add rice washed and drained and fry for about 10 minutes.
4. Add tomato juice, fried onions and chillies and cook until rice is grainy.
5. Just 10 minutes before removing from the fire stir in the fried chicken or meat and peas.

56. SPANISH RICE SPECIAL - 3

Ingredients for 8 *portions.*

½ lb. rice

½ a small chicken (weight to be under 2 ½ lb.) meat to be cut up into small pieces.

½ lb. prawns, small size shelled.

meat of one small lobster boiled and cut into small pieces.

1 chicken liver cut up or 2 oz. liver cut

¼ lb. of red capsicum chillies cut into cubes.

2 onions chopped, 4 cloves of garlic chopped

½ lb. peas, 4 oz. olive oil, 1 ¾ - 2 pints chicken stock

1 tomato chopped

a pinch of Spanish saffron

1 teaspoon salt

Method

1. Heat oil, add chicken and allow to sauté until meat is half done.

2. Add the garlic, onions, liver, lobster, prawns and cook for a few minutes. Add rice and cook until most of the oil is absorbed.

3. Add chillies. Add stock with saffron threads, salt and bring to boil.

4. Arrange prawns, chillies, etc. on top and add the fresh peas and bake in an oven after removing contents into a casserole dish. If deep frying pan is used the pan may be put into the oven. Add more stock if necessary.

5. Serve in the dish in which it has been baked.

57. SULTANA RICE

Ingredients for 8 *portions.*

1 ½ lb. rice	1 lb. sultanas
3 teaspoons salt	4 hard boiled eggs
6 cardamoms powdered	4 cloves
2″ cinnamon	2″ rampe

2 sprigs curry leaves	2 oz. onions chopped
2 oz. oil	2 oz. onions sliced
1 oz. oil	3 ¼ - 4 pints stock
1″ sera	

Method

1. Heat 1 oz. oil. Add chopped onions, curry leaves, rampe, sera and fry until onions are golden brown.
2. Add rice and ½ sultanas. Fry for a few minutes.
3. Add stock, salt and powdered cardamoms. Cook until rice is fluffy and grainy.
4. Heat 2 oz. oil, add sliced onions and fry until light golden brown. Add balance sultanas and fry until slightly puffed out.
5. Add rice, stir well. Mix in chopped hard boiled eggs.
6. Garnish with parsely, potato chips or pappadam, fried in thin strips.

Accompaniments for Sultana Rice

Prawn Pickle

Khorma Curry

Chutney

Brinjal Potato Curry

Fricadells

58. TURKISH RICE

Ingredients for 8 *portions*

1 lb. rice	1 dessertspoon salt

1 lb. mutton	¼ teaspoon pepper
¼ lb. bacon	1 tin peas
3 Bombay onions	1 ¼ - 1 ¾ pints stock
2 cloves garlic finely chopped	3-4 dessertspoons oil

Method

1. Wash and allow rice to dry. Cut meat into cubes.
2. Fry bacan, and remove. Add oil if necessary. Then add meat and fry, remove and add onion and brown, and lastly the rice.
3. Arrange the meat, then bacon, then onions and rice and pour the stock heated over this and cover well and cook until soft or arrange in a baking dish. Bake at 300^{0} F for about 1 hour until soft and cooked. Tomato juice may be added with part of stock.

59. YELLOW RICE -1

Ingredients for 8 *portions.*

2 lb. rice	4 oz. Bombay or red onions chopped
2 dessertspoons oil	
1″ rampe	1 teaspoon salt
	a sprig of curry leaves
6 cardamoms	20 pepper corns bruised
5 cloves	11/2 - 1 oz. maldive fish(if desired)
4 cloves garlic	½ - ¾ teaspoon turmeric

3 - 3 ¾ 1st and 2nd extracts of coconut milk or stock.

Spice Bundle

6 cardamoms	1″ cinnamon
3 cloves	10-15 pepper corns bruised

Method - 1

1. Heat oil, fry onions until light brown. Add spices and maldive fish. Add rice, fry for a few minutes. Add coconut milk and turmeric and bring to boil on very high heat, for 5-7 minutes and reduce heat to a very low fire until rice is done. If spice is used in a bundle add bundle with the coconut milk and omit spices at the start.

Method - 2

1. Heat the oil, fry onions with the garlic and curry leaves. When onions are brown add the coconut milk and bring to boil. Add rice and boil for a few minutes. Reduce heat and cook until done.
2. Garnish with hard boiled eggs and parsley or deep fried kathurumurunga leaves.

60. YELLOW RICE - 2

Ingredients for 8 *portions*

1 ½ lb. rice	3 ¾ pints stock
2 oz. coconut ground into a fine paste	
2 sprigs curry leaves	2 oz. chopped onions
2 oz. ghee	

Spice Bundle

6 cardamoms

1″ cinnamon

3 cloves

10-15 pepper corns bruised

Method

1. Wash rice. Set aside. Heat oil and curry leaves and fry until light golden brown.
2. Add rice fry for a few seconds. Add turmeric to give a very light colour..
3. Add stock, mixed with finely ground coconut. Add salt and cook until rice is fluffy and grainy. Increase turmeric if necessary to get the desired yellow colour.

N.B. These rice recipes are all not typically Sri Lankan, but they are popularly used.

FISH PREPARATIONS

61. AMBUL THIAL - 1

Ingredients for 8 *portions.*

1 lb. tuna or any blood fish
6-8 pieces goraka
6-8 cloves
a thin slice ginger
3 teaspoons salt
1 teaspoon pepper powder
2 dessertspoons chillie powder
4-5 cloves garlic
a sprig of curry leaves
½ pint water

Method

1. Cut the fish into 8 pieces and wash well using lime and put into a pan which will take a single layer of fish.
2. Soak the goraka for ½ hour or boil in water and grind fine. Mix the chillie powder, pepper salt into a paste with a little water.
3 Mix this well into the fish, add the rest of the ingredients and ½ pint water and bring to boil, simmer until al of the gravy has disappeared and the pieces are quite dry.

62. AMBUL THIAL - 2

1 lb. tuna fish
6 pieces goraka ground fine
½ dessertspoon pepper powder
2 sprigs curry leaves

2 dessertspoons chillie powder ½ teaspoon cummin powder ½ teaspoon sweet cummin powder 1 teaspoon coriander powder	Roasted to a dark colour without burning
2 teaspoon fenugreek	
8 cloves garlic chopped fine	9-10 red onion chopped
1 slice ginger ground	1 clove
1 cardamom	1″ cinnamon
3 teaspoon salt	8-10 oz. water

Method

1. Cut and wash fish
2. Mix all ingredients with fish. Add water.
3. Bring to boil and simmer until gravy is dry.

63. AMBUL THIAL - 3

Ingredients for 8 *portions.*

1 lb. tuna or any fish	(finely ground goraka size of 2 limes) (finely ground pepper the size of 1 lime)	increase or decrease according to taste.

Method

1 Wash fish after cutting into convenient pieces, using lime juice or goraka. Drain out water.

2. Mix the ground goraka, pepper and salt well into the pieces of fish taking care to keep the pieces intact.

3. Arrange pieces of fish neatly in a pan that will take a single layer of fish. Set pan with fish on a low heat and place another chatty filled with burning char-coal on top and cook till fish is slightly done. Shake the pot to prevent burning at the bottom.

4. Put out the fire, almost completely, at the bottom but retain burning char-coal chatty on top and cook the fish till dry.

5. Use a dry spoon to serve. This may be kept for a week.

64. AMBUL THIAL - 4

Ingredients for 8 *portions.*

1 lb. fish
roasted and ground cummin sweet cummin, coriander about the size of a lime
3-4 red onions chopped
1″ piece of rampe
3 dessertspoons coconut oil
roasted and ground dry red, chillies about the size of a lime
3-2 cloves garlic chopped
a sprig of curry leaves
salt
a pinch of turmeric
5-6 pieces goraka

Method

1. Wash and cut fish into convenient sizes, using lime juice and goraka wash fish. Do not damage the fish. Drain water. Mix with ground chillie and curry stuffs

2. Take a dry chatty. Put some oil and turn the chatty to get the bottom well coated with oil. Then arrange the fish. Put a little water, mix the remaining ingredients except the oil Pour it over the fish. Sprinkle the remaining oil and cook as in variation - 3.

65. AMBUL THIAL - 5

Ingredients for 8 *portions.*

1 lb. fish
2 oz. olive oil or corn oil
5-6 pieces goraka
juice of 1 lime
salt

Method

1. Wash and cut fish into convenient sizes. Then wash fish with lime juice. Do not damage fish.
2. Cut the goraka into very fine pieces. Powder the salt or use table salt.
3. Take a dry chatty and rub 1 oz, of olive, sprinkle some of the cut goraka over it and then sprinkle salt over it.
4. Arrange a few slices of fish. Proceed as before until the remaining fish has been arranged. Sprinkle the remaining 1 oz. of olive oil over the arranged layer and cook as in recipe 3.

66. FISH BOLLE CURRY

Ingredients for 8 *portions.*

1 lb. minced raw fish (1 ¼ lbs. with bones and skins etc.)
a sprig of curry leaves
½ oz. green chillies
½ oz. garlic
¼ oz. ginger
1 teaspoon salt
2 oz. finely chopped onions

Method

1. Cut the fish into small pieces, wash and dry well and pass through mincer together with the green chillies, and curry

leaves. Chop garlic ginger and onions very fine.

2. Make 16 balls with the minced fish. Put into the centre of each ball a pinch of chopped garlic ginger and press well together till smooth and free of cracks.

3. Add to boiling gravy.

Gravy

1. Boil skin, bones to obtain stock (12 oz.) strain

2. To stock add 3 teaspoons coriander powder, 2 teaspoons fenugreek, 4 cloves garlic chopped, 1 onion ground, 2-3 red chillies chopped, 2 cloves, 2 cardamoms, 2 oz. 1st extract of coconut milk. 2 sprigs curry leaves. Cook until onions and garlic are done.Add fish balls and simmer for 10 minutes.

67. CUTTLE FISH - 1

Ingredients for 8 *portions.*

1 lb. cuttle fish small size 2 ½″-3″

1 oz. onions chopped

3 teaspoons chillie powder

1 teaspoon sweet cummin powder

2 teaspoons fenugreek

4 cloves garlic

2 cardamoms

16 oz. 2nd and 3rd extracts of coconut milk

1 piece goraka

3 teaspoons coriander powder

2 teaspoons cummin powder

2 green chillies

2 sprigs curry leaves

1 clove

4 oz. 1st extract of coconut milk

salt

Filling

¼ lb. Green gram roasted and broken into bits (not powdered)

1 teaspoon coriander

1 teaspoon chillie powder | 1 teaspoon salt

2 cloves garlic chopped | 1/3 teaspoon turmeric

Method

1. Clean and wash cuttle fish well. Wipe dry.
2. Mix filling ingredients together and stuff cuttle fish and fix ekels or tooth picks.
3. Mix all ingredients except 1st extract of coconut milk. Add stuffed cuttle fish and bring to boil and cook on low heat until green gram is done and fish tender.
4. Add 1st extract of coconut milk and cook until gravy is thick.

68. CUTTLE FISH - 2

Ingredients for 8 *portions.*

1 lb. cuttle fish

2 dessertspoons chillie powder

2 teaspoons salt

6-8 cloves garlic ground

2 slices ginger ground

1 teaspoon pepper powder

2 teaspoon fenugreek

½ teaspoon cummin powder

½ teaspoon sweet cummin powder

1 ½ teaspoons coriander powder

a sprig of curry leaves

3-4 green chillies chopped

2-3 teaspoons lime juice

1 oz. red onions, chopped

2 dessertspoons oil

12 oz. 2nd extract of coconut milk

4 oz. 1st extract of coconut milk

Method

1. Clean cuttle fish. Cut into 1" pieces.
2. Mix with all the powdered ingredients and salt.
3. Heat oil. Add curry leaves onions and fry for a few minutes.
4. Add cuttle fish and left over ingredients and cook for 5-7 minutes.
5. Add 2nd extract of coconut milk and cook until done.
6. Add 1st extract of coconut milk. Bring to boil add lime juice and take off fire.

69. FISH CUTLETS

Ingredients for 8 *portions*

¾ lb. boiled fish free from skin and bone

½ oz. green chillies	4-6 potatoes boiled
2 oz. onions	½ teaspoon pepper powder
1 sprig enduru or curry leaves	1 teaspoon salt
	¼ teaspoon cummin powder
batter and bread crumbs	Oil for deep frying

Method

1. Chop the onions and chillies and curry leaves. Pass the fish and potatoes through fine mincer. Heat 1 dessertspoon oil in a pan, add onions, curry leaves and fry till light brown, add fish and potatoes.
2. Add pepper, salt and cummin and mix well. Divide into 16 portions. Flatten out and shape into cutlets.

4. Dip in batter, crumb. Allow to rest for a few minutes before deep frying in hot oil.

70. DRY-FISH-Tempered

Ingredients for 8 *portions.*

6 oz. dry-fish	2 sprigs curry leaves
4 oz. onions chopped	4 oz. water
4 cloves garlic chopped	1 dessertspoon chillie powder
1 teaspoon fenugreek	1 clove, 1 cardamom
1 tomato chopped	1″ cinnamon
1 piece goraka	2 oz. oil

Method

1. Cut and wash dry-fish
2. Heat oil. Add all ingredients mixed well except water. Fry for about 10 minutes.
3. Add water and reduce heat and cook until dry-fish is done and gravy dries up.

71.DRY FISH DRY CURRY

Ingredients for 8 *portions.*

1 lb. katta dry fish	¾ oz. chopped garlic
¼ oz. ginger sliced	2 dessertspoons coarse chillie powder
½ teaspoon fenugreek	
rampe, curry leaves	2 dessertspoons oil
4 pieces goraka	10 oz. 1st extract of coconut milk

Method

1. Wash and cut up dry fish into ¾″ cubes.

2. Chop the ginger and garlic fine.

3. Add all the ingredients including the oil. Bring to boil and simmer until the curry is dry. Can be kept for some time.

72. FISH CURRY (COLD METHOD)

Ingredients for 8 *portions.*

1 lb. fish	1 oz. onions
2 clove garlic	a slice of ginger
½ teaspoon fenugreek	1 dessertspoon chillie powder
2 teaspoons coriander powder	¼ teaspoon sweet cummin
½ teaspoon cummin powder	1″ cinnamon
a sprig of curry leaves	2-3 pieces goraka
1 teaspoon salt	6 oz, 2nd & 3rd extracts of coconut milk
4 oz. 1st extract of coconut milk	

Method

1. Cut the fish into 8 portions. Wash very well using lime juice.

2. Chop the onions, garlic, green chillies.

3. Put all the ingredients into a pan with the fish and the 2nd extract of coconut milk and bring to the boil and cook till done.

4. Add the 1st extract of coconut milk and bring to the boil. Simmer for a few minutes and take off fire.

73. FRICADELLS

Ingredients for 8 *portions.*

1 tin fish (15 oz.) flaked
¼ lb. onions
curry leaves
salt
batter, crumbs
½ lb. boiled potatoes
1 oz. green chillies chopped
1 teaspoon lime juice
1 ½ dessertspoons oil
oil for deep frying

pepper

Method

1. Chop the onions and green chillies. Boil potatoes and mash.
2. Heat oil in a pan and when very hot add the curry leaves, onions and chillies and fry till light brown. Add the flaked fish and toss for a few minutes. Add potatoes. Season with pepper, salt, and lime juice.
3. Shape into 1" diameter balls. Dip in batter crumb and deep fry (36 fricadells).

74. HEAD CURRY

Ingredients for 8 *portions*

Cut up one seer head, or about one pound of fish

1 ½ teaspoons of fenugreek

2-3 green chillies and 2 teaspoons chilly powder

a pinch of turmeric

1 teaspoon cummin or sweet cummin (optional)

1 oz. red onions, or 1 oz. Bombay onions

a sprig of curry leave, 1″ of cinnamon

2 teaspoons lime juice or a small tomato

½ pint 2nd extract of coconut milk

8-12 oz. 1st extract of coconut milk

1 teaspoon salt

Method

1. Cut up fish head into large pieces depending on size (1lb. into six) and wash well using lime juice.
2. Chop the green chillie, onions and tomato if used.
3. Add all the ingredients except the lime juice and 1st extract of coconut milk. Mix well and bring to boil and simmer, till onions are done.
4. Add 1st extract of coconut milk and lime or tomato if used. Bring to boil and take off fire.

75. KALU POL (SHARK)

Ingredients for 8 *portions*

1 lb. fish

2 slices ginger

1 teaspoon chillie powder

2 teaspoons cummin powder

½″ cinnamon

2 pieces goraka

2 oz. water

3 cloves garlic

1 ½ oz. coconut grated

2 teaspoons coriander powder

½ teaspoon sweet cummin powder

1 teaspoon salt

2 dessertspoons oil

Method

1. Cut the fish into 1 - 1 ½ pieces. Chop the garlic and ginger fine. Grind the goraka after soaking or boiling in a little water. Roast the coconut and curry powder till dark brown and grind to a fine paste.

2. Mix all the ingredients, except the oil and water with the fish and leave for about an hour.

3. Heat oil in a small pan and when very hot add the fish. Toss for 2-3 minutes, add the water. Bring to boil and cook till done.

76. MIRIS MALU - 1

Ingredients for 8 *portions*

1 lb. fish
2 cloves
1 teaspoon fenugreek
¼ pint water
1″ rampe
2 teaspoons coriander powder
8 teaspoons chillie powder
2 cloves garlic
a sprig of curry leaves
1 piece goraka

Method

1. Cut fish into 8 portions and wash well using lime juice. Chop the garlic.

2. Put the fish into a pan with all the ingredients. Bring to the boil and simmer till done.

77. MIRIS MALU - 2

Ingredients for 8 *portions*

1 lb. fish	2 pieces goraka
1 teaspoon fenugreek	5 teaspoons chillie powder
¼ teaspoon turmeric	¼ pint water
2 cloves	1 teaspoon cummin powder
2 cardamoms	2 cloves garlic
½″ rampe	a sprig of curry leaves
1 teaspoon pepper powder	3 teaspoons salt

Method

1. Cut fish into 8 portions and wash well using lime juice.
2. Grind the goraka.
3. Put all the ingredients together into a pan. Bring to boil and simmer till done.

78. MIRIS MALU - 3

Ingredients for 8 *portions*

1 lb. fish (seer)	5 teaspoons chillie powder
2 teaspoons coriander powder	
1 teaspoon cummin powder	1 teaspoon sweet cummin powder
4 pieces goraka	
2 cloves garlic	a thin piece of ginger
2 cloves	2 cardamoms
1″ cinnamon	½ teaspoon fenugreek
¼ teaspoon pepper	1 teaspoon salt
6-8 oz. water	a sprig of curry leaves.

Method

1. Wash and cut the fish into 16 pieces. Roast the chillie coriander, cummin and sweet cummin till dark golden brown. Grind the goraka, pepper, garlic and ginger to a fine paste.

2. Add all the ingredients to the fish. Add the water and mix well (use a small pan so that the liquid covers the fish). Bring to boil and simmer steadily till done and gravy is thick.

79. MIRIS MALU - 4

Ingredients for 8 *portions*

1 lb. fish or small fish

5 teaspoons chillie powder	1 ½ teaspoons salt
3-4 pieces goraka	8-10 oz. water
a thin slice of ginger	4 cloves garlic

¼ teaspoon pepper

Method

1. Cut the fish into convenient pieces and wash well using lime.

2. Soak the goraka, or boil in water and grind well. Grind the ginger garlic and pepper. Roast chillie powder.

3. Mix the ground ingredients with salt and water. Arrange the pieces of fish in a small pan Add the liquid. Bring to boil and simmer till gravy is thick.

80. MIRIS MALU - 5

Ingredients for 4 *portions.*

1 lb. fish
3-4 pieces goraka ground
6-8 clove garlic ground
2 cloves
2 cardamoms
2 sprigs curry leaves
1 ¼ -2 teaspoons salt
1 teaspoon lime juice
1 oz. onions chopped
5 teaspoons chillie powder
3-4 thin slices ginger
1 teaspoon pepper powder ground
1″ cinnamon
2″ rampe
6-8 oz. water
2 dessertspoons oil

Method

1. Cut and wash fish well.
2. Mix all powdered and ground ingredients and salt with fish. Set aside 5-10 minutes.
3. Heat oil. Add remaining ingredients, except water and fry until onions are golden brown.
4. Add fish. Toss for a few minutes taking care not to break fish.
5. Add water. Bring to boil and simmer until gravy is thick.

81. MIRIS MALU - 6

Ingredients for 8 *portions.*

1 lb. fish
1 dessertspoon chillie powder
1 teaspoon pepper powder
2 pieces goraka, 4 cloves garlic, 1 slice ginger } ground fine

2 teaspoons coriander powder
1 teaspoon cummin powder
1 teaspoon sweet cummin powder
1″ cinnamon
1″ rampe
2 teaspoons salt
2 oz. onions
2 teaspoons fenugreek
2 cloves
2 cardamoms
a sprig of curry leaves
8 oz. 1st & 2nd extracts of coconut milk

Method

1. Cut and wash fish.
2. Mix all ingredients with coconut milk.
3. Bring to boil and simmer until gravy is thick.

82. FISH MOILEE

Ingredients for 8 *portions.*

1 lb. fish
2 oz. Bombay onions
4 oz. 1st extract of coconut milk
6 slices ginger
¼ teaspoon turmeric
2 teaspoons salt
1 dessertspoon lime juice
3-4 dessertspoons oil for frying
1 dessertspoon vinegar
8-12 oz. 2nd and 3rd extract of coconut milk
2 sprigs curry leaves
6 green chillies
6 cloves garlic
1/2 lb. potatoes

Method

1. Cut the fish into 8 portions, wash well using lime.
2. Slice the onions garlic and green chillies. Peel, wash and cut potatoes into 1" cubes. Chop the ginger.
3. Heat the oil in a pan and when very hot add the curry leaves and onions and fry till tender but not brown.
4. Add the potatoes, fish and the rest of the ingredients except the coconut milk, lime and vinegar. Keep tossing for just a few minutes.
5. Add the 2nd and 3rd extracts of coconut milk, bring to boil and simmer till potatoes are tender and liquid reduced.
6. Add the first extract of coconut milk, bring to boil. Add the lime juice and vinegar and take off fire.

83. FISH WHITE CURRY WITH MUSTARD

Ingredients for 8 *portions.*

1 lb. fish	4 teaspoons mustard ground
2 oz. red onions	fine with ½ oz. of vinegar
1 ¼ teaspoons salt	¼ teaspoon turmeric
½ oz. garlic	2 cloves, 2 cardamoms
12-15 oz. 2nd extract of coconut milk	4 oz. 1st extract coconut milk
2" piece cinnamon	2 teaspoons lime juice

Method

1. Cut the fish into pieces and wash well using lime juice.

2. Chop the onions and garlic fine.

3. Mix all the ingredients together except the 1st extract of coconut milk, mustard and lime. Bring to boil and cook till onions are soft.

4. Add the 1st extract of coconut milk, mixed with the mustard and bring to boil. Simmer for a few minutes and add lime and take off the fire.

84. SMALL FISH (HURULLO) 1

Ingredients for 8 *portions.*

1 lb. fish	½ oz. onions
3 cloves garlic	1 slice ginger
2″ cinnamon	3 dessertspoons vinegar
2 teaspoons pepper powder	pinch of turmeric
1 teaspoon cummin powder	2 dessertspoons oil
1 ½ teaspoons salt	

Method

1. Clean and wash fish very well.

2. Chop the onions, garlic, and ginger.

3. Mix all the ingredients together, except the oil.

4. Put the oil in a pan. Place the fish in a single layer. Bake at 350^0 F, till liquid has all dried up and fish is done.

5. This can also be cooked on the stove with a pan of coals placed over.

85. SMALL FISH

Ingredients for 8 *portions.*

1 lb. fish
3 cloves garlic
1 clove
1″ cinnamon
½ teaspoon pepper powder
1 oz. tamarind
½ oz. onions
1 slice ginger
1 cardamom
3 teaspoons chillie powder
1 teaspoon salt
2 dessertspoons oil
1 oz. water.

Method

1. Clean and wash fish well.
2. Chop the onions, garlic, ginger. Squeeze tamarind in 1 oz. water.
3. Mix all the ingredients well with the fish except oil.
4. Put oil into a flat cake pan and place the fish in a single layer. Bake in the oven at 350 G till it is quite dry.
5. This can also be cooked on slow flame with coals above pan.

86. SPRATS FRESH DRY CURRY

Ingredients for 8 *portions.*

1 lb. sprats with heads & intestines cleaned
4 cloves garlic finely chopped
1 ½ teaspoons salt
3 teaspoons chillie powder
3 dessertspoons coconut oil
the juice of ½ lime
6 oz. water.

Method

1. Clean sprats very well to remove all traces of sand and wash several times.

2. Mix all ingredients and cook on a slow fire until the liquid had reduced to about 1/3.

3. Add the sprats in the final stages of cooking. The oil may be sprinkled over the fish. Place the fish in a casserole dish and close it and put it to bake at any temperature between 350^{0} F - 400^{0} F. One more teaspoon of chillie powder may be added if a hotter curry is desired.

87. SPRATS DRIED WITH TOMATOES

Ingredients for 8 *portions.*

¼ lb. dried sprats
2 oz. onions chopped
4 cloves garlic chopped fine
2 teaspoons salt
¼ lb. tomatoes chopped well
a sprig of curry leaves
2 dessertspoons oil
4 teaspoons chillie powder (coarse)
½″ piece of ginger

Method

1. Remove sprats heads wash several times to remove sand and drain well.

2. Heat oil and when very hot, add the onions, curry leaves, sprats and salt. Toss well. Add the garlic, ginger and chillie powder and cook on a fairly hot fire for about 5 minutes.

3. Add tomatoes, stir on a hot fire for a few minutes, then reduce heat and simmer for a further 15 minutes.

88. SPRATS DRIED WITH POTATOES

Ingredients for 8 *portions*

Method

1. Use recipe as for dried sprats with tomato.
2. Add 1/2lb. peeled potatoes, cut into pieces with tomato.
3. Add 12 oz. 1st and 2nd extracts of coconut milk. Cook until potatoes are done.

89. SPRATS (DRIED) TEMPERED

Ingredients for 8 *portions.*

¼ lb. sprats	2 clove garlic chopped fine
2 oz. Bombay onions	3 oz. oil
3 teaspoons chillie powder	2 teaspoons salt
a sprig of curry leaves	2 pieces goraka

Method

1. Remove sprats heads and wash well several times with the two pieces of goraka.
2. Heat oil, add all ingredients mixed together and fry for about 5 minutes on high flame. Lower temperature and allow to simmer in oil for another 10-15 minutes. Add more salt if necessary. Quantity of chillie powder may be increased according to taste.

90. SPRATS BOLA AMBUL

Ingredients for 8 *portions.*

½ lb. dried sprats
a pinch of turmeric
1 ¼ pints coconut milk
curry leaves
10-15 green chillies
2 oz. red onions chopped
salt
1 dessertspoon flour
¼ teaspoon chillie powder
a few cloves garlic
¼ coconut cut in pieces and ground very fine
lime juice

Method

1. Clean and soak the sprats. Wash well.
2. Grind it to a paste with garlic, mix the flour, a little salt and ¼ teaspoon of chillie powder, and lime juice to taste and the ground sprats.
3. Shape into small balls and fry till brown and drain.
4. Split the green chillies and fry lightly.
5. Cook the other ingredients in the coconut milk and when it is half boiled add the fried chillies and sprat balls.
6. Add lime juice and salt to taste. Cook till the gravy is further reduced.

91. FISH TOMATO CURRY

Ingredients for 8 *portions.*

1 lb. fish
½ lb. tomatoes cut fine
2 teaspoons chillie powder
2 ½ teaspoons salt

2 cloves
2 cardamoms
a piece of cinnamon
¼ lb. onions sliced
¼ onion ground
3 teaspoons mustard
3 dessertspoons oil
¼ teaspoons turmeric
1 small bunch of coriander leaves ground fine (omit if not wanted)
1 teaspoon sweet cummin powder
½ oz. garlic ground
3 oz. curd
oil for shallow frying

Method

1. Cut the fish into 8 pieces. Wash well with lime. Dry well to take off all moisture, rub a little salt and turmeric and shallow fry in about ½″ oil.
2. Heat the oil in a pan and when very hot add the sliced onions and fry till golden brown. Add all other ingredients except fried fish, tomatoes and curd. Stir and fry for a few minutes.
3. Add the beaten curd tomato and salt and cook for a few minutes.
4. Add the fried fish, bring to boil and take off fire.

92. FISH WHITE CURRY - 1

Ingredients for 8 *portions.*

1 lb. fish
2-3 green chillies
2 teaspoons fenugreek
1 sprig curry leaves
2 oz. 1st extract of coconut milk
1 oz. onions
1 tomato
1 teaspoon salt
8 oz. 2nd & 3rd extracts of coconut milk

Method

1. Cut the fish into 8 portions and wash well using lime.
2. Wash and chop onion and chillies. Soak the 2 teaspoons fenugreek in a little water for ½ an hour.
3. Put all the ingredients except fish with 2nd and 3rd extracts of coconut milk in a pan, and bring to boil.
4. Put in the fish and simmer for a few minutes.
5. Add the 1st extract of coconut milk, bring to boil and take off fire.

93. FISH WHITE CURRY - 2

Ingredients for 8 *portions.*

1 lb. fish	4 green chillies
1 oz. coconut	3 cloves garlic
1 oz. onion	1 teaspoon salt
¼ teaspoon turmeric powder	½ teaspoon fenugreek
1 ¼ teaspoons lime juice	6 oz. 2nd & 3rd extracts of coconut milk
4 oz. 1st extract of coconut milk	

Method

1. Wash and cut fish into 8 pieces. Chop the onions. Grind the chillies, coconut and garlic into a fine paste.
2. Add all the ingredients to the fish with the 2ns and 3rd extracts of coconut milk. Bring to boil and cook till done.
3. Add the first extract of coconut milk. Bring to boil, take off fire. Add the lime juice.

94. FISH WHITE CURRY - 3

Ingredients for 8 *portions.*

1 lb. fish
1 piece goraka
2″ cinnamon
½ teaspoon turmeric powder
2 sprigs curry leaves
2 oz. onions chopped
1 small tomato chopped
4 oz. 1st extract of coconut milk
4-5 green chillies
3 teaspoons fenugreek
1 cardamom
1 clove garlic chopped
1 ½ teaspoons salt
2-3 teaspoons lime juice
12 oz. and 3rd extracts of coconut milk

Method

1. Cut and wash fish.
2. Add all ingredients except fish, 1st extract of coconut milk and lime juice. Bring to boil and simmer until liquid is reduced to half and onions pulpy.
3. Add fish and 1st extract of coconut milk and simmer until fish is done 7-10 minutes. Add lime juice.

SHELL FISH PREPARATIONS

95. BADUM - PRAWN

Ingredients for 8 *portions.*

1 lb. prawns	¼ lb. Bombay onions
¼ oz. garlic	2 dessertspoons chillies pounded coarsely
¼ teaspoon turmeric	
a few sprigs of curry leaves	2″ piece of rampe
1 ¾ teaspoons salt	1 teaspoon lime juice
1″ piece cinnamon	5 dessertspoons oil
2 cloves	2 cardamoms

Method

1. Wash, devein and wash prawns well.
2. Slice onions evenly, chop the garlic fine, cut rampe into ¼″ piece.
3. Heat the oil and when very hot add the curry leaves and rampe. Then the onions. Toss until the onions are turning brown.
4. Add the rest of the ingredients and toss till the prawns are well cooked and hard.
5. This can be kept for a few days.

96. PRAWNS TEMPERED

Ingredients for 8 *portions.*

1 lb. prawns	2 oz. onions

¼ oz. garlic
½ teaspoon coriander
1 sprig curry leaves
1″ cinnamon
3 dessertspoons oil

3 teaspoons chillie powder
¼ teaspoon turmeric
1″ rampe
1 ½ teaspoons salt

Method

1. Wash, shell, devein and wash prawns, leaving tails on.
2. Grind the heads and shells very fine and squeeze out the extract.
3. Chop the onions, and cut the rampe into smaller pieces.
4. Heat the oil in a pan and when very hot, add the curry leaves and rampe. Add the onions and cinnamon and toss till onions are lightly brown.
5. Add the prawns with the rest of the ingredients and keep tossing till firm.
6. Add the prawn extract. Toss for a few minutes, till almost dry. Take off fire.

97. PRAWN OR CRAB OMELETTE

Ingredients for 8 *portions.*

4 large eggs
4 oz. prawn or crab meat finely flaked
Oil for frying

1 oz. each of finely shredded carrot, leeks, cabbage, celery Bombay onions and capsicum chillies

Method

1. Beat the eggs very lightly, add salt to taste. Add the shredded vegetable and flaked crab or prawn meat.

2. Heat a pan about 5″ diameter. Add oil and when hot add 1/8 of mixture and allow to set. Turn over other side of the omelette for just a minute or two only. Cut into wedges or serve whole. Prepare 8 omelettes.

N.B:- Murunga leaves are added to shell fish, crabs, prawns to prevent any allergic conditions. Murunga leaves washed pounded, extract removed and consumed at least half cup juice helps to relieve allergies on consuming shell fish.

98. PRAWN CURRY

Ingredients for 8 *portions.*

1 lb. prawns
2 teaspoons chillie powder
4-6 cloves of garlic
1″ piece cinnamon
1 ¼ teaspoons salt
1 teaspoon lime juice
1 tomato
2 dessertspoons oil
1 good pinch of turmeric
1-2 oz. red onions

2 cloves, 2 cardamoms
a thin slice of ginger
a sprig of curry leaves
½ teaspoon fenugreek
3-4 green chillie
4 oz. 1st extract of coconut milk
4-6 oz. 2nd and 3rd extracts of coconut milk

Method

1. Wash shell, devein and wash prawns well.
2. Grind the heads, legs and tails with the least amount of water, or 3rd extract of coconut milk. Mix with the 1st extract of coconut milk.
3. Chop the onions, garlic and ginger, green chillies, if used and tomato if used.
4. Heat the oil in a pan and when very hot add the curry leaves, then all the other ingredients mixed well with the prawns, except the 1st extract of coconut milk and tomato if used. Toss for about 5 minutes. Add tomatoes if used. Toss for a few minutes.
5. Then add the 1st extract of coconut milk with the ground extract of prawns. Simmer gently for 7-10 minutes. Murunga leaves may be added.

99. PRAWN CURRY - 2

Ingredients for 4 *portions.*

1 lb. prawns, with shells and only heads removed.

3 teaspoons chillie powder	1 oz. onions
2 oz. coconut	½ teaspoon fenugreek
1 sprig curry leaves	½″ of sera or omit
6 cloves of garlic	2 cardamoms
2 cloves	a dash of grated nutmeg
3 teaspoons coriander	a pinch of turmeric
1 ½ teaspoons salt	1 teaspoon lime juice

½ pint 2nd and 3rd extracts of coconut milk

4 oz. extract of coconut milk

Murunga leaves from 2-3 sprigs

Method

1. Wash and remove only the heads from the prawn.
2. Slice the onions and garlic. Roast the coconut and grind fine.
3. Mix all the ingredients except the juice and 1st extract of coconut milk, with the prawns, add the 2nd and 3rd extracts of coconut milk and bring to boil, simmer for 15 minutes.
4. Add the 1st extract of coconut milk and lime, bring to boil, simmer and take off fire.
5. Murunga leaves may be added from the start.

100. PRAWN CURRY - 3

Ingredients for 8 *portions.*

1 lb. prawns

5-6 dry chillies

1 teaspoon fenugreek

½″ cinnamon

1 dessertspoon coriander

1 teaspoon cummin

1 cloves, 1 cardamom

1 sprig of curry leaves

1″ rampe, sera

Method

1. Roast all ingredients until a deep brown colour is obtained.
2. Pound or grind the roasted ingredients. Mix with the following ingredients and the 1st and 2nd extracts of coconut milk and cook until prawns are done.

1 Bombay onion chopped

2 thin slices of ginger

3-4 cloves garlic

2-3 green chillies chopped

12 oz. 1st and 2nd extract coconut milk

Lime juice or goraka or both

101. PRAWN WHITE CURRY

Ingredients for 8 *portions.*

1 lb. prawns	¼ oz. green chillies
1 sprig curry leaves	1 oz. onions
3 cloves garlic	1 thin slice ginger
1 teaspoon salt	1 teaspoon lemon juice
½ teaspoon fenugreek	¼ teaspoon turmeric

½ pint 2nd extract of coconut milk

1 tomato

Method

1. Wash shell devein prawns and wash leaving the tails on if small.

2. Wash the shells and heads and grind them fine and squeeze out the liquid.

3. Chop the onions chillies ginger and garlic and the tomato. Put all the ingredients into a pan with the 2nd extract of coconut milk, except the prawns, extract of prawns and bring to the boil and simmer till liquid has reduced and the ingredients reduced to pulp.

4. Add the prawns and the prawn extract and cook till prawns are done and gravy is thick.

5. Add the lime juice and take off fire.

MEAT PREPARATIONS

102. BEEF BREADFRUIT CURRY

Ingredients for 8 *portions.*

1 ½ lb. beef, breast with bones

1 small bread fruit

Beef Ingredients

3-4 green chillies sliced
2 teaspoons chillie powder
a sprig of curry leaves
2 dessertspoons oil
1 teaspoon fenugreek
tamarind the size of 1/2 a lime mixed well in meat
1 ½ teaspoons curry powder
1 Bombay onion sliced.

2-3 cloves garlic
1 slice ginger sliced fine
1 clove, 1 cardamom
16-24 oz. 2nd and 3rd extracts of coconut milk & sufficient water to cover meat, depending on the size of the pan
8 oz. 1st extract of coconut milk

Bread Fruit Ingredients

2 teaspoons coriander
1 teaspoon cummin
1 clove, 1 cardamom
1″ cinnamon

6-8 dry chillies
½ teaspoon sweet cummin
a sprig of curry leaves
rampe, sera.

Method

1. Wash and cut beef into 2″ chunks.
2. Heat oil. Add onions and curry leaves, rampe sera and fry until onions are light golden in colour

3. Mix meat with tamarind and all the other ingredients. Add to fried onions. Fry for 5-10 minutes. Add 2nd extract of coconut milk and water to cover and pressure cook for 30-40 minutes or cook until meat is well tender and comes off the bone. All ingredients to be added during second stage of cooking.

Method

1. Roast coriander, cummin, dry chillies, sweet cummin, cloves, cardamoms, cinnamon until dark in colour.
2. Pound or grind well and set aside.
3. When meat is almost done, mix curry powders with 1st extract of coconut milk. Mix with the breadfruit, cut into 2″ chunks, and add to meat mixture.
4. Cook until breadfruit is just done.

103. BLACK MEAT CURRY

Ingredients for 8 *portions.*

1 lb. meat	1 oz. coconut
1 oz. rice	¼ oz. garlic
3 slices ginger	2 oz. onions
1 oz. thick tamarind pulp	1 ½ dessertspoons chillie powder
extract with 2 ozs. coconut milk of water	1 teaspoon sweet cummin powder
1 teaspoon cummin powder	1 ¼ teaspoons salt
a pinch of turmeric	rampe, sera
curry leaves	2 dessertspoons oil
1 ½ dessertspoons coriander powder	16 oz. 1st and 2nd extracts of coconut milk

Method

1. Wash and cut the meat into ¾″ cubes.
2. Chop half the onions and slice half of them. Chop garlic and ginger fine.
3. Roast the coconut and rice till brown and grind to a fine paste with water. Roast the curry powder till dark. (like coffee)
4. Mix all the ingredients together except the curry leaves, rampe, sera and sliced onions. Add the meat.Bring to boil and take off fire.
5. Heat the oil in a pan, when very hot add the curry leaves, rampe, sera and onions. Fry till golden brown. Add the meat. Bring to boil and take off fire.

104. BOLLE CURRY

Ingredients for 8 *portions.*

1 lb. minced beef	1 oz. onions
¼ oz. green chillies	1 teaspoon salt

Method

1. Chop the onions and green chillies. Add to the minced beef with the salt and make into small balls (24 balls).
2. Bring the gravy (see page 207) to boil. Add the meat balls simmer till gravy is thick.

105. CORIANDER MEAT CURRY - 1

Ingredients for 8 *portions.*

1 lb. meat	4 oz. onions
4 dessertspoons coriander	2 teaspoons mustard
a thin slice ginger	2 teaspoons pepper powder
1 sprig curry leaves	1" rampe
1 oz. coriander leaves	1" cinnamon
2 cloves	2 cardamoms
4 cloves garlic	½ teaspoon turmeric
2 teaspoons salt	1 teaspoon lime juice
4 dessertspoons oil	10 oz. 1st extract of coconut milk

Method

1. Wash and cut the meat into slices or cubes 1 ½" and put into a pan.
2. Grind the mustard, half the onions, pepper, coriander, ginger and garlic, coriander leaves. Rub well into the meat.
3. Add the rest of the ingredients, except curry leaves,spices and half the onions.
4. Heat the oil in a pan and when very hot add the sliced onions, curry leaves and spices and fry for a few minutes.
5. Add the meat and fry for a few minutes till meat is brown. Allow to cook in its liquid for a few minutes.
6. Add the coconut milk, bring to boil, reduce and simmer till tender. Add the lime juice just before taking off the fire.

106. CORIANDER MEAT CURRY - 2

Ingredients for 8 *portions.*

1 lb. meat
1 dessertspoon cummin powder
¼ oz. green chillies
2 slices ginger
2 sprigs curry leaves
1 teaspoon fenugreek
2 teaspoons lime juice
4 dessertspoons oil
2 ½ dessertspoons coriander powder
2 teaspoons pepper powder
¼ oz. cloves of garlic
2 oz. onions
rampe
1 ½ teaspoons salt
3 teaspoons vinegar
12 oz. 1st & 2nd extracts of coconut milk

Method

1. Wash and cut the meat into cubes or slices.
2. Slice the chillies, chop the onions and chop the garlic and ginger finely.
3. Heat the oil in a pan and when hot add the curry leaves, rampe and onions and fry till onions are golden brown. Add the garlic, ginger and green chillies.
4. Add all the powdered ingredients and fenugreek and lastly the meat, salt, lime juice and vinegar and fry until meat gets slightly browned.
5. Add coconut milk, bring to boil, cove r with lid and simmer until meat is tender.

107. FENUGREEK MEAT CURRY - 1

Ingredients for 8 *portions.*

1 lb. meat sliced thin
1 bundle fresh fenugreek leaves
3-5 green chillies
2 cloves garlic
2 cardamoms crushed
1″ cinnamon
1 teaspoon curry powder
8 oz. 1st and 2nd extracts coconut milk
1 oz. Bombay onions chopped
½ teaspoon chillie powder
2 teaspoons raw rice
a slice of ginger
2 teaspoons raw coconut
2 cloves
1 sprig curry leaves
2 teaspoons fenugreek
1 ¼ teaspoons salt
2 dessertspoons oil

Method

1. Grind fenugreek leaves, garlic, ginger, green chillies, raw rice and fresh coconut very fine.
2. Heat oil, add onions, curry leaves, cinnamon, cloves and cardamoms, fenugreek and fry for a few seconds only. Add ground ingredients and fry for a few minutes.
3. Add coconut milk and bring to boil. Add meat and simmer until meat is tender.

108. FENUGREEK MEAT CURRY - 2

Ingredients for 8 *portions.*

1 lb. meat cut into thin slices
1 bundle fresh fenugreek leaves
2 teaspoons pepper corns
½ teaspoon chillie powder

1 ½ teaspoons salt
3 teaspoons fresh coconut lightly roasted with
2 teaspoons raw rice
4-5 cadjunuts
1″ cinnamon
2 dessertspoons oil
2 cloves garlic
2 cardamoms crushed
2 teaspoons fenugreek
1 oz. chopped onions
12-15 oz. 1st and 2nd extracts of coconut milk
a pinch of turmeric.

Method

1. Grind fenugreek leaves, pepper corns, garlic, cadjunuts, rice and rub well into meat with turmeric, chillie powder and salt.
2. Heat oil, add cardamoms, cinnamon, onions and meat and fry until meat is lightly browned.
3. Add coconut milk and fenugreek and simmer until tender and gravy almost dry

109. HOT MEAT CURRY

Ingredients for 8 *portions.*

1 lb. beef
1 teaspoon sweet cummin powder
1 teaspoon coriander powder
2 cardamoms
½″ cinnamon
2 cloves
½″ rampe
½ pint 1st & 2nd extracts of coconut milk or water
1 teaspoon cummin powder
1 oz. red onions
½ teaspoon fenugreek
1-2 slices ginger
1 ½-3 teaspoons chillie powder
1 sprig curry leaves
1/4-1/2 teaspoon pepper powder
2-3 dessertspoons oil
1- 1 ½ teaspoons salt

Method

1. Wash and cut up meat into cubes against grain
2. Add all the powdered ingredients except oil, liquid, garlic, onions and curry leaves and mix well.
3. Heat oil until very hot. Add garlic, onions, curry leaves and fry just a minute or two at the most.
4. Add the meat with the spices and keep tossing or stirring until the meat is slightly browned. Add the coconut milk or water, and bring to boil. Reduce heat at once and simmer until soft.

110. KHORMA - 1

Ingredients for 8 *portions.*

1 lb. meat	1 oz. grated coconut
1 oz. cadjunuts	1dessertspoon coriander powder
1 sprig coriander leaves	2 green chillies
(or use a sprig of parsley)	2 teaspoons chillie powder
½″ cinnamon	3 cloves garlic
2 cloves	1 ½ teaspoons salt
2 oz. onions	a thin slice ginger
8 oz. curd (Yoghurt)	3 cardamoms
1-2 teaspoons lime juice	3 dessertspoon ghee or oil
1 tomato	

Method

1. Wash and dry meat, cut into cubes. Soak meat in curd with salt for 15-20 minutes.
2. Grind the coconut, green chillies, ginger, garlic and cadjunuts very fine.
3. Chop the onions and tomato.
4. Heat the oil in a pan till very hot and fry the onions, coriander leaves, ground ingredients and curry powders.
5. Add the meat and keep tossing till brown.
6. Add the chopped tomato. Lower flame and simmer till meat is tender. Add the lime juice before taking off the fire.

111 KHORMA - 2

Ingredients for 8 *portions.*

1 lb. of meat to be cut into 8 pieces

12 oz. of curd

1 cardamom crushed

1″ cinnamon

2 teaspoons pepper powder

1 clove

1 teaspoon salt

Mix above ingredients and set aside for half an hour and simmer until meat is tender. Drain stock and set aside.

Gravy

1 dessertspoon poppy seeds or khus-khus

2 dessertspoons lightly roasted coconut

2 teaspoons lightly roasted rice

2 teaspoons lightly roasted sweet cummin seeds

1 teaspoon cummin powder

1 dessertspoon coriander powder

2 teaspoons chillie powder

2 clove garlic finely chopped

1 slice of ginger chopped

4oz. chopped onions

2 oz. sliced onions

2 medium sized tomatoes blanched and chopped fine

2 sprigs coriander leaves

1 teaspoon lime juice

1 teaspoon salt

1 dessertspoon ghee

Method

1. Grind to a fine paste coconut, poppy seeds, rice nuts, coriander leaves, chopped onions and cummin seeds.

2. Mix rest of the ingredients with ground ingredients, except sliced onions and ghee.

3. Heat ghee, add curry leaves and sliced onions and fry until dark brown and crisp. Add all the other ingredients and fry for a few minutes.

4. Add meat and fry for a few more minutes. Add stock and cook only until it comes to boil and take off fire.

112. LAMPREY CURRY

Ingredients for 8 *portions*

- 10 red onions chopped
- 2 thin slices of ginger
- ¼ teaspoon sweet cummin powder
- 1 teaspoon each coriander and cummin powder
- 2-4 dessertspoons chillie powder
- 16 oz. 1st and 2nd extracts of coconut milk
- ¼ lb. each of mutton, pork and beef
- 2-4 cloves garlic
- ½ teaspoon fenugreek
- 4 dessertspoons dried roasted prawn powder
- ¼ teaspoon turmeric
- 2 dessertspoons oil

Method

1. Cover the meat with sufficient water. Add salt, cardamoms, cinnamon, cloves and boil. Use this stock for boiling the rice for ghee rice.

2. Cut the meats into very small pieces. Mix with all the ingredients and set aside.

3. Heat 2 dessertspoons oil and fry the onions and curry leaves. After a few minutes add the meat and cook for about 5 minutes. Add the coconut milk and simmer until the coconut milk has reduced and is just moist.

113. MEAT CURRY (COLD METHOD)

Ingredients for 8 *portions.*

1 lb. beef	2 cloves
1 oz. onions	2 cardamoms
2 cloves garlic	1 dessertspoon chillie powder (roasted)
1″ rampe	1 dessertspoon coriander powder (roasted)
½″ sera	¼ teaspoon sweet cummin powder (roasted)
curry leaves	1″ cinnamon (roasted)
1 ½ teaspoons salt	¾ teaspoon fenugreek (roasted)
4 oz. 1st extract of coconut milk	

8 oz. 2nd and 3rd extracts of coconut milk

Method

1. Wash and cut the beef into small pieces against the grain and put into a pan.

2. Roast the chillie powder, coriander, cummin, sweet cummin, cinnamon, cardamom and cloves and fenugreek till dark brown in colour. Add to meat.

3. Chop the onions, garlic and ginger. Add to meat with the rest of the ingredients and the 2nd extract of coconut milk. Bring to boil and reduce flame and cook till meat is done.

4. Add the 1st extract of coconut milk bring to the boil. Simmer for a few minutes and take off fire.

114. MEAT CUTLETS

Ingredients for 8 *portions.*

1 lb. minced beef	2 oz. onions
½ oz. green chillies	a sprig of celery
½-3/4 teaspoon pepper	1-1 ½ teaspoon salt
bread crumbs	batter-flour and water

Method

1. Chop the onions, chillies and celery fine.
2. Mix well with all the ingredients. Divide into 16 portions.
3. Form into cutlets. Dip into batter and crumbs. Allow to rest for a while and deep fry until golden brown.

115. MINCE BEEF CURRY

Ingredients for 8 *portions*

1 lb. minced beef	¼ lb. onions
¼ lb. potatoes	1 oz. green chillies
1 sprig curry leaves	1″ rampe
3 cloves garlic	2 cloves
2 cardamoms	1″ cinnamon
a thin slice ginger	1 teaspoon pepper
2 teaspoon salt	4 dessertspoons oil
1 teaspoon coriander powder	3 teaspoons chillie powder
½ teaspoon cummin powder	½ pt. 1st and 2nd extracts of coconut milk

Method

1. Chop the chillies, onions, garlic and ginger. Peel and cube the potatoes into a little less than ½″ cubes and leave in water.

2. Mix the beef with the curry powders, salt, pepper and ginger.

3. Heat the oil in a pan when very hot drain the potatoes and fry it lightly. Add the curry leaves, onions, chillies, garlic, spices and fry till onions are light brown in colour.

4. Add the beef and fry for 10 minutes longer till meat is browned.

5. Add the coconut milk. Bring to boil and simmer till liquid has reduced to required amount.

116. MUSTARD MEAT CURRY

Ingredients for 8 *portions.*

1 lb. beef
2 teaspoons coriander powder
1 teaspoon sweet cummin powder
2 slices ginger
a piece of rampe
4 oz. 1st extract of coconut milk
1 ½ teaspoons salt
2 dessertspoons mustard ground fine
1 dessertspoon chillie powder
1 teaspoon cummin powder
1/4 oz. garlic
2 sprigs curry leaves
a thin slice sera
1 pt. 2nd and 3rd extracts of coconut milk
3 oz. onions
1-2 teaspoons lime juice
2 dessertspoons oil

Method

1. Wash and cut beef into ½ cubes.
2. Chop 1 oz. and slice 2 oz. onions, chop garlic and ginger fine. Grind the mustard fine.
3. Add all the ingredients except 1st extract of coconut milk, mustard, sliced onions, curry leaves and oil. bring to boil and cook till meat is tender.
4. Mix mustard with 1st extract of coconut milk and add to meat. Bring to boil and remove from fire.
5. Heat the oil in a pan and when very hot add the curry leaves and sliced onions and fry till crisp and dry.
6. Add the meat. Bring to boil and simmer for about 5minutes. Take off fire and add lime juice and stir.

117.PEPPER CURRY - 1

Ingredients for 8 *portions*

1 lb. meat	1 teaspoon salt
2 teaspoons mustard	1 teaspoon lemon juice
4 oz. onion	a thin slice of ginger
2 dessertspoons of white or black pepper ground fine	2 cardamoms, 2 cloves
	1″ cinnamon
1 teaspoon coriander	1 sprig curry leaves
½ teaspoon turmeric powder	1″ rampe
4 cloves garlic	2 dessertspoons oil

10 oz. 1st extract of coconut milk

Method

1. Wash and cut meat into slices.
2. Grind the pepper, mustard, garlic and ginger fine and mix well with the meat.
3. Chop the onions. Heat the oil in a pan and when it is very hot add the onions, curry leaves and rampe and fry for a few minutes. Add all the other ingredients, except coconut milk, with the meat and keep tossing for a few minutes.
4. Add the coconut milk. Bring to boil and simmer till tender.

118. PEPPER CURRY - 2

Ingredients for 8 *portions.*

1 lb. meat in one piece	1 teaspoon salt
4 teaspoons black pepper powder	½ teaspoon turmeric powder
	1 dessertspoon ghee
6 red onions sliced or	2 cloves
1 Bombay onion	1″ piece cinnamon
2 cardamoms	1 teaspoon lemon juice
4 oz. 1st extract of coconut milk	a thin slice ginger ground
	1″ piece rampe
a sprig of curry leaves	½ oz. garlic ground

Method

1. Add 1 teaspoon pepper, turmeric, salt, cardamoms, cloves, cinnamon and sufficient water to cover meat and boil until tender.
2. Slice meat and rub well into pieces of meat the garlic,

ginger, pepper crushed or ground together with half the onions.

3. Heat the ghee and add curry leaves, rampe, and half onion chopped. Fry until golden brown and add meat, fry for a few minutes.

4. Add the 1st extract of coconut milk and any gravy left over after boiling meat. Cook on a steady fire until liquid is almost evaporated.

119. PEPPER CURRY - 3

Ingredients for 8 *portions.*

1 lb. meat cut into thin slices

¼ lb. Bombay onions if small cut into 2 and if medium cut into 4. If red onions are used do not cut them.

6-8 cloves garlic cut into 2 only

6 thin slices ginger	3-4 teaspoons pepper powder
1 dessertspoon vinegar	1 ½ teaspoons salt
a pinch of turmeric	2 teaspoons cummin powder
4 cardamoms crushed	4 cloves
1″ cinnamon	1 sprig curry leaves
rampe, sera	10-12 green chillies cut into two
16 oz. 1st extract of coconut milk	8 oz. 2nd and 3rd extracts of coconut milk

2 dessertspoons oil

Method

1. Boil meat with onions, vinegar, turmeric, salt ginger and garlic. Do not add water. Strain stock and set aside.

2. Heat oil, fry curry leaves, rampe, chillies, sera, cloves, cardamoms and cinnamon for a few minutes. Then add meat and fry for 5-10 minutes.

3. Add stock, 1st and 2nd extracts of coconut milk and allow to simmer until meat is tender and gravy thick.

Variations

½ lb. of boiled peeled potatoes cut into pieces may be added a few minutes before taking off fire. Add ½ teaspoon of extra salt.

120. PEPPER CURRY - 4

Ingredients for 8 *portions.*

1 lb. meat cut into slices and flattened out with a meat hammer or the grinding stone.

4-5 teaspoons pepper powder	2 dessertspoons curd
1 cloves powdered	2 cardamoms powdered
1 teaspoon lime juice	1 piece sera
curry leaves	1″ rampe
1 dessertspoon oil	1 medium Bombay onion sliced
12 oz. 2nd extract of coconut milk	3-4 cloves garlic
	1″ cinnamon

4 oz. 1st extract of coconut milk

salt

Method

1. Mix pepper, cloves, cardamoms, cinnamon, curd, salt with flattened out slices of meat.

2. Heat oil. Add sliced onions, rampe, curry leaves, fry until onions are light golden brown.

3. Add meat, fry for 5-7 minutes. Add 2nd extract of coconut milk and simmer until meat is tender and gravy is almost dry.

4. Add 1st extract of coconut milk. Bring to boil. Add lime juice.

121. POL KIRI BADUM (MUTTON CURRY)

Ingredients for 8 *portions.*

1 lb. mutton		1 dessertspoon chillie powder
2 teaspoons cummin powder	roasted	½″ lemon grass
2 teaspoons sweet cummin powder	roasted	1 sprig curry leaves
½ teaspoon fenugreek	roasted	2 cloves
		1″ cinnamon
		4 dessertspoons vinegar
2 cloves garlic		15oz. 2nd and 3rd extracts of coconut milk
2 slices ginger		
1 ½ teaspoons salt		5 oz. 1st extract of coconut milk
2 dessertspoons oil		
1 ½ dessertspoons coriander		1 oz. onions

Method

1. Wash and cut meat into 1″ cubes and pound with meat hammer.

2. Chop onions, garlic, ginger. Roast the coriander, cummin and sweet cummin powder. Add all the ingredients with half the chopped onions and the 2nd and 3rd extracts of

coconut milk. Bring to boil and simmer till gravy is thick and meat tender.

3. Heat oil in pan and when very hot add the onions and fry till brown. Add the meat and 1st extract of coconut milk. Bring to boil and simmer till dry and gravy is thick.

122. SATE CURRY - 1

Ingredients for 8 *portions.*

1-2 lb. beef	2 teaspoons cummin powder
1 teaspoon sweet cummin powder	2 bay leaves
	2 cloves
4 teaspoons coriander	2 cardamoms
4-5 curry leaves	1″ cinnamon
2 pieces aromatic ginger	1 dessertspoon tamarind dissolved in 4 ozs. coconut milk or water
8 oz. 1st and 2nd extracts of coconut milk	
1 oz. garlic	oil for frying
1 ½ teaspoons salt	1 big or 2 small capsicum chillies
Ekels for skewering meat	

Method

1. Cut the meat into ½″ cubes. Dry well. Sprinkle ½ teaspoon salt and fry in ¼″ oil till brown.

2. Cut the onions and capsicum into squares, slice the ginger and garlic. Dissolve tamarind in coconut milk.

3. Thread on ekels a piece of meat, a slice of garlic, piece of capsicum, onion and ginger. Repeat in this order till there are 3 or 4 pieces of meat, beginning and ending with meat.

4. Mix all the other ingredients with the coconut milk, add the skewered meat. Bring to boil. Add tamarind juice and simmer till tender.

123. SATE CURRY - 2

Ingredients for 8 *portions.*

1 lb. meat	3-4 dessertspoons oil
4 oz. Bombay onions	1 oz. garlic (reduce according to taste)
6 oz. curd	
2″ piece ginger	1 medium sized tomato
1 large capsicum chillie	3 teaspoons cummin powder
4 teaspoons coriander powder	½ teaspoon turmeric powder

2-4 teaspoons chillie powder according to taste.

Ekels 3-4″ long

Method

1. Boil meat until tender, cut into small squares ½″
2. Cut the capsicum into squares and onions into 4 pieces. Slice ginger and garlic. Crush left over pieces of ginger and garlic and add a little water and extract juice. Chop the tomato.
3. Thread on ekels a piece of meat, then garlic, capsicum, onion and lastly ginger and repeat in this order till there are 3 or 4 pieces of meat beginning and ending with meat.
4. Heat oil and brown the onions not used. Add all the curry powders and fry well. Add the ginger-garlic juice rained, the chopped tomato and lastly the curd beaten and mix well.

5. Arrange the sate sticks neatly in the gravy. Allow to simmer for 10-15 minutes.

124. SATE CURRY - 3

Ingredients for 8 *portions.*

1 lb. meat
½ oz. ginger
1 teaspoon cummin powder
1 teaspoon fenugreek
½ teaspoon turmeric powder
3 teaspoon chillie powder
1 oz. grated coconut
½ oz. garlic
10 oz. 1st and 2nd extracts of coconut milk
a sprig of curry leaves
2 oz. onions
1 dessertspoon coriander powder
2 cloves
1 teaspoon khus-khus (poppy seeds)
1 oz. cadjunuts
2 dessertspoons oil
1 ½ teaspoon salt
1 teaspoon lime juice
2 dessertspoons dhal

Method

1. Wash and cut meat into ½ cubes. Dry well.
2. Grind ginger, garlic, ½ the onions, coconut, cadjunuts, khus-khus and dhal.
3. Mix with rest of the ingredients and then with meat. Thread meat on ekels, 4-5 pieces of meat per ekel, 24 ekels in all 3 portions.
4. Heat oil, add curry leaves, onions and fry for a few minutes. Add skewered meat and cook for a few minutes.

Add 1st and 2nd extracts of coconut milk and simmer until meat is done.

125. SATE CURRY WITH BROWN GRAVY - 4

Ingredients for 8 *portions*

1 lb. beef cut into 1″ squares

¼ teaspoon turmeric powder — 1 teaspoon salt

2-3 teaspoons chillie powder — 1 dessertspoon oil

Method

1. Mix ingredients well, heat oil, add meat and cook meat with a small quantity of oil, and in its own gravy, until done. No liquid is to be added.

2. Meat should be of a dark brown colour when done. String cooked meat alternatively with ginger, onion and garlic.

Gravy Ingredients

1 medium size Bombay onion or 10-12 red onions

2 green chillies — 4 cloves garlic

3-4 slice of ginger — 2″ piece of rampe

a sprig of curry leaves } 1″ piece of sera

1 dessertspoon oil } ¼ cup tamarind juice

½ cup 1st extract of coconut milk

2 cups 2nd extract of coconut milk

2 teaspoons of raw rice — roasted and ground

1 teaspoon of white cummin

Method

1. Heat oil. Add all ingredients except 1st & 2nd extracts of coconut milk, tamarind and ground ingredients, Fry for 5-7 minutes.
2. Add 2nd extract of coconut milk, tamarind and cook until it reaches boiling point.
3. Then add the meat, 1st extract of coconut milk, ground ingredients and simmer until gravy thickens.

126. SMORE

Ingredients for 8 *portions.*

1 piece meat (3-4 lbs.)	½ lime pickle	
2 oz. chopped onions	1 dessertspoon chillie powder	
2 dessertspoons coriander powder	1 slice ginger	
1 sprig curry leaves	2 teaspoons cummin powder	roasted
½″ sera	2 teaps. sweet cummin powder	roasted
2 cloves	½ teaspoon fenugreek	roasted
2 cloves garlic	1″ cinnamon	
4 dessertspoons vinegar	1 ½ teaspoons salt	
1 ½ oz. 2nd and 3rd extracts of coconut milk	2 dessertspoons oil	

4 oz. 1st extract of coconut milk

Method

1. Remove all gristle from meat and wash and dry it. Prick or pound meat with hammer and rub the lime pickle well into it. Put it into a small pan.

2. Chop the onions, garlic, ginger. Roast the coriander, cummin and sweet cummin. Add all the ingredients to the meat with half the chopped onions. Add the 2nd and 3rd extracts of coconut milk and if it does not cover the meat, add more milk. (Do not use too large a pan)

3. Bring to boil and simmer till meat is tender and gravy has almost dried up. If there is any gravy left drain it off and remove meat.

4. Heat oil and when it is very hot add the remaining onions and fry until brown. Add the 1st extract of coconut milk, then the gravy and bring to boil. Add meat. Slice and serve with thick gravy.

127. TAMARIND MEAT CURRY

Ingredients for 4 *portions*

1 lb. beef	2 oz. onion chopped
2 teaspoons chillie powder	1 teaspoon coriander
1 teaspoon fenugreek	3 cloves
3 cardamoms	1″ cinnamon
4 cloves garlic	a slice of ginger
1 teaspoon pepper	a sprig of curry leaves
1″ rampe	½ sera
2 teaspoons salt	4 dessertspoons oil
2 oz. tamarind	8 oz. 2nd and 3rd extracts of coconut milk

Method

1. Wash and cut beef into large slices and flatten well. Squeeze the tamarind in the milk. Mix in the marind, spices

and all the other ingredients except onion, curry leaves, and oil. Soak meat for 1 hour.

2. Heat the oil in a pan and when very hot fry the onions and curry leaves until onions are golden brown.

3. Add the meat and fry for about 10 minutes. Reduce heat and simmer till meat is tender.

128. VINDALOO

Ingredients for 8 *portions.*

1 lb. meat	1 teaspoon cummin powder
1 teaspoon turmeric powder	4 dessertspoons vinegar
6 cloves garlic	1″ rampe
4 teaspoons chillie powder	3 dessertspoons oil
2 oz. onions	1 teaspoon salt
4 oz. 2nd extract of coconut	2 teaspoons mustard

milk, or water

Method

1. Wash and cube meat ¾ - 1″, slice onions.

2. Grind the garlic and mustard in vinegar.

3. Heat the oil in a pan and when very hot add the curry leaves and onions and fry for a few minutes. Add the ground ingredients and the other ingredients except the meat and coconut milk and cook for 5-7 minutes.

4. Add the remaining vinegar and meat and keep frying for a few minutes.

5. Add the coconut milk. Bring to boil and reduce heat and simmer until meat is tender.

129. WHITE MEAT CURRY

Ingredients for 8 *portions.*

1 lb. meat
¼ teaspoon turmeric
1 ½ teaspoons salt
1 oz. rice
½ oz. cadjunuts
2 teaspoons fenugreek
2 slices ginger
a thin slice of sera
2 cloves
¾ oz. green chillies
1 oz. onions
2 teaspoons lime juice
1 oz. coconut
16 oz. 1st and 2nd extracts of coconut milk
1/4 oz. garlic
a sprig of curry leaves
2 cardamoms crushed
1″ cinnamon

Method

1. Wash and cut meat into 1/2″ cubes.
2. Slice the green chillies and onions, chop the ginger and garlic fine.
3. Grind the coconut, rice and cadjunuts to a fine paste.
4. Mix all the ingredients. Bring to boil, cover with lid and simmer until meat is tender and gravy thick.

130. PORK CURRY WITH GORAKA

Ingredients for 8 *portions.*

1 lb. pork
2 teaspoons salt
3 pieces goraka ground fine
10 oz. water

1 dessertspoon chillie powder 1 teaspoon cummin powder 1 teaspoon sweet cummin powder 2 teaspoons coriander powder a sprig of curry leaves 2 cloves garlic chopped 6 cloves 2 teaspoons pepper powder	} roasted to a dark colour

2″ piece of sera

Method

1. Wash and cut pork into small pieces.
2. Mix all ingredients well with pork. Add water.
3. Bring to boil. Simmer until gravy is thick and meat tender.
4. Flavour of curry increases with keeping. Should be made and kept overnight or a few hours.

131. CHICKEN CURRY

Ingredients for 8 *portions.*

1 chicken (2 ½ lb.)	2 teaspoons sweet cummin powder
2 dessertspoons coriander	2 teaspoons cummin powder
½ dessertspoon chillie powder	½ teaspoon fenugreek
2 oz. red onion	1-2 green chillies
2 thin slices ginger	½″ cinnamon
3 cardamoms	1″ rampe

1-1 ¼ teaspoons salt
2 small tomatoes chopped
1 oz. cadju
1 dessertspoon rice } roasted
2 dessertspoons coconut } roasted
2-3 dessertspoons oil
8-12 oz. 1st and 2nd extracts of coconut milk

Method

1. Cut the chicken into 8 portions. Chop onions and green chillies. Grind the cadju, garlic, rice and roasted coconut, cloves, cardamoms into a fine paste.

2. Add all the powdered and ground ingredients, and salt to the chicken and mix well and leave for 15-20 minutes.

3. Heat oil in a pan till very hot. Add the rampe and onions and fry till light brown. Add the chicken and toss for 5-7 minutes. Add the coconut milk. Bring to boil and simmer till done.

132. CHICKEN KHROMA

Ingredients for 8 *portions.*

1 chicken (2 ½ lbs.)
1 ½ oz. cadjunuts
1 sprig coriander leaves
a sprig of parsley
½″ cinnamon
2 oz. onion
2 cloves
8 oz. curd (Yoghurt)
1 oz. grated coconut
1 dessertspoon coriander powder
2 green chillies
2 teaspoons chillie powder
3 cloves garlic
1 ½ teaspoons salt
a thin slice of ginger
3 cardamoms

1-2 teaspoons lime juice 3 dessertspoons oil

1 tomato

Method

1. Wash and dry meat, cut into cubes.
2. Grind the coconut, green chillies, ginger, garlic and cadjunuts very fine. Add to meat with the curd and salt and soak for 15-20 minutes.
3. Chop the onions and tomatoes.
4. Heat the oil in a pan till very hot and fry the onions, coriander leaves and curry powders.
5. Add the meat and keep tossing till brown.
6. Add the chopped tomato and simmer till meat is tender. Add lime juice before taking off fire.

LIVER PREPARATIONS

133. LIVER BADUM - 1

Ingredients for 8 *portions.*

1 lb. liver	3 teaspoons chillie powder
2 teaspoons coriander powder	1 teaspoon cummin powder
¼ teaspoon sweet cummin powder	¼ teaspoon turmeric powder
1 oz. onion	2 cloves garlic
a slice ginger	1″ cinnamon
1″ rampe	a sprig of curry leaves
2 cloves	2 cardamoms
3 dessertspoons oil	4 oz. 1st extract of coconut milk
	2 dessertspoons vinegar
	1 teaspoon salt

Method

1. Wash and cut liver into slices or cubes.
2. Wash and chop onions, ginger and garlic and add tothe liver with the spices, curry powders, curry leaves, salt and vinegar and mix well.
3. Heat the oil in a pan and when hot, add the liver, and keep tossing till onions are done and liver is slightly fried.
4. Add the coconut milk bring to the boil and simmer, till done.

134. LIVER BADUM - 2

Ingredients for 8 *portions.*

1 lb. liver
2 oz. onions chopped
1 teaspoon lime juice
1 oz. onion
1 teaspoon salt
1 cardamom
1/2″ sera
a sprig of curry leaves
6-8 oz. curd
2 cloves garlic chopped
pepper to taste
1 teaspoon coriander powder
1 clove
1″ cinnamon
1/2″ rampe
3 dessertspoons oil

Method

1. Wash and cut liver into 1″cubes. Add curd, salt, pepper, curry powder, ginger, garlic, spices, mix well and leave aside.

2. Heat oil in a pan add curry leaves, rampe, sera and onions. Fry till light golden brown. Add the liver and toss till liver is done. Take off the fire and add lime juice to taste.

135. LIVER HATH MAALU

Ingredients for 8 *portions.*

¼ lb capsicum chillies
¼ lb. big red onions
¼ lb. ash plantains
¾ lb. liver
1 teaspoon pepper powder
1 ½ teaspoons coriander powder
¼ lb. potatoes
¼ lb. brinjals
¼ lb. tomato
3 teaspoon chillie powder
1 teaspoon mustard seeds crushed

	¼ oz. cloves of garlic finely chopped
4 teaspoons vinegar	
3 teaspoons salt	6 oz. coconut milk
1/2 teaspoon fenugreek	a sprig of curry leaves
1″ piece cinnamon	1 cardamom, 1 clove
oil for deep frying	1 teaspoon turmeric powder
3 dessertspoons oil	2 oz. Bombay onions, sliced.

Method

1. Peel red onions and wash and set aside. Peel ash plantains and cut into ½″ cubes and set aside, with turmeric rubbed on it. Wash, dry and cut brinjals into ¼″ cubes and set aside. Cut capsicum chillies if they are large, into four, if they are small into two or three (ripe chillies are nicer if available). Wash and scrub potatoes and cut them into ½″ cubes and rub turmeric and set aside. Cut tomatoes into four if they are small or into eight if they are large. Wash liver and remove skin and cut into ½″ cubes.

2. Heat oil for deep frying. Deep fry potatoes, brinjals and plantains separately until they are light brown.

3. Dip red onion, chillies, tomatoes in the deep fat and take out immediately. These may be fried all together in a frying basket. Drain well.

4. Heat oil, add sliced onions, curry leaves, liver, garlic, cloves, cardamoms and cinnamon and allow to cook for about 8-10 minutes. Then add coconut milk, curry powders, salt, pepper, vinegar, fenugreek and mustard.

   Cook for a further few minutes.

5. Add the fried vegetables. Simmer for 10 more minutes. This curry may be served with yellow rice or ghee rice.

136. LIVER HOT CURRY

Ingredients for 8 *portions.*

¾ lb. liver
1 oz. onion
3 cloves garlic
1 teaspoon coriander powder
½″ teaspoon sweet cummin powder
¼ teaspoon fenugreek
1″ cinnamon
1 ½ teaspoons chillie powder
2 green chillies
a thin slice ginger
1 teaspoon cummin powder
¼ teaspoon turmeric powder
1 dessertspoon vinegar
1 teaspoon salt
a sprig of curry leaves
8 oz. 1st and 2nd extracts of coconut milk.

Method

1. Remove membrane and wash liver quickly. Cut into small pieces. Chop the onions, chillies, garlic and ginger.
2. Mix all the ingredients together well. Add the coconut milk. Bring to boil and simmer till done. Do not over cook as liver will be tough.

137. LIVER, PEAS, CADJU IN CURRY

Ingredients for 8 *portions.*

½ lb. liver
¼ lb. cadju
2 teaspoons coriander powder
2 cardamoms
2 Bombay onions chopped
1 ¼ teaspoons salt
½ lb. peas
½ teaspoon cummin powder
½ teaspoon pepper powder
6 oz. 2nd and 3rd extract coconut milk

1 teaspoon chillie powder
½″ cinnamon
2 cloves garlic chopped
2 oz. 1st extract of coconut milk
2 dessertspoons oil

Method

1. Soak cadju if dry ones are used in boiling water to which ½ teaspoon bicarbonate of soda is added,overnight or 2-3 hours. If fresh cadju is used boil for 5-10 minutes and remove skins.

2. Shell peas and set aside.

3. Wash liver. Remove membrane and cut into cubes ¾ -1″ x ½″ and set aside.

4. Heat oil. Add garlic and cardamoms. Fry 3-5 minutes, remove from pan and set aside.

5. Add cadju, peas and all other ingredients except coconut milk. Fry for 3-5 minutes.

6. Add 2nd and 3rd extracts of coconut milk, simmer until cadju is almost done.

7. Add 1st extract of coconut milk, and fried liver and remove when liver is just cooked through.

8. Add ½ teaspoon vinegar if desired.

   N.B. Kidney may be used in pace of liver. Follow instructions for cleaning kidney. Slice kidney and cut into strips. Cook along with cadju as kidney takes longer to cook.

138. LIVER PEPPER CURRY

Ingredients for 8 *portions.*

¾ lb. liver
1 teaspoon coriander powder
1" cinnamon
1 medium onion finely sliced
1 teaspoon salt
1 ½ dessertspoons oil
3 teaspoons pepper powder
3-4 cloves garlic finely chopped
1 cardamom
rampe, sera, curry leaves
1 teaspoon fenugreek
a pinch of turmeric
12 oz. 1st and 2nd extracts of coconut milk.

Method

1. Wash liver, remove membrane and cut liver into pieces.
2. Mix all the ingredients except coconut milk with the liver.
3. Heat 1 ½ dessertspoons oil until very hot. Add liver with the ingredients fry a few minutes tossing all the time to prevent it sticking.

139. LIVER AND TOMATO

Ingredients for 8 *portions.*

¾ lb. liver
4 oz. tomatoes
2 cloves garlic
1 teaspoon cummin powder
1 dessertspoon vinegar
a sprig of curry leaves
4 green chillies
3 oz. Bombay onions
2 teaspoons chillie powder
1 teaspoon coriander powder
¼ teaspoon pepper powder
1 ¼ teaspoons salt
1" piece of rampe
4 dessertspoons oil

Method

1. Remove membrane and wash liver. Cut into 1″ slices.
2. Slice the onions and tomato and chillies into four lengthwise. Chop garlic.
3. Heat oil in a pan and when very hot add the curry leaves and rampe, and onions and toss. When slightly coloured add the tomato and the liver, mixed with all the other ingredients. Keep tossing till liver is cooked through. Do not over cook.

140. LIVER WHITE CURRY

Ingredients for 8 *portions.*

3/4 lb. liver	4-5 green chillies
¼ teaspoon turmeric	1 capsicum chillie
1 teaspoon coriander powder	3-4 cloves of garlic
	1″ cinnamon
1 clove, 1 cardamom	1 medium onion chopped
rampe, sera	4 oz. 3rd extract of coconut milk

8 oz. 2nd extract of coconut milk

4 oz. 1st extract of coconut milk.

Method

1. Wash liver, remove membrane and cut liver into pieces.
2. Add all the ingredients except the liver and the 1st and 2nd extracts of coconut milk. Cook the ingredients until the onions are partially done.
3. Add the liver and the 1st and 2nd extracts of coconut milk and cook until liver is done. Do not over cook. Add lime juice to taste.

EGG PREPARATIONS

141. EGG CURRY

Ingredients for 8 *portions.*

8 eggs	2 green chillies chopped
1″ rampe	2 oz. onions chopped
2 teanspoons chillie powder	1 ¼ teaspoons salt
½ teaspoon cummin powder	1 teaspoon coriander powder
¼ teaspoon turmeric powder	¼ teaspoon sweet cummin powder
½ pint 1st and 2nd extracts of coconut milk	1″ cinnamon

Method

1. Boil the eggs, shell, prick with skewer, deep fry until light golden brown.
2. Put into a pan the coconut milk and all the other ingredients.
3. Bring to boil, simmer until onions are soft and pulpy. Add fried eggs slit half way up to the yolk to allow gravy to season egg.

142. WHITE EGG CURRY

Ingredients for 8 *portions.*

8 eggs hard boiled	kirihodi (Recipe No.155)

Method

1. When kirihodi is prepared add eggs, slit half way.
2. Cook a further 2-3 minutes

143. EGG CUTLETS

Ingredients for 8 *portions.*

12 oz. raw minced beef, minced very fine or ground on grinding stone

4 hard boiled eggs

2 teaspoons chillie powder

1 ½ teaspoons salt

1 teaspoon coriander powder

¼ teaspoon cummin powder

1 dessertspoon flour

1/2 teaspoon mixed spices (cloves, cardamoms, cinnamon powdered)

1 portion gravy (Recipe No.150 or159)

Method

1. Mix meat and all powdered ingredients and divide into 4 portions.
2. Prick lightly, boiled eggs with fork or skewer and roll in flour.
3. Flatten each portion of meat and place egg in centre and cover meat mixture to seal egg.
4. Place egg cutlets in prepared boiling gravy. Reduce heat and cook 10-15 minutes on low heat turning eggs so that gravy is absorbed by meat.
5. Cut into two just before serving. Serve with gravy.

144. OMELETTE CURRY

Ingredients for 8 *portions.*

6 eggs
1 dessertspoon chopped green chillies
fat for frying
1 portion gravy (Recipe No. 146,147 or 149)
½ oz. finely chopped Bombay onion
2 teaspoons salt
2 dessertspoons chopped tomatoes

Method

1. Beat egg mixture with all ingredients and prepare two omelettes.
2. Cut each omelette into four portions.
3. Prepare gravy and when done add the omelette and cook for 5-7 minutes.

145. EGG RULOUNG

Ingredients for 8 *portions.*

6 eggs
2 oz. sliced red onions
2-4 oz. bacon cut into ¼″ - ½″ cubes
2 capsicum chillies cut into ½″ cubes
6 dessertspoons oil
6 dessertspoons milk
pepper and salt

Method

1. Whisk egg whites and yolks until very stiff. Add pepper and salt.

2. Heat half the quantity of oil and fry bacon. Drain and set aside.

3. Add balance oil, add onions and chillies and cook but do not allow onions and chillies to fry.

4. Add bacon, well beaten eggs and milk. Stir all the time until the egg begins to set.

5. Remove from fire before the eggs set completely as the heat in the pan is sufficient to cook the egg and the egg must be moist for Egg Ruloung.

GRAVY PREPARATIONS

146. KALU HODHI

Ingredients for 8 *portions.*

2 oz. 3rd extract milk
1 teaspoon coriander powder
a sprig of curry leaves
1 clove, 1 cardamom
1 teaspoon fenugreek
2 teaspoons rice
12 oz. 1st and 2nd extracts of coconut milk
1 teaspoon cummin
1 piece ginger
1 medium onion chopped
½ a piece of goraka ground
1 teaspoon chillie powder

Method

1. Roast chillie powder and rice until very dark.
2. All ingredients should be either pounded fine or ground fine.
3. Add all ingredients to the 3rd extract of coconut milk and cook until onions are soft and done.
4. Add 1st and 2nd extracts of coconut milk, and bring to boil.

147. GRAVY FOR CAPSICUM CHILLIES FILLED WITH BEEF - 1

Ingredients for 8 *portions.*

1 oz. onion
3 cloves garlic
¼ oz. green chillies
2 teaspoons chillie powder

½ teaspoon fenugreek	3 teaspoons coriander powder
½ teaspoon cummin powder	2 cloves
2 cardamoms	½″ cinnamon
1 ¼ teaspoons salt	8 oz. 1st extract of coconut milk
4 oz. 2nd extract of coconut milk	

Method

1. Chop the onions, chillies, garlic and put into a pan.
2. Add all the other ingredients except the 1st extract of coconut milk.
3. Bring to boil and reduce flame and cook till onions are very tender. Smash the ingredient with the back of the spoon.
4. Add the 1st extract of coconut milk. Bring to the boil and simmer for a few minutes.
5. Add the fried filled chillies. Bring to boil and take off fire.

148. GRAVY FOR CAPSICUM CHILLIES FILLED WITH FISH - 2

Ingredients for 8 *portions.*

1 oz. onion	¼ oz. green chillies
2 teaspoons fenugreek	¼ teaspoon turmeric powder
1 clove	2 cardamoms
1/2″ cinnamon	1 ¼ teaspoons salt
4 oz. 2nd extract of milk	8 oz. 1st extract of coconut milk

Method

1. Chop the onions, chillies and add to the 2nd extract of coconut milk with all the other ingredients except the 1st extract of coconut milk.
2. Bring to boil and simmer till the onion is very tender and liquid reduced.
3. Smash the ingredients with the back of the spoon and add the 1st extract of coconut milk. Bring to boil and simmer till done.
4. Add the filled chillies. Bring to boil, simmer for a few minutes and take off fire.

149. GRAVY FOR CAPSICUM CHILLIES FILLED WITH VEGETABLE - 3

Ingredients for 8 *portions.*

1 oz. onion	a sprig of curry leaves
1 small tomato	1 teaspoon maldive fish
1 teaspoon chillie powder	¼ teaspoon turmeric powder
½ teaspoon fenugreek	1 teaspoon coriander powder
¼ teaspoon cummin powder	2 cloves
2 cardamoms	½″ cinnamon
1 ¼ teaspoons salt	6 oz. 2nd extract of coconut milk

4 oz. 1st extract of coconut milk

Method

1. Chop the onions, tomato and put into a pan with all the other ingredients except the 1st extract of coconut milk.

2. Bring to boil and simmer till onions are very tender and pulpy.

3. Smash with the back of the spoon.

4. Add the 1st extract of coconut milk, bring to boil and simmer for a few minutes.

5. Add the filled chillies, bring to the boil, simmer for a few minutes and take off fire.

Note - These gravies may be interchanged for the three different preparations of capsicum fillings.

150. GRAVY FOR BOLLE CURRY

Ingredients for 8 *portions.*

¼ oz. green chillies	1 ½ oz. onions
4 cloves garlic	a thin slice of ginger
1 sprig curry leaves	1″ lemon grass
2 cloves	2 cardamoms
½″ cinnamon	¼ teaspoon turmeric powder
1 ½ teaspoons salt	1 teaspoon lime juice
4 oz. 1st extract of coconut milk	1 small tomato chopped (optional)

½ pint 2nd extract of coconut milk

2 teaspoons coriander powder	roasted
½ teaspoon cummin powder	
1 teaspoon sweet cummin powder	
3 teaspoons chillie powder	
½ teaspoon fenugreek	

Method:

1. Chop the onion, garlic, ginger and chillies. Roast together the coriander, cummin, sweet cummin, chillie powder and fenugreek, till dark brown in colour.

2. Put all the ingredients except the 1st extract of coconut milk into a pan. Bring to boil and simmer till onions are soft.

3. Add the 1st extract of coconut milk, bring to boil, simmer. Then add the meat balls, Bring to boil and simmer till gravy is thick. Take off fire.

151. GRAVY FOR FISH BOLLE CURRY - 1

Ingredients for 8 portions.

*16 oz. stock	1 oz. onion
2 oz. green chillies	1 1/2 teaspoons chillie powder
1 teaspoon coriander powder	1 teaspoon cummin powder
	a pinch of turmeric powder
1/2 teaspoon sweet cummin powder	1 teaspoon salt or less, if already added to stock
a sprig of curry leaves	4oz. 1st extract of coconut milk

1/4 oz. coriander leaves ground (optional)

Method

1. Chop onions and green chillies. Add to stock with all the other ingredients. Bring to boil and simmer till onions are soft.

---

* *Stock to be made from fish bones, skins and head.*

2. Add the 1st extract of coconut milk. Bring to boil, add the fish balls. Simmer until fish balls are cooked through 5-7 mins.

152. GRAVY FOR FISH BOLLE CURRY -2

Ingredients for 8 *portions.*

Same ingredients as for Gravy 1 Recipe No.151

Method

1. Roast and grind extra 2 oz. coconut.
2. Roast the chillie, cummin, coriander and sweet cummin and add to the stock instead of adding the 1st extract of coconut milk.
3. Cook all ingredients together until onions are soft. Omit 1st extract of coconut milk.

153. GRAVY FOR STUFFED CABBAGE

Ingredients for 8 *portions.*

½ pt. 1st and 2nd extracts of coconut milk
a sprig of curry leaves
2 cardamoms
1 clove garlic
1 oz. onion
2 cloves
1″ cinnamon
1 dessertspoon oil

1 teaspoon coriander powder
1 teaspoon cummin powder
½ teaspoon sweet cummin powder
} roasted

Method

1. Roast powdered ingredients and spices. Chop onions and garlic.
2. Heat oil in pan and when very hot fry the onions and curry leaves. Then add the roasted ingredients and coconut milk. Bring to boil.
3. Add stuffed cabbage, stem side down. Bring to boil, and simmer with lid on till done and gravy is thick.

Note:- Use a pan which will be just enough to hold cabbage.

154. DIYA HODHI

Ingredients for 8 *portions.*

12 oz. 1st and 2nd extracts of coconut milk

2-3 green chillies cut

3-4 dry chillies broken up

10-15 red onions finely sliced

salt to taste

a dash of lime juice

Method

1. Mix all the ingredients with the coconut milk and serve.

Variation

Temper all ingredients in very little oil. Add to the coconut milk.

155. KIRI HODHI

Ingredients for 8 *portions.*

4 teaspoons fenugreek soaked in water

3 oz. onions chopped	3-4 green chillies
a sprig of curry leaves	2 cardamoms
1″ cinnamon	2-3 teaspoons maldive fish (optional)
12 oz. 2nd and 3rd extracts of coconut milk	lime juice to taste
12 oz. 1st extract of coconut milk	1/8-1/4 teaspoon turmeric powder to give a desired colour
1 teaspoon rice flour	

Method

1. Cook 2nd and 3rd extract of coconut milk and all ingredients, except lime juice and 1st extract of coconut milk, until onions are soft. This should be done on a slow fire.
2. Mix very well, to bring out the thickening effect from the fenugreek. Add 1 teaspoon salt.
3. Add 1st extract of coconut milk. Keep stirring all the while. Bring to boil, add lime juice. Remove from fire.

Variation

1 small tomato chopped 2-3 slices of potato finely chopped

may be added right from the start

156. THAMBUN HODHI - 1

Ingredients for 8 *portions.*

1 teaspoon cummin	3 teaspoons coriander powder
8-10 red onions	4-5 cloves of garlic
2 green chillies	a sprig of curry leaves
tamarind about the size of a lime	5-6 pepper corns
	1 teaspoon maldive fish (optional)

Method

1. Bruise or chop slightly, all ingredients except the tamarind.
2. Add the tamarind and salt with 1 ¼ - 1 ¾ pints water. Bring to boil and simmer till done.

157. THAMBUN HODHI - 2

Ingredients for 8 *portions.*

2 teaspoons cummin	6-8 red onions
1 dry red chillie broken	5 dessertspoons coriander powder
a sprig of curry leaves	4-5 cloves garlic
pepper corns	1 cardamom
½" cinnamon	tamarind about the size of ½ a lime

Method

1. Heat pan, add all ingredients except tamarind and onions and keep tossing the ingredients in the heated pan until an oily texture is noticed in the condiments. and an aroma of the condiments.

2. Add 4-5 cups of water with tamarind and onions and reduce to 2-3 cups and cook until onions and garlic become soft.

158. MIRIS HODHI

Ingredients for 8 *portions.*

1 teaspoon cummin	2 teaspoons coriander powder
3-4 cloves garlic	5-6 red onions
3-4 dry chillies	1 ¼ - 1 ¾ pints water
1 teaspoon salt	a dash of lime juice
curry leaves	1 clove
pepper corns	1 cardamom
1″ cinnamon	tamarind about the size of ½ a lime

Method

1. Grind garlic, cummin, coriander, chillies.
2. Add whole red onions, tamarind, cloves, cardamom, cinnamon, curry leaves, salt.
3. Add water bring to boil and simmer until the required strength is obtained.
4. Should give 12 oz. - 16 oz. of fairly strong Miris Hodhi.

159. HOT CURRY

Ingredients for 8 *portions.*

1 onion ground	4 teaspoons chillie powder
2 teaspoons rice	2 teaspoons coriander powder

2 teaspoons coconut
1 small tomato chopped
1″ cinnamon
1 green chillie
4 oz. 3rd extract of coconut milk
2 teaspoons fenugreek
rampe, curry leaves, sera
3-4 cloves garlic, finely chopped
2 dessertspoons coconut oil
16 oz. 1st and 2nd extracts of coconut milk

Method

1. Roast and grind 2 teaspoons of rice and 2 teaspoons of coconut until light golden brown.
2. Heat oil. Add all powdered and ground ingredients. Fry for a few minutes.
3. Add 3rd extract of coconut milk. Cook on a slow fire until onions are soft.
4. Add 1st and 2nd extracts of coconut milk. Bring to boil on a slow fire, allow to boil for a few minutes. Take off the fire.

N.B.- Hard boiled eggs, boiled potatoes, boiled prawns, boiled fish, boiled meat or egg cutlets may be served with this gravy.

160. PRAWN SHELL GRAVY

Ingredients for 8 *portions.*

Shells from 1 ½ lbs. of prawns
1 teaspoon chillie powder
1 teaspoon fenugreek
a thin slice of ginger
1 medium sized onion chopped
¼ teaspoon turmeric
4-6 cloves garlic
a sprig of curry leaves

rampe, sera
*Prawn shell should be ground and extract to be taken with
8 oz. 3rd extract of coconut milk
16 oz. 2nd & 3rd extracts of coconut milk

2 tsps. rice, 1 teaspoon of coconut, 2-3 dry chillies } roast till golden brown & powder or grind
4 oz. 1st extract extract of coconut milk
1 teaspoon lime juice

Method

1. Add all the ingredients except the 1st extract of coconut milk and lime juice.
2. Bring to boil. When onions are soft, add the first extract of coconut milk. bring to boil, add lime juice stirring all the while.

N.B:- Boiled eggs, boiled potatoes or capsicum chillies filled with prawns may be served with this gravy.

**All prawn heads and shells when used should be washed in several changes of water, before the extraction of juice. A mincer, mortar, liquidizer or grinding stone may be used. The shells and heads may be washed well dried in the sun or oven, and powdered. This powder may be used for curries or sambols.*

VEGETABLE PREPARATIONS

161. ASH PLANTAIN RED CURRY

Ingredients for 8 *portions.*

1 lb. ash plantains
2 teaspoons coriander powder
1″ cinnamon
1 clove
a sprig of curry leaves
8 oz. 1st and 2nd extracts of coconut milk.
3 teaspoons chillie powder
½ teaspoon cummin powder
1 cardamom
1 oz. onion 1″ rampe
3 dessertspoons oil
1 ½ teaspoons salt

Method

1. Peel and cut ash plantain into 1 ½ - 2″ finger lengths. Place in water. Chop the onions.
2. Heat oil and when very hot, add the curry leaves, rampe and onions and toss till onions are light brown.
3. Mix all the ingredients with the plantains. Fry for a few minutes till curry powder darkens.
4. Add the coconut milk and simmer till plantains are done.

162. ASH PLANTAIN BLACK CURRY

Ingredients for 8 *portions.*

1 lb. ash plantains,
1 ½ teaspoons chillie powder
1 teaspoon cummin powder
2 oz. onions,
1½ teaspoons coriander
¼ teaspoon sweet cummin

¼ teaspoon pepper powder
1 ½ teaspoons salt
1″ cinnamon
2 dessertspoons oil

12 oz. 1st & 2nd extract of coconut milk,

a sprig of curry leaves

Method

1. Peel and cut plantains into 4 and then into 1 ½″ lengths. Chop the onions. Roast the curry powders until dark brown.

2. Heat the oil in a pan. Add the curry leaves and chopped onions, fry until light brown. Add the plantains mixed with all the ingredients toss for a few minutes.

3. Add the coconut milk. Bring to boil and cook until gravy has reduced and plantains cooked.

163. ASH PLANTAIN FRIED AND CURRIED

Ingredients for 8 *portions.*

1 lb. ash plantains,
1 ½ teaspoons chillie powder

1 ½ teaspoons coriander powder

½ teaspoon sweet cummin powder

1 ½ teaspoons cummin powder

½ teaspoon fenugreek

2 green chillies
1 ½ teaspoons salt
1″ cinnamon
1 cardamom
a sprig of curry leaves
2 oz. onions
1 medium sized tomato or
3 teaspoons lime juice
½ rampe
oil for deep frying

10 oz. 1st and 2nd extracts of coconut milk.

Method

1. Peel and cut the ash plantains into finger lengths. 1 ½" long. Rub salt and turmeric and deep fry until golden brown.

2. Chop the onions, green chillies and tomato. Add all the ingredients to the coconut milk except plantains and bring to boil, and cook till onions are done and gravy is thick. Add the fried plantains, bring to boil and simmer for 5-7 minutes.

164. ASH PLANTAIN (WHITE CURRY) - 1

Ingredients for 8 *portions.*

1 lb. ash plantain,	2 oz. onions,
2 green chillies	½ teaspoon fenugreek
a sprig of curry leaves	1 ¼ teaspoons salt
2 oz. 1st extract of coconut milk	¼ teaspoon turmeric powder

8-10 oz. 2nd and 3rd extracts of coconut milk.

Method

1. Peel wash and cut the plantains into ¼" thick slices on the slant and put into the 2nd & 3rd extracts of coconut milk. Chop the onions and chillies.

2. Add all the ingredients with the 2nd & 3rd extracts of coconut milk and cook till done and gravy has reduced.

3. Add the 1st extract of coconut milk, bring to boil and take off fire.

165. ASH PLANTAIN (WHITE CURRY) - 2

Ingredients for 8 *portions.*

1 lb. ash plantains,	2 oz. onions,
½ oz. green chillies,	¼ teaspoon turmeric powder
2 teaspoons fenugreek	1 dessertspoon maldive fish
1 ½ teaspoons salt,	½ teaspoon cummin powder,
a sprig curry leaves,	½″ rampe
4 oz. 1st extract of coconut milk	15 oz. 2nd & 3rd extracts of coconut milk

Method

1. Peel plantains, wash and slice. Place in a pan with the 2nd and 3rd extracts of coconut milk. Soak the fenugreek in a little water for some time.

2. Slice the onions, green chillies. Add to the plantains together with all the other ingredients except 1st extract of coconut milk. Bring to the boil and simmer till done.

3. Add the 1st extract of coconut milk, bring to boil and take off fire.

N.B:- As a plantain skins may be boiled 1/2 lb. Water drained and ground into a fine paste with 3 cloves of garlic 1-2 green chillies, 10-15 pepper, a slice of ginger. Mix well and add salt and lime juice.

---

* *N.B. Ash plantain skins may be boiled 1/2 lb. Water drained and ground into a fine paste with 3 cloves of garlic 1-2 green chillies, 10-15 pepper, s slice of ginger. Mix well and add salt and lime juice.*

166. ASH PLANTAIN SKINS TEMPERED

Ingredients for 8 *portions.*

5 oz. skin shredded (from 1 lb. ash plantains).

1 oz. dried prawns
1/8 teaspoon turmeric powder
¾ teaspoon salt
a sprig of curry leaves for tempering
1 oz. onion for tempering
1 teaspoon chillie powder
8 oz. water
1 ½ dessertspoons oil.

Method

1. Boil shredded skins with water, turmeric, salt and prawns. Take off fire when plantain skins are cooked.
2. Heat oil in a pan, when very hot, add the curry leaves and chopped onions. Toss till onions are light brown in colour.
3. Add the boiled skins and prawns. Fry for 5 - 7 minutes.

167. BEAN AND POTATO CURRY - 1

Ingredients for 8 *portions.*

¼ lb. potatoes medium sized
½ lb. beans
½ teaspoon fenugreek
a pinch of turmeric
1 ½ dessertspoons coriander powder
1 teaspoon cummin powder
2 teaspoons chillie powder
½ teaspoon sweet cummin powder
a sprig of curry leaves.
2-3 green chillies
¼ teaspoon salt
2 dessertspoons oil
6 oz. chopped onions
8 oz. 1st and 2nd extracts of coconut milk

Method

1. Peel wash and cut potatoes and leave in water. String, wash and cut beans into ¼″ pieces on the slant. Chop the onions and green chillies.

2. Heat pan and add coriander, cummin, sweet cummin and chillie powder and roast until golden brown.

3. Mix the potatoes, beans, roasted curry powders, salt, fenugreek, turmeric and green chillies.

4. Heat the oil in a pan when very hot, add the curry leaves and onions. Fry till onions are light brown. Add the mixed vegetables and keep tossing for 5-7 minutes.

5. Add the coconut milk, bring to boil and simmer till potatoes are done and gravy is thick.

168. BEAN POTATO CURRY - 2

Ingredients for 8 *portions.*

½ lb. potatoes,	½ lb. beans,
2 oz. onions,	5-6 green chillies
½ teaspoon turmeric powder	2 teaspoons fenugreek
½ oz. coconut	1 teaspoons mustard
a sprig of curry leaves	2 teaspoons salt,

12 oz. 1st and 2nd extracts of coconut milk,

lime juice (optional)

Method

1. Peel wash and cut potatoes and leave in water. String wash and cut beans into ¼″ pieces. Chop the onions and green chilles.

2. Grind coconut with half the quantity of onions and mustard.

3. Mix all ingredients, except ground ingredients, with the potatoes and cook until almost done.

4. Add ground ingredients mixed with a little gravy from curry.

5. Add lime juice just before taking off fire.

169. BEAN CURRY TEMPERED

Ingredients for 8 *portions.*

1 lb. beans
¼ teaspoon turmeric powder
1 ½ teaspoons chillie powder
1 teaspoon coriander powder
½ teaspoon cummin powder
pinch of sweet cummin powder
¼ teaspoon fenugreek
1 dessertspoon maldive fish
2 dessertspoons oil.

4 oz. onions
2 sprigs of curry leaves
1-2 teaspoons salt
4 oz. 1st extract of coconut milk

Method

1. String the beans wash and cut into convenient pieces, either on the slant or straight.

2. Place in a pan the beans, chillie powder, sliced or chopped onions, curry leaves, green chillies, fenugreek and curry powders, maldive fish, salt and mix.

3. Heat the oil until very hot in pan, add the beans and keep tossing for 3-5 minutes.

4. Add the 1st extract of coconut milk and cook in an open pan till done.

Note: In preparing beans, in this manner, the colour is retained, ladies fingers, carrots, radish, leeks or beetroot leaves may be prepared in this manner.

This may be prepared by using the cold method i.e.,by mixing all the ingredients together with 8 oz. 1st & 2nd extracts of coconut milk and cooking till done. The green colour of the vegetable is not retained when using this method.

170. BEETROOT LEAVES TEMPERED

Ingredients for 8 *portions.*

¾ lb. beetroot leaves (1 ¾ beetroots),

3-4 teaspoons chillie powder	4 dessertspoons coconut oil
2 oz. Bombay onions	a spring of curry leaves
½ teaspoon fenugreek	½ teaspoon salt

½ teaspoon lime juice (optional)

Method

1. Wash and dry the beetroot leaves, shred fine.
2. Chop the onions.
3. Heat oil and when very hot add the curry leaves and onions and fry for a few minutes.
4. Add the beetroot leaves mixed with chillie powder, salt and fenugreek to half fried onions and cook for a few minutes on a hot flame. Reduce heat and let it simmer for 10-15 minutes.

5. Add ½ teaspoon of lime juice before taking off the fire.

Note:- Carrot leaves, leeks may be prepared this way.

171. BEETROOT CURRY (TEMPERED)

Ingredients for 8 *portions.*

1 lb. beetroots,	1 oz. onions,
2-3 green chilles,	2 teaspoons chillie powder
1 teaspoon coriander,	1 teaspoon sugar,
3 teaspoons vinegar	2 dessertspoons oil
2 ½ teaspoons salt,	12 oz. 1st and 2nd extracts of coconut milk.

Method

1. Peel and grate beetroots with coarse side of cheese grater or slice and cut into fine strips.
2. Slice onions and green chillies.
3. Heat oil and curry leaves, onions and chillies. Add the beetroot mixed with all ingredients. Fry for a few minutes.
4. Add the coconut milk and cook until beetroot is done.

Note:- Carrots, knoll kol, radish, turnips may be done in this manner.

172. BILLING CURRIED

Ingredients for 8 *portions.*

1 lb. billing,	2 oz. onions,
4 green chillies	a sprig of curry leaves
2 teaspoons chillie powder	1 ½ teaspoons coriander powder

¼ teaspoon turmeric powder 2 teaspoons salt

2 oz. 1st extract of coconut 2 dessertspoons oil.

Method

1. Wash and slice the billing fine. Cover with water adding 2 teaspoons salt and leave for ½ - 1 hour. Wash and chop the onions and green chillies.

2. Add all the ingredients except coconut milk to the billing well squeezed out.

3. Heat the oil until very hot in pan, and add the billing. Fry 5 - 7 minutes. Stir.

4. Add the coconut milk, bring to the boil and simmer.

173. BREADFRUIT STUFFED

Ingredients for 8 *portions.*

1 breadfruit (2 ¾ lbs)	½ lb. minced beef
¼ lb. onions	½ oz. green chillies
1 - 1 ¼ teaspoons salt	1 teaspoon cummin powder
1 dessertspoon oil	¼ teaspoon pepper powder
½ teaspoon chillie powder	Fat-Margarine
2 oz. beef stock	3 oz. of scraped breadfruit ground.

Method

1. Wash the breadfruit well without bruising skin. Cut a lid off the stem end and scoop out the breadfruit leaving about ¾″ all round. Grind or finely chop scooped out breadfruit.

2. Chop the onions and chillies. Heat oil in a pan add the onions. Fry for a few minutes. Add the minced beef, green chillies, cummin, chillie, pepper and salt, ground breadfruit and fry for 5 minutes more, add stock bring to boil and take off fire.

3. Sprinkle about ½ teaspoon pepper and salt into the cavity and fill with the minced beef mixture. Cover with the lid and smear fat lightly all over the fruit.

4. Place the breadfruit in a baking tin on a ring and bake at 350^0 F till soft.

174. BREADFRUIT - BLACK CURRY

Ingredients for 8 *portions.*

1 lb. breadfruit
2 green chillies
1 teaspoon coriander powder
a pinch of turmeric powder
1″ cinnamon
4 oz. 1st extract of coconut milk
2 oz. Bombay onions
a sprig of curry leaves
1 teaspoon cummin powder
1/4 teaspoon pepper
10 oz. 2nd & 3rd extracts of coconut milk

Method

1. Peel and cut breadfruit into convenient pieces. Chop the onions and chillies.

2. Roast the curry powders till dark brown. Mix all the ingredients together with the 2nd and 3rd extracts of coconut milk. Bring to boil and simmer till done. Add the 1st extract of coconut milk bring to boil and simmer till thick and take off fire.

175. BREADFRUIT HOT TEMPERED

Ingredients for 8 *portions.*

1 ½ lb. breadfruit
2 teaspoons salt
1″ rampe
1 dessertspoon maldive fish
3 oz. Bombay onions
1 ½ dessertspoons coarse chillie powder
a sprig of curry leaves
a pinch of turmeric
3 dessertspoons oil.

Method

1. Peel and cut breadfruit into 2″ pieces. Cover with water add turmeric powder and 1 ½ teaspoons salt and boil till tender. Drain water if necessary and leave on fire for a few minutes to get fluffy. Chop onions.

2. Heat oil until very hot in a pan and add the curry leaves and onions and fry till light brown. Add the chillie powder, maldive fish and boiled breadfruit and salt. Mix well leave for 2-3 minutes and take off fire.

176. BRINJAL CURRY (FRIED AND COOKED)

Ingredients for 8 *portions.*

1 lb. brinjal
a sprig of curry leaves
2 oz. onions
2 teaspoons coriander powder
¼ teaspoon sweet cummin powder
2 green chillies
2 dessertspoons vinegar
1½ teaspoons cummin powder
1 ½ teaspoons salt
3 clove garlic
¼ teaspoon turmeric
1″ piece rampe

2″ piece cinnamon
8 oz. 1st & 2nd extracts
of coconut milk
1 ½ dessertspoons mustard
ground fine
2 teaspoons sugar.

Method

1. Wash and cut the brinjals lengthwise into 2" pieces. Rub with turmeric and deep fry till golden brown.
2. Wash and cut the onions, chillies and garlic and put into a pan with all the other ingredients and the coconut milk.
3. Bring to boil and simmer till gravy is thick. Add fried brinjals and simmer till liquid has reduced.

177. BRINJAL CURRIED

Ingredients for 8 *portions.*

1 lb. brinjal
2 teaspoons chillie powder
1 teaspoon cummin powder
½ teaspoon turmeric powder
1″rampe
2 teaspoons salt
4 teaspoons lime juice
1 oz. 1st extract of
coconut milk.
2 oz. onions
1 teaspoon coriander
½ teaspoon sweet cummin
a sprig of curry leaves
½″ cinnamon
2 teaspoons mustard ground
fine
6 dessertspoons oil

Method

1. Wash and cut brinjals into ¼″ slices on the slant.
2. Heat oil until very hot in a pan add curry leaves and onions, the brinjals mixed with all the ingredients except coconut milk and mustard. Fry till brinjals are cooked.

Add the coconut milk with the mustard. Bring to boil and simmer for 10 minutes and take off fire.

Note:- This may be prepared using the cold method i.e. putting in all the ingredients with 8 oz. 1st & 2nd extracts of coconut milk and omitting chillie powder and oil. Cook till gravy is thick. If desired, temper with 1 dessertspoon oil, 1 oz. chopped onion, a sprig of curry leaves.

178. BRINJALS POTATO AND ASH PLANTAIN CURRY

Ingredients for 8 *portions.*

6 oz. brinjals
6 oz. potatoes
1 ½ teaspoons coriander powder
½ teaspoon fenugreek
2 oz. onions
2 dessertspoons vinegar
a sprig of curry leaves
1″ cinnamon
6 oz. ash plantains
1 ½ teaspoons chillie powder
1 teaspoon cummin powder
2 green chillies
1 ½ teaspoons salt
oil for deep frying
10 oz. 1st & 2nd extracts of coconut milk
1″ rampe
1 dessertspoon mustard ground fine.

Method

1. Wash and cut brinjal into ¾″ cubes. Peel wash and cut the plantains and potatoes into ¾″ cubes. Rub turmeric and salt and deep fry until golden brown.

2. Chop onions, green chillies. Mix all the ingredients together with the coconut milk, except fried vegetables and bring to boil and simmer till thick.

3. Add the fried vegetables and cook for a few minutes and take off fire.

179. BRINJAL CAPSICUM CHILLIES & ASH PLANTAIN CURRY

Ingredients for 8 *portions.*

6 oz. brinjals	6 oz. ash plantains
6 oz. capsiucm	2 teaspoons chillie powder
1 teaspoon cummin	1 ½ dessertspoon coriander powder
½ teaspoon fenugreek	1 ½ teaspoons salt
2 oz. onions chopped	oil for deep frying
2 dessertspoons vinegar	14 oz. 1st & 2nd extracts of coconut milk
a sprig of curry leaves	1″ rampe
1″ cinnamon	1 dessertspoon ground mustard
2 oz. red onions whole	1 cardamom
1 clove	

Method

1. Wash and cut brinjals into ¾″ cubes. Peel wash and cut the plantains into ¾″ cubes. Rub turmeric and salt and deep fry until golden brown. Slit end of chillies and deep fry with red onions for a minute only.
2. Mix all the ingredients together with the coconut milk and bring the gravy to boil. Simmer till onions are cooked.
3. Add the fried vegetables and cook for a few minutes and take off fire.

180. BIG ONIONS CURRIED

Ingredients for 8 *portions.*

¾ lb. Big onions
1 teaspoon coriander powder
1″ cinnamon
2 cardamoms
1 ripe chillie
1 teaspoon fenugreek
½ teaspoon turmeric
6 oz. 1st and 2nd extracts of coconut milk.
2 teaspoons chillie powder
½ teaspoon cummin powder
¼ teaspoon sweet cummin powder
1 clove
1 teaspoon maldive fish
a sprig of curry leaves
½″ rampe
1 teaspoon salt

Method

1. Cut the big onions into quarters or keep them whole if small.
2. Put all the ingredients with the big onions into a pan and cook for 10-15 min. or until onions are cooked, but not too soft.

181. BIG ONIONS TEMPERED

Ingredients for 8 *portions.*

¾ lb. Big onions sliced fine
2 teaspoons maldive fish or dried prawn powder
a sprig of curry leaves
3 teaspoons chillie powder
¼ teaspoon turmeric powder
1″ cinnamon

2 dessertspoons tamarind 1 ½ teaspoons salt	dissolved in 1 oz. water

½″ rampe

4 dessertspoons oil

Method

1. Heat the oil. Add all the ingredients and fry for a few minutes till onions are half done.

2. Add tamarind.

3. Fry till onions are cooked, but not too soft.

182. BITTER GOURD CURRIED

Ingredients for 8 *portions.*

¾ lb. bitter gourd	1 small tomato
1 oz. onions	2 green chillies
2 sprigs of curry leaves	2 teaspoons chillie powder
½ teaspoon cummin powder	¼ teaspoon sweet cummin powder
½ teaspoon fenugreek	
1 teaspoon salt	½″ cinnamon

8 oz. 1st & 2nd extracts of coconut milk.

Method

1. Wash and cut bitter gourd into four. Then into 1 ½″ lengths. Add 2 pieces goraka, ½ teaspoon salt and boil till soft.

2. Chop the onions, green chillies and tomato.

3. Mix all the ingredients except bitter gourd, with the coconut milk. Bring to boil and simmer till onions are soft.

4. Add boiled bitter gourd, cook for a further 10 minutes and take off fire.

N.B.:- Bitter Gourd Sambol.

Bitter gourd may be grated after washing with the coarse side of grater. This is mixed with sliced onions, green chillies. Add lime juice and salt to taste. 1-2 tablespoons of thick coconut milk may be added. A chopped tomato may also be added.

183. BITTER GOURD FRIED AND CURRIED

Ingredients for 8 *portions.*

¾ lb. bitter gourd.

Gravy

8oz. 1st and 2nd extracts of coconut milk

2 teaspoons mustard ground	1 teaspoon chillie powder
1 teaspoon coriander powder	½ teaspoon cummin powder
	2 oz. big onions
¼ teaspoon sweet cummin powder	2 cloves garlic
	2 cardamoms
1 teaspoon maldive fish	½″ cinnamon
1 clove, 1 piece goraka	1 ¼ teaspoons salt.

Method

1. Wash and cut the bitter gourd into finger lengths. Rub turmeric and salt and deep fry. Chop onions, green chillies and garlic.

2. Add all the ingredients with the coconut milk. Bring to boil and simmer till onions are soft.

3. Add the fried bitter gourd. Bring to boil and simmer till gravy is thick.

184. CABBAGE CURRY (Tempered)

Ingredients for 8 *portions.*

1 lb. cabbage	1 oz. red onions,
2-3 green chillies	1 teaspoon maldive fish
2 sprigs of curry leaves	¼ teaspoon turmeric powder
2 teaspoons coriander powder	1 teaspoon cummin powder
	2 teaspoon chillie powder
½ teaspoon sweet cummin	2 dessertspoons oil

2 teaspoons salt

4 oz. 1st extract of coconut milk, (for dry curry)

8 oz. 1st extract of coconut milk (for curry with gravy)

Method

1. Wash and cut up cabbage into rough pieces taking care to slice stalks finely.

2. Mix cabbage with all the ingredients except oil and coconut milk.

3. Heat oil in a pan until very hot and add the cabbage and stir occasionally till cabbage is done (test thick stalks) and very little gravy left.

4. Add the coconut milk, bring to boil allow to simmer for a few minutes.

5. For cold method, all ingredients can be added together with 10 oz. 1st and 2nd extract of coconut milk and cooked till done.

185. CABBAGE CURRIED WHOLE

Ingredients for 8 *portions.*

1 cabbage (1 lb)
2 green chillies
2 teaspoons chillie powder
1 teaspoons cummin powder
¼ teaspoon turmeric powder
1 cardamon
2 dessertspoons maldive fish
2-3 oz. onions
2 sprigs of curry leaves
2 teaspoons coriander powder
½ teaspoon sweet cummin powder
1 clove
2″ cinnamon
1 dessertspoon oil
½ pint 2nd extract of coconut milk
4 oz. 1st extract of coconut milk

Method

1. Wash cabbage well under running water. Chop onions and chillies.

2. Put all the ingredients together, except 1/3 onions and a sprig of curry leaves and 1st extract of coconut milk. Bring to boil and simmer till cabbage is soft. Test thick part of stalk.

3. Take out cabbage from gravy. Heat oil in a pan. Add remaining onions and curry leaves. Allow to brown. Add gravy. Then add 1st extract of coconut milk. Bring to boil, put back cabbage and simmer for a few minutes more, till gravy is thick.

186. CABBAGE STUFFED CURRIED

Ingredients for 8 *portions.*

1 cabbage (1 lb)

3 oz. onions

a sprig of curry leaves

½ teaspoon pepper

1 portion recipe No.153

¾ lb. minced beef

2 green chillies

½ teaspoon chillie powder

1 teaspoon salt

Method

1. Steam cabbage for about 10 minutes, with stem side up. Drain.

2. Chop chillies, onions, add to meat with the rest of the ingredients and mix well.

3. Open out cabbage very carefully and remove the centre with the very tiny leaves. Put meat stuffing and close up first round of leaves. Put more stuffing to close up second round of leaves and so on till stuffing is all used up. Tie up cabbage with thread to keep in place. Cook in gravy for stuffed cabbage (Recipe No.153).

187. CABBAGE WHITE CURRY

Ingredients for 8 *portions.*

1 lb. cabbage
2 green chillies
½ teaspoon fenugreek
½ teaspoon turmeric powder
1 dessertspoon oil
3-4 oz 1st extract of coconut milk
1 oz. onions
1 teaspoon mustard seeds for tempering
1 oz. onions
1 teaspoon maldive fish
1 ¼ teaspoons salt
8 oz. 2nd and 3rd extracts of coconut milk
a sprig of curry leaves

Method

1. Wash and cut cabbage into 1″ pieces. Cut stalks, finely chop onions and chillies.
2. Mix all the ingredients except 1st extract of coconut milk and cook till done and gravy has reduced.
3. Heat oil in a pan and when very hot add curry leaves and onions. Cook till onions are golden brown. Add mustard and the 1st extract of coconut milk, bring to boil. Add the cooked cabbage, simmer for a few minutes and take off fire.

188. CABBAGE RED CURRY

Ingredients for 8 *portions.*

1 lb. cabbage
2 green chillies
a sprig of curry leaves
2-3 teaspoons chillie powder
¼ teaspoon turmeric powder
1 ½ - 2 teaspoons salt

8oz. 1st and 2nd extracts of coconut milk

oz. onions.

Method

1. Wash and cut the cabbage coarsely, taking care to slice the stalks finely.

2. Mix all the ingredients together with the coconut milk. Bring to boil and simmer till done.

189. CABBAGE BROWN CURRY

Ingredients for 8 *portions.*

1 lb. cabbage	2 oz. onions
½ teaspoon fenugreek	a sprig of curry leaves
½ teaspoon cummin powder	½ teaspoon sweet cummin powder
1 ½ teaspoons chillie powder	
1 teaspoon ground mustard	2 teaspoons coriander powder
2 teaspoons salt	2 teaspoons coconut grated

8 oz. 1st and 2nd extracts of coconut milk.

Method

1. Wash and chop cabbage coarsely, slice the stalk finely. Chop onions.

2. Roast the curry powders and coconut until dark brown in colour and grind the mustard and roasted ingredients.

3. Heat oil in a pan. Add onions and curry leaves fry for 2-3 minutes. Add the roasted ingredients and the cabbage. Fry for a few minutes.

4. Add the coconut milk. Bring to boil and simmer till done.

190. CARROT CABBAGE AND BEAN CURRY

Ingredients for 8 *portions.*

6 oz. cabbage
6 oz. carrots
½ pint 1st extract of coconut milk
1 teaspoon cummin powder
1 dessertspoon chillie powder
2 oz. chopped onions
a sprig of curry leaves
2 teaspoons maldive fish
1 cardamom crushed
1 teaspoon mustard seeds
6 oz. beans
½ pint 2nd extract of of coconut milk
1 teaspoon coriander powder
½ teaspoon sweet cummin powder
2 teaspoons fenugreek
¼ oz. green chillies
¼ teaspoon turmeric powder
½″ cinnamon
2 teaspoons salt
2 dessertspoons oil

Method

1. Wash and shred cabbage, coarsely, peel carrots, wash and cut into ½″ cubes. String wash and cut beams into 1″ pieces.
2. Chop the onions and green chillies.
3. Add all the ingredients except half the onions, curry leaves and mustard and 1st extract of coconut milk, and cook till the carrots and beans are done but not over-boiled.
4. Heat the oil until very hot in a pan, add the remaining onions, curry leaves and toss till onions are golden brown. Add the mustard seeds and fry for a few seconds longer. Add the cooked vegetables, toss for a few minutes.

5. Add the 1st extract of coconut milk, bring to the boil reduce heat, cook for a few minutes longer.

191. CARROT CURRY (BROWN)

Ingredients for 8 *portions.*

1 lb. carrots	2 oz. onions
2 green chillies	a sprig of curry leaves
2 teaspoons chillie powder	1 teaspoon coriander powder
1 teaspoon cummin powder	½ teaspoon sweet cummin powder
½ teaspoon turmeric powder	
2 dessertspoons oil	1 teaspoon salt

6 oz. 1st and 2nd extracts of coconut milk

Method

1. Peel, wash and cut carrot into 1″ x ¼″ x ¼″ strips. Chop onions and green chillies.
2. Heat oil until very hot in a pan, and the carrot mixed well with all the ingredients except the coconut milk. Keep tossing for 5-7 minutes. Add the coconut milk. Bring to boil and simmer till done.

192. CARROT WHITE CURRY

Ingredients for 8 *portions.*

1 lb. carrots	4 green chillies
2 oz. big onions	½ teaspoon fenugreek
a sprig of curry leaves	¼ teaspoon turmeric powder
1 teaspoon maldive fish	2 teaspoons salt

2 oz. 1st extract of coconut milk

10 oz. 2nd and 3rd extracts of coconut milk

½″ cinnamon

Method

1. Wash, cut or grate carrot with coarse side of grater.Chop the onions and green chillies.
2. Cook with all the ingredients except 1st extract of coconut milk until done.
3. Add 1st extract of coconut milk, bring to boil stirring all the time.

193. CADJU CURRY - 1

Ingredients for 8 *portions.*

½ lb. dried cadjunuts

1 teaspoon fenugreek

3-4 teaspoons chillie powder

2 oz. onions chopped

8 oz. 1st and 2nd extracts of coconut milk

1 cardamom

1″ cinnamon

2 teaspoons coriander powder

1 teaspoon cummin powder

¼ teaspoon turmeric powder

a sprig of curry leaves

1 clove

1 - 1 ¼ teaspoon salt

Method

1. Cover cadjunuts with boiling water add 1 teaspoon of bicarbonate soda. Soak overnight if possible or several hours. Wash in several changes of water. Boil until tender but do not make cadju soft. Wash in cold water after boiling.

2. Heat oil in a pan and when very hot add the curry leaves and onions and fry till onions are light brown.

3. Add the cadjunuts mixed well with all the powdered ingredients and salt. Cook for 5-10 minutes.

4. Add the coconut milk. bring to boil and simmer till done.

Note: Omit chillie powder if a white curry is desired and add 2-4 green chillies chopped.

194. STUFFED CAPSICUM CHILLIES WITH VEGETABLE FILLING

Ingredients for 8 *portions.*

½ lb. capsicum chillies (2″ - 16 Chillies)	2 oz. onions
	1 ½ dessertspoons maldive fish
a sprig of curry leaves	¾ teaspoon salt
1 teaspoon chillie powder	2 dessertspoons oil
½ lb. potatoes (boiled)	1 portion Recipe No.149

Method

1. Chop the onions and cut the potato into ½″ cubes.

2. Heat the oil in a pan and when very hot add the onions, curry leaves, maldive fish, chillie powder, and salt and toss for a few minutes, till light brown.

3. Add the potatoes and toss lightly for a few minutes and take off fire.

4. Slit the chillies on a side, remove the seeds and fill with the mixture.

5. Heat oil in a pan and when very hot toss the chillies for 5-7 minutes.

6. Cook stuffed chillie in gravy (Recipe No.149). Bring gravy to boil. Cook till thick. Add stuffed chillies. Simmer for a few minutes and take off fire.

195. STUFFED CAPSICUM CHILLIES WITH BEEF FILLING

Ingredients for 8 *portions.*

½ lb. capsicum chillies (2-16 chillies)	2 oz. onions
	a sprig of curry leaves
6 oz. beef minced	1 teaspoon pepper powder
½ oz. green chillie	1 clove garlic
2 oz. potatoes (boiled)	2 dessertspoons oil
1 teaspoon salt	1 portion Recipe No.147
a thin slice ginger	

Method

1. Chop the onions, green chillies, garlic and ginger and cut the potato into ¼″ cubes.

2. Heat the oil in a pan and when very hot add the curry leaves, onions and garlic and toss for a few minutes.

3. Add the beef, ginger, pepper and salt and toss for a few minutes, till beef is cooked, then add the potatoes, toss for a few minutes, take off fire.

4. Slit the chillies on a side and remove the seeds. Fill with the beef mixture.

5. Heat 2 dessertspoons oil in a shallow frying pan and when very hot put the filled chillies and toss them for about 5-7 minutes. Cook in gravy (Recipe No.147). Bring gravy to boil, simmer. Add the stuffed chillies. Cook for just a few minutes.

196. CAPSICUM CHILLIES - FILLING WITH FISH

Ingredients for 8 *portions.*

½ lb. capsicum chillies (2-16 chillies)	2 oz. onions
	¼ oz. green chillies
6 oz. fish (boiled and flaked)	2 oz. potatoes (boiled)
a sprig of curry leaves	1 teaspoon pepper powder
1 teaspoon salt	2 dessertspoons oil
1 clove garlic	1 portion Recipe No.148

Method

1. Chop the onions, green chillies, garlic and cut the potatoes into ¼″ cubes.

2. Heat the oil in a pan and when very hot add the curry leaves, onions, chillies and garlic and toss for a few minutes.

3. Add the flaked fish, pepper and salt and cook for a few minutes and take off fire.

4. Slit the chillies on one side, take out seeds and fill with the fish mixture.

5. Cook stuffed chillies in gravy (Recipe No.148). Bring gravy to boil, simmer 5-10 minutes. Add the stuffed chillies. Cook for a few minutes and take off fire.

197. CAPSICUM CHILLIES WHITE CURRY

Ingredients for 8 *portions.*

1 lb. capsicum chillies	2 oz. onions
1 dessertspoon maldive fish	¼ teaspoon turmeric
1 teaspoon salt	½ teaspoon fenugreek
a sprig of curry leaves	6 oz. 2nd extract of coconut milk
2 oz. 1st extract of coconut milk	1 tomato (optional)

Capsicum chillies may be dipped in boiling water for just a minute or two and water allowed to drain. Then wipe dry and stuff with any one of the fillings.

Method

1. Wash and slit the chillies half way from the bottom end. Chop the onions and tomato if used.
2. Add all the ingredients together, mix well and bring to boil till done and gravy has reduced.
3. Add the 1st extract of coconut milk. Bring to boil and take off fire.

198. CAPSICUM CHILLIES RED CURRY

Ingredients for 8 *portions*

1 lb. capsicum chillies	2 oz. onions
1 dessertspoon maldive fish	1 teaspoon chillie powder
1 teaspoon coriander powder	3 dessertspoon oil
½ teaspoon cummin powder	a sprig of curry leaves
1 teaspoon salt	6 oz. 1st extract of coconut milk

Method

1. Wash and slit the chillies half way, from the bottom end. Chop the onions.
2. Heat oil in a pan. Add the curry leaves and onions and fry till light brown, add the capsicum chillies mixed with all the ingredients except coconut milk. Toss till done.
3. Add the coconut milk. Bring to boil and simmer for 5-7 minutes.

199. CUCUMBER WHITE CURRY

Ingredients for 8 *portions.*

1 lb. cucumber	2 green chillies
1 oz. red onions	a sprig of curry leaves
a pinch of turmeric	1 teaspoon mustard ground
1 ½ teaspoons salt	½ teaspoon fenugreek
3 oz. 2nd and 3rd extracts of coconut milk	1 oz. 1st extract of coconut milk

Method

1. Peel and cut cucumber into small even pieces. Chop the onions and green chillies. Mix with all the ingredients and cook in the 2nd and 3rd extracts of coconut milk till done and gravy has reduced.
2. Mix the mustard and the 1st extract of coconut milk and add to curry. Bring to boil and take off fire.

200. CUCUMBER MEAT CURRY TYPE

Ingredients for 8 *portions.*

1 lb. cucumber	2 green chillies
1 oz. red onions	a sprig of curry leaves
2 teaspoons chillie powder, 1 teaspoon coriander powder, ½ teaspoon cummin powder } roasted	
2 dessertspoons roasted coconut ground	
½ teaspoon sweet cummin	a pinch of turmeric powder
½″ cinnamon	4 oz. 1st and 2nd extracts of coconut milk
1 teaspoon salt	

Method

1. Wash, peel and cut cucumber into big pieces, score skin side lightly.
2. Chop chillies and onions. Roast the coconut and curry powders till dark brown.
3. Add all the ingredients to the cucumber with the coconut milk, bring to boil and simmer till done.

201. MADU DALU (CYCAS) - 1 - (CURRIED)

Ingredients for 8 *portions*

1 lb. madu dalu	2 oz. onions
½ oz. green chillies	½ sprig of curry leaves
3-4 teaspoons chillie powder	1 teaspoon coriander powder
1 teaspoon cummin powder	½ teaspoon sweet cummin powder

2 cloves garlic
1 dessertspoon maldive fish
16 oz. 1st and 2nd extracts of coconut milk
2 pieces goraka
1 teaspoon salt

Method

1. Peel off skin from thick end of madu dalu. Wash well and cut into ¼″ pieces.
2. Chop the onions, green chillies and garlic.
3. Put all the ingredients together with the coconut milk into a pan. Bring to boil and simmer till done and gravy has reduced.

202. DHAL WHITE CURRY

Ingredients for 8 *portions.*

½ lb. dhal
2 green chillies
1 ½ teaspoons salt
¼ pint 1st extract of coconut milk
1 ¼ oz. onions
¼ teaspoon turmeric powder
1 pint 2nd and 3rd extracts of coconut milk

For tempering:
2 dessertspoons oil
1 teaspoon mustard seeds
5-6 dry chillies
2 sprigs of curry leaves
3 cloves garlic

Method

1. Clean and wash dhal. Slice the onions.

2. Place in a pan with ½ the curry leaves, chillies and ½ oz of sliced onions, turmeric and 2nd and 3rd extracts of coconut milk and cook till done. Stir occasionally.

3. Add the salt, stir and remove dhal to another container.

4. Heat the oil till very hot add the remaining curry leaves, sliced onions, dry chillies cut up roughly, mustard and crushed garlic. Keep stiring till onions are golden brown and mustard crackles.

5. Add the dhal. Stir. Add the first extract of coconut milk bring to boil and remove from fire.

Note:- Add ½ pint 1st extract of coconut milk if curry is with gravy. If dry curry is required add ¼ pint coconut milk.

203. DHAL CURRY - (Tempered)

Ingredients for 8 *portions.*

½ lb. dhal	2 oz. onions
2-3 dry chillies	1″ rampe
a sprig of curry leaves	2 teaspoons chillie powder
1 teaspoon coriander powder	2 clove garlic
	2 dessertspoons oil
½ teaspoon salt	1 pint 1st and 2nd extracts of coconut milk
1 ¼ - 1 ½ pints 1st and 2nd extracts of coconut milk	for more gravy

Method

1. Wash and soak the dhal in water for an hour.

2. Slice the onions, chillies and chop garlic.

3. Heat the oil till very hot in a pan, add the curry leaves, onions, chillies, garlic and the drained dhal and keep tossing till dhal is cooked.

4. Add the rest of the ingredients and the coconut milk. Bring to boil and simmer till done.

Note:- Add I pint 1st and 2nd extracts of coconut milk if dry curry is required, 1 ¼ or 1 ½ pints of 1st and 2nd extracts of coconut milk if more gravy is needed.

204. DHAL, DRY CURRY

Ingredients for 8 *portions.*

Same as Dhal White Curry, but allow dhal to get dry after 1st and 2nd extracts of coconut milk is added before tempering.

205. DHAL CUTLETS

Ingredients for 8 *portions.*

3 oz. dhal
1 teaspoon maldive fish
a sprig of celery or curry leaves chopped
3 dessertspoons oil
¼ teaspoon pepper powder
4 green chillies chopped
2 oz. Bombay onions chopped
½ teaspoon cummin powder
¼ teaspoon salt
1 teaspoon chillie powder
oil for deep frying

batter and crumbs for coating.

Method

1. Soak dhal in water for several hours. Cook till soft.

2. Heat oil in pan and add onions, chillies, curry leaves and temper for a few minutes.

3. Then add dhal and the rest of the ingredients and cook till dry.

4. Form into cutlets, dip in batter and crumbs. Deep fry.

206. DHAL RED CURRY

Ingredients for 8 *portions*

4 oz. dhal	½ teaspoons salt
2 oz. onions	2 ripe chillies
2 teaspoons chillie powder	1 teaspoon maldive fish
2 teaspoons coriander powder	¼ teaspoon turmeric powder
	1 teaspoon cummin powder
a sprig of curry leaves	½″ cinnamon
½″ rampe	1 ¼ dessertspoons oil for tempering

16 oz. 2nd extract of coconut milk or water.

Method

1. Clean and wash the dhal. Chop the onions, slice the green chillies.

2. Boil dhal in water or coconut milk, add all ingredients except half the onions, curry leaves, rampe, salt and turmeric.

3. Add turmeric and salt when done, simmer down gravy. Heat oil until very hot in a pan, add the remaining onions, curry leaves and rampe.

4. When onions are browning add cooked dhal mixture. Bring to the boil and take off fire.

207. DHAL AND SPINACH

Ingredients for 8 portions.

¾ lb. spinach	2 oz. dhal
2 oz. onions	2 green chillies
1 clove garlic	a sprig of curry leaves
8 oz. 1st and 2nd extracts coconut milk	½ teaspoons salt
	2 dessertspoons oil

Method

1. Pick and wash the spinach well. Cut the leaves into big pieces. Cut the tender stalks fine. Wash the dhal removing all stones.
2. Chop the onions and green chillies.
3. Heat oil till very hot in a pan, add the dhall with the onions and curry leaves and fry for a few minutes. Add garlic and chillie and fry for a few minutes more. Add the coconut milk and turmeric. Bring to boil and simmer till dhal is done. Add the salt.
4. Add the spinach to the cooked dhal and cook till stalks are tender.

208. DRUMSTICK CURRY - FRIED AND COOKED

Ingredients for 8 *portions*

1 lb. drumsticks	a sprig of curry leaves

½' rampe
1 teaspoon salt
1 teaspoon mustard
4 dessertspoons oil
½ pint 1st and 2nd extracts of coconut milk
1 dessertspoon tamarind juice
½ teaspoon turmeric powder
2 teaspoons chillie powder
1 teaspoon cummin powder
2 teaspoons coriander powder
1 teaspoon fenugreek
2 oz. onions
½ teaspoon sweet cummin powder

Method

1. Heat oil till very hot in a pan, add onions and curry leaves and fry for a few minutes. Add mustard and fry till onions are golden brown. Add drumsticks and all the ingredients except coconut milk and cook on a low flame till done.
2. Add the coconut milk, bring to boil and take off fire.

209.GREEN GRAM - MEAT CURRY TYPE (Moong ata)

Ingredients for 8 *portions.*

8 oz. green gram
3 teaspoons chillie powder
1 teaspoon coriander powder
½ teaspoon sweet cummin powder
1 pint 1st and 2nd extracts of coconut milk
2 oz. onions
1 green chillie
1 teaspoon cummin powder
¼ teaspoon turmeric powder
4 dessertspoons oil
1 teaspoon salt

Method

1. Wash and dry green gram.
2. Roast green gram slightly and pound or roll with rolling pin on a board. Winnow to remove skin.
3. Chop onions and green chillies.
4. Heat oil in a pan, add onions and curry leaves and cook till onions are light brown. Add green gram with all the other ingredients except coconut milk. Keep frying for 5-7 minutes.
5. Add coconut milk, bring to boil and simmer till done.

210. GREEN GRAM - COLD METHOD

Ingredients for 8 *portions.*

8 oz. green gram	2 oz. onions
2 green chillies	2 teaspoons chillie powder
1 teaspoon coriander powder	½ teaspoon cummin powder
	¼ teaspoon turmeric powder
a sprig of curry leaves	1 pint 2nd and 3rd extracts of coconut milk or water
1 teaspoon salt	

6-8oz. 1st extract of coconut milk

Method

1. Wash and remove stones from green gram, chop onions and chillies.
2. Put all the ingredients into a pan with the 2nd and 3rd extracts of coconut milk, bring to boil and cook till done.
3. Add 1st extract of coconut milk. Bring to boil and take off fire.

211. INNALA - WHITE CURRY

Ingredients for 8 *portions.*

1 lb. innala	2 oz. onions
2 green chillies	½ teaspoon turmeric powder
½ teaspoon fenugreek	1 teaspoon salt
16 oz. 2nd extract of coconut milk	4 oz. 1st extract of coconut milk.

Method

1. Remove skin from innala by putting into a sack and beating against the floor, or soak for a few hours and scrape with a small knife. Wash well.
2. Add all the ingredients with 2nd and 3rd extracts of coconut milk. Bring to boil and cook till tender, and gravy has reduced.
3. Add the 1st extract of coconut milk. Bring to boil and simmer for a few minutes, take off fire.

212. INNALA TEMPERED

Ingredients for 8 *portions.*

1 lb. innala	3 teaspoons chillie powder (coarse)
4 dessertspoons oil	
¼ teaspoon turmeric powder	a sprig of curry leaves
½ teaspoon fenugreek	2 oz. onions

1 teaspoon salt.

Method

1. Wash and put innala in a pan, cover with water and boil till soft.

2. Heat oil in a pan and when very hot add onions and curry leaves and fry till light brown. Add innala with all the other ingredients and keep frying for a few minutes and take off fire.

213. INNALA HOT CURRY

Ingredients for 8 *portions.*

1 lb. innala	1 teaspoon coriander
¼ teaspoon turmeric powder	1 teaspoon cummin
a sprig of curry leaves	1 dessertspoon maldive fish (optional)
1/2 " rampe	3 teaspoons chillie powder
2 dessertspoons oil	2 oz. 1st extract of coconut milk
1 teaspoon salt	

Method

1. Soak the innala and scrub well to remove skin. Cover with water, add 1 teaspoon salt and boil till done and water has absorbed.

2. Heat oil till very hot in a pan, add the curry leaves, rampe and onions. Fry till onions are light brown. Add the innala, chillie powder, turmeric, salt and keep tossing a for 5-7 minutes.

3. Add the first extract of coconut milk, bring to boil and remove from fire.

214. JAK SEED CURRY - 1

Ingredients for 8 *portions.*

1 lb. jak seeds	1 teaspoon salt
2 oz. coconut roasted to a dark colour	2 teaspoons coriander
	2 teaspoons chillie powder
1 pint 2nd extract of coconut milk	1 piece goraka

Method

1. Wash the seeds. Cover with cold water, add 1 teaspoon salt and boil till tender. Remove the outer skin.
2. Add all the ingredients and simmer for about ½ an hour till gravy has rediced and thick.

215. JAK SEED - 2

Ingredients for 8 *portions.*

1 lb. or 100 jak seeds	4 teaspoons chillie powder
1 teaspoon cummin powder	2 teaspoons coriander powder
¼ teaspoon turmeric	1 ½ teaspoons fenugreek
1″ cinnamon	1 clove
1 cardamom	1 teaspoon salt
a sprig of curry leaves	1 pint 2nd extract of coconut milk

Method

1. Crack jak seeds with a hard object to break skin. Boil, do not make it pulpy.

2. Mix all the ingredients with coconut milk. Add boiled jak seeds with skins removed and cook until gravy is thick.

3. Reduce gravy to ½ or less. Curry to be cooked on a slow fire from step No.2. Slow fire is preferred to the end.

216. JAK WHITE CURRY

Ingredients for 8 *portions.*

1 lb. jak pericarps and seeds

1 teaspoon pepper	2 oz onions
1 teaspoon salt	½ teaspoon turmeric
2 cardamoms	1 teaspoon fenugreek
½ dessertspoon maldive fish	1″ cinnamon
10 oz 2nd extract of coconut milk	½ oz. green chillies

4 oz. 1st extract of coconut milk

Method

1. Cut pericarps into strips. Clean seeds, Wash well.
2. Chop onions and green chillies.
3. Boil seeds till partially cooked with all the ingredients except 1st extract of coconut milk.
4. Add pericarps and cook on a slow fire till tender.
5. Add 1st extract of coconut milk. Bring to boil, cook for 5 minutes till done.

217. JAK TEMPERED

Ingredients for 8 *portions.*

1 lb. jak pericarps
¼ teaspoon turmeric
2 oz. onions
a sprig of curry leaves
4 dessertspoons oil
3 teaspoons chillie powder
1 teaspoons salt
2 green chillies
1″ rampe

Method

1. Wash and cut jak pericarps into strips. Chop the onions and green chillies.
2. Heat the oil till very hot in a pan, add the rampe, curry leaves and onions.
3. Mix all the other ingredients with jak, pericarps, and when the onions are light brown keep tossing until cooked. Cover with lid and lower heat. Stir occasionally till done.

218. JAK RED CURRY

Ingredients for 8 *portions.*

1 lb. jak pericarps without seeds
2 green chillies
2 teaspoons chillie powder
1 teaspoon salt
1 pint 2nd and 3rd extracts of coconut milk
¼ teaspoon turmeric
a sprig of curry leaves
2 cloves garlic
1 teaspoon cumin powder
1 teaspoon sweet cummin powder
1 teaspoon fenugreek
4 oz. 1st extract of coconut milk
2 oz. onions.

Method

1. Wash and cut jak pericarps into strips. Chop the onions and chillies. Add all the ingredients with the 2nd and 3rd extracts of coconut milk. Bring to boil and cook till done.

2. Add the 1st extract of coconut milk. Bring to boil and simmer for five minutes.

219. KOHILA STEMS - CURRIED

Ingredients for 8 *portions.*

1 lb. kohila
2 teaspoons coriander powder
2 teaspoons chillie powder
¼ teaspoon turmeric
2 oz. onions
¼ oz. green chillies
a sprig of curry leaves
2 pieces goraka or 5 billing (fresh or dried). Combination of acids may be used e.g. tomato and billing
¼ teaspoon fenugreek
1 teaspoon salt
3 dessertspoons oil
1 dessertspoon maldive fish

6oz. 1st extract of coconut milk

Method

1. Break off the leaves and the tender parts of the stems. Peel off skins from thicker stems and break into pieces. Wash and squeeze out the water.

2. Chop the onions, green chillies. Mix all the ingredients with the kohila except curry leaves, onions and coconut milk.

3. Heat the oil till very hot in a pan, add the curry leaves, onions and fry till onions are light brown. Add the kohila and toss for 5-6 minutes.

4. Add the coconut milk, bring to boil, simmer till gravy is reduced and kohila is cooked.

220. KOHILA TEMPERED (YAMS OR ALA)

Ingredients for 8 *portions.*

¾ lb. kohila yams	2 oz. onions
2 green chillies	2 teaspoons chillie powder
1 teaspoon coriander powder	1 teaspoon cummin powder
1 teaspoon mustard	¼ teaspoon turmeric powder
a sprig of curry leaves	3 dessertspoons oil
1 ½ teaspoon salt	1 tomato or 2-3 billings or a piece of goraka
12 oz. 1st and 2nd extracts of coconut milk	

Method

1. Wash and cut kohila into 1″ pieces, then shred into fine strips. Chop the onions and green chillies.

2. Heat oil in a pan and when very hot add the curry leaves and onions, add mustard and curry powder and fry for a minute or two. Add the kohila with the rest of the ingredients except coconut milk and fry for 5 minutes. Add the coconut milk and bring to boil. Simmer till done.

221. KOHILA CUTLETS (YAMS OR ALA)

Ingredients for 8 *portions.*

¾ lb. kohila ala	3 oz. onions
½ oz. green chillies	2 teaspoons maldive fish

a sprig of curry leaves

¼ teaspoon cummin powder ½ teaspoon chillie powder

1 dessertspoon oil batter and crumbs

oil for deep frying

Method

1. Wash and cut the kohila into big pieces. Cover with water, add 1 ½ teaspoons salt and boil till soft. Mince coarsely.
2. Chop the onions and green chillies.
3. Heat oil till very hot, add the curry leaves and onions, fry till light brown. Then add the rest of the ingredients and the kohila. Fry for a few minutes and take off fire.
4. Form into cutlets. Dip in batter and crumbs. Deep fry.

222. KANKUN TEMPERED

Ingredients for 8 *portions.*

1 lb. kankun leaves a sprig of curry leaves

2 oz. onions chopped 1 teaspoon salt

1 dessertspoon chillie powder (coarse). 4 dessertspoons oil

Method

1. Pick, clean and wash the kankun leaves.
2. Heat oil till very hot in pan add the onions, curry leaves and chillie powder. Fry till onions are done.
3. Add leaves and salt. Toss for 5-10 minutes and take off fire.

223. LADY'S FINGERS - TEMPERED

Ingredients for 8 *portions.*

1 lb. lady's fingers
2 green chillies
1-1 ½ teaspoons chillie powder
¼ teaspoon turmeric
2 oz. 1st extract of coconut milk
1 ½ - 2 oz. onions
a sprig of curry leaves
½ teaspoon fenugreek
1 dessertspoon maldive fish
3 dessertspoons oil
1 teaspoon salt

Method

1. Wash, trim and cut lady's fingers into 1″ pieces.
2. Slice the chillies and onions.
3. Put into a pan with all the ingredients and mix well.
4. Heat the oil till very hot in a pan, add the lady's fingers. Keep tossing for 5-7 minutes.
5. Add the coconut milk, bring to boil and simmer.

224. LADY'S FINGERS WHITE CURRY

Ingredients for 8 *portions.*

1 lb. lady's fingers
1 green chillie
1 teaspoon maldive fish
a sprig of curry leaves
2 oz. 1st extract of coconut milk
3 dessertspoons oil
½ oz. red onions
½ teaspoon turmeric
1 teaspoon salt
10 oz. 2nd and 3rd extracts of coconut milk
½ teaspoon fenugreek

Method

1. Wash, trim and cut lady's fingers into 1" pieces.
2. Slice the chillies and chop onions.
3. Put into a pan the lady's fingers with all the ingredients except 1st extract of coconut milk and mix well.
4. Heat the oil till very hot in pan, add the lady's fingers, keep tossing for 5-7 minutes.
5. Add the 1st extract of coconut milk, bring to boil and simmer until done.

Note:-The cold method may also be used. Cook the lady's fingers with all the ingredients and 10 oz.2nd and 3rd extracts of coconut milk. Cook till tender. Add 2 oz of 1st extract of coconut milk, simmer and take off fire.

225. LADY'S FINGERS FRIED AND COOKED

Ingredients for 8 *portions.*

1 lb. lady's fingers	2 green chillies
a sprig of curry leaves	1 oz. onions
1 ½ teaspoons chillie powder	½ teaspoon coriander powder
½ teaspoon cummin powder	½" cinnamon
1 teaspoon maldive fish	1 teaspoon salt

8 oz. 1st & 2nd extracts of coconut milk

Method

1. Wash and cut lady's fingers into 1" lengths on the slant. Rub turmeric and deep fry till light brown.

2. Chop the onions and green chillies. Mix all the ingredients together except fried lady's fingers and bring to boil and simmer till onions are cooked and soft. Add the fried lady's fingers. Bring to boil and take off fire.

226. LADY'S FINGERS RED CURRY TEMPERED

Ingredients for 8 *portions.*

1 lb. lady's fingers
1-2 green chillies
½ teaspoon coriander powder
¼ teaspoon sweet cummin powder
a pinch of turmeric
1 teaspoon maldive fish
1 oz. onions
2 teaspoons chillie powder
½ teaspoon cummin powder
1 teaspoon salt
a sprig of curry leaves
½″ cinnamon
4 oz. 1st extract of coconut milk
1 ½ dessertspoons oil

Method

1. Chop onions and green chillies.
2. Heat oil till very hot in a pan, add curry leaves and onions. Fry till onions are light brown.
3. Mix all the ingredients with the lady's fingers, add to oil and temper. Then add coconut milk and simmer till done.

227. LADY'S FINGERS (COLD METHOD)

Ingredients for 8 *portions.*

1 lb. lady's fingers
¼ oz. green chillies
1 oz. onions
½ teaspoon turmeric powder

1 teaspoon salt
1 teaspoon maldive fish
½ pint 2nd extract of coconut milk
¼ teaspoon fenugreek
a sprig of curry leaves
2 oz. 1st extract of coconut milk

Method

1. Trim, wash and cut lady's fingers into 1" pieces and place in a pan.
2. Add the chopped onions and green chillies and all the other ingredients with the 2nd extract of coconut milk. Bring to boil. Siammer till tender and liquid has reduced.
3. Add the 1st extract of coconut milk. Bring to boil. Simmer for a few minutes and take off fire.

228. LEEKS WHITE CURRY

Ingredients for 8 *portions.*

1 lb. leeks
½ teaspoon turmeric
½ teaspoon fenugreek
6 oz. 2nd & 3rd extracts of coconut milk
2 oz. onions
2 green chillies
1 teaspoon salt
4 oz. 1st extract of coconut milk
a sprig of curry leaves

Method

1. Wash and cut leeks into ½" pieces. The stalk into ¼"pieces. Chop onions and green chillies.
2. Add all the ingredients together except the 1st extract of coconut milk. Bring to boil and cook steadily till done and gravy has reduced.

3. Add the 1st extract of coconut milk. Bring to boil and take off fire.

229. MANGO CURRIED - 1

Ingredients for 8 *portions*

1 lb. mature mango but not ripe.

1 teaspoon mustard	10 dry chillies broken into small pieces
2 slices ginger	1″ rampe
5 cloves garlic	1″ sera
a sprig of curry leaves	1 dessertspoon coriander powder
1 dessertspoon of chillie powder	1 teaspoon sweet cummin powder
1 teaspoon cummin powder	1 teaspoon salt
1 dessertspoon vineger	2 oz. onions
3 dessertspoons oil	1 dessertspoon maldive fish or dried prawn powder
1 dessertspoon sugar	

¾ pint 1st & 2nd extracts of coconut milk

Method

1. Peel and cut mango into slices prick with fork. Add 1 dessertspoon of salt and cover with water and allow to soak for about ½ an hour.

2. Chop onions, ginger, garlic and cut the chillies into small pieces.

3. Heat oil in a pan till very hot, add the onions, chillies, mustard, curry leaves, rampe, sera and fry for a few minutes.

4. Wash and drain mango and add together with the vineger, salt and sugar. Fry for a few minutes.

5. Add the maldive fish, ginger, garlic, fry for a minute or two. Add the coconut milk, bring to boil and simmer till tender.

6. Roast the coriander, cummin and sweet cummin powder till golden brown and add to partially cooked curry.

7. Cook till gravy thickens. May be kept for 8-10 days.

230. MANGO CURRY - 2

Ingredients for 8 *portions.*

1 lb. mango (green)
2 clove garlic
2 dessertspoons mustard ground with vinegar
2 teaspoons coriander powder
8 oz. 1st extract of coconut milk
3 teaspoons chillie powder
1 slice ginger
1″ cinnamon
2 ripe chillies
½ teaspoon cummin powder
4oz. 2nd extract of coconut
1 oz. vinegar
1 teaspoon salt

Method

1. Peel and cut mango into four pieces. Chop the garlic, ginger and chillies.

2. Grind mustard with a little of the vinegar.

3. Mix all the ingredients with the 2nd extract of coconut milk. Bring to the boil and cook till mango is tender.

4. Add the mustard dissolved in the 1st extract of coconut milk. Bring to the boil and cook till done.

231. MA BEAN - CURRIED

Ingredients for 8 *portions.*

1 lb. ma beans	2 oz. onions
2 green chillies	a sprig of curry leaves
2 teaspoons chillie powder	¼ teaspoon turmeric powder
1 ½ teaspoons coriander powder	1 teaspoon cummin powder
	3 dessertspoon oil
1 teaspoon salt	4 oz. 1st extract of coconut milk

Method

1. Wash and break the beans into 1 ½ - 2″ lengths. Chop the onions and green chillies.
2. Heat the oil in a pan and when very hot add the curry leaves and onions. Add all the ingredients except the coconut milk and mix well with the beans, and keep tossing for 5-7 minutes.
3. Add the coconut milk bring to boil and simmer till done.

232. MA BEAN TEMPERED (RED)

Ingredients for 8 *portions.*

1 lb. ma beans	4 oz. onions
¼ teaspoon turmeric powder	2 sprigs of curry leaves
1 ½ teaspoons chillie powder	1 teaspoon coriander powder
½ teaspoon cummin powder	1 pinch of sweet cummin powder
½ teaspoon fenugreek	1 teaspoon salt
1 dessertspoon maldive fish	4 oz. 1st extract of coconut milk
2 dessertspoons oil	

Method

1. String the beans, wash and break into convenient pieces.
2. Mix together the beans, chillie powder, sliced or chopped onions, curry leaves, green chillies, fenugreek, curry powder and maldive fish.
3. Heat the oil in a pan and when it is very hot, add the beans and keeptossing for a few minutes until cooked.
4. Add the coconut milk and allow to cook till done.

Note:- In preparing beans in this manner, the colour is retained. Lady's fingers, carrots, raddish, leeks or beetroot leaves, may be prepared in this manner. Keep pan open.

233. MUKUNUWENNA TEMPERED

Ingredients for 8 *portions.*

1 lb. mukunuwenna (waste 4 ½ oz.)

2 green chillies	2 oz. onions
3 dessertspoons oil	3 dessertspoons maldive fish
1 teaspoon salt	1 ½ dessertspoons coarse
chillie powder	a spring of curry leaves

a pinch of turmeric

Method

1. Pick, clean and wash the mukunuwenna leaves. Chop onions and chillies.
2. Heat the oil when very hot add the curry leaves and onions and chillies and fry for a few minutes. Add the chillie powder, maldive fish and toss for a few minutes.

3. Add the leaves, salt, turmeric and keep tossing till done.

234. ONION LEAVES TEMPERED

Ingredients for 8 *portions.*

1 lb. onion leaves	1 oz. Bombay onions
¼ oz. green chillies	2 ½ teaspoons coarse chillie powder
2 dessertspoons maldive fish	
5 dessertspoons oil	1 teaspoon salt
¼ teaspoon turmeric powder	a sprig of curry leaves

Method

1. Clean, wash and cut onion leaves into ¾″ pieces and put into a pan.
2. Chop the onions and chillies and add to the onion leaves with all the other ingredients. Mix well together.
3. Heat the oil in a pan and when very hot add the onion leaves and keep tossing till done.

235. POTATOES TEMPERED

Ingredients for 8 *portions.*

1 lb. boiled potatoes	½ lb. Bombay onions
a sprig of curry leaves	2 dessertspoons chillie powder
¼ teaspoon turmeric	1 teaspoon salt
1-2 dessertspoons maldive fish (optional)	4 dessertspoons oil

Method

1. Peel and cut potatoes into even sizes. Add salt, turmeric, chilliepowder and mix well.
2. Heat oil and when it is very hot add the curry leaves and onions sliced fine. Fry till golden brown
3. Add the potatoes and keep tossing with the onions for a few minutes till done.

Variation 1.

1. Mix potatoes with turmeric and salt.
2. Heat about ¼″ oil in a pan and fry potatoes until a crust begins to form.
3. Add the onions sliced, and fry until brown.
4. Add the chillies and drain off excess oil. Keeps well.

Variation 2.

1. Mix the potatoes with salt only.
2. Mix the sliced onions with chillie powder, salt and lemon juice.
3. Heat 4 dessertspoon oil and toss the curry leaves and onions and cook for a few minutes. Add the potatoes.
4. Or add the cooked onions to the potatoes and toss them off the fire. This method is used for very large quantity of potatoes. Keeping qualities are poor.

236. POTATO WHITE CURRY - 1

Ingredients for 8 *portions.*

1 lb. potatoes
3 dessertspoons oil
1 oz. onion
a sprig of curry leaves
2 green chillies
2 teaspoons coriander powder
1 teaspoon chillie powder
¼ teaspoon turmeric powder
1 teaspoon salt
½" cinnamon
½ pint 1st & 2nd extracts of coconut milk

Method

1. Chop the onions and greenchillies. Peel and cut potatoes into convenient sizes.
2. Heat oil till very hot add the onions, curry leaves and cinnamon. When the onions are light brown, add the potatoes and salt and fry lightly for 5-7 minutes.
3. Add the curry powders and keep tossing for a minute or two.
4. Add the 1st & 2nd extracts of coconut milk and cook till done.

237. POTATO WHITE CURRY - 2

Ingredients for 8 *portions*

1 lb. potatoes
5-6 red onions
2 green chillies
2 teaspoons maldive fish
2 sprigs curry leaves
½ teaspoon turmeric
¼ teaspoon fenugreek
1 teaspoon salt
½ pint 2nd & 3rd extracts of coconut milk
2 oz. 1st extract of coconut milk

Method

1. Wash and peel potatoes. Cut into convenient sizes and add into the 2nd & 3rd extracts of coconut milk to prevent discolouration.
2. Add to this, the onions and chillies sliced, curry leaves, all indredients except 1st extract of coconut milk. Cook until potatoes are boiled.
3. Add the 1st extract of coconut milk. Bring to boil, and take off fire.

238. POTATO MUSTARD CURRY

Ingredients for 8 *portions.*

Cook as for Potato White Curry, and add 1 teaspoon ground mustard and a pinch of pepper mixed with the 1st extract of coconut milk.

239. POTATO CURRY (FRIED)

Ingredients for 8 *portions.*

1 lb. potatoes	¼ lb. onions
1″ piece cinnamon	a sprig of curry leaves
2-3 teaspoons maldive fish or prawn powder	4-5 green chillies
4 oz. 1st extract of coconut milk	8 oz. 2nd & 3rd extracts of coconut milk
1 cardamom crushed	¼ teaspoon turmeric
lime juice	1 teaspoon salt
	4 dessertspoon oil

Method

1. Wash potatoes with skins and cut into rather thick slices.
2. Slice the onions and green chillies.
3. Heat oil and when very hot add the potatoes, and toss till half cooked. Keep tossing all the time. Take off fire.
4. Put all the ingredients into a pan except the 1st extract of coconut milk, lime juice and potatoes and bring to the boil. Reduce heat and cook till onions are done.
5. Add the fried potatoes and the 1st extract of coconut milk and cook for 5-10 minutes.

240. POTATO BROWN CURRY

Ingredients for 8 *portions.*

1 lb. potatoes	2 dessertspoons coriander powder
2 teaspoons cummin powder	1 teaspoon sweet cummin powder
2 teaspoons fenugreek	2 teaspoons mustard (optional)
a pinch of turmeric	2 cloves garlic
1 dessertspoon chillie powder	2 oz. coconut
16 oz. 1st & 2nd extracts of coconut milk	2 oz. onions
a sprig of curry leaves	2 dessertspoons oil
1 teaspoon salt.	

Method

1. Peel and cut potatoes into 1″ pieces.
2. Chop the onions and garlic. Roast the coconut till dark in colour and grind to a paste.

3. Heat oil in a pan. Add all the curry powders and ground coconut and fry for a few minutes. Add mustard and fry for a few seconds.

4. Add potatoes and fry for 1-2 minutes. Add coconut milk and cook until potatoes are done and gravy is thick and reduced.

241. POTATO RED CURRY

Ingredients for 8 *portions.*

1 lb. potatoes
a sprig of curry leaves
a pinch of turmeric
1 teaspoon coriander powder
1 clove
1 cardamom
2 teaspoons maldive fish
2 oz. 1st extract of coconut milk
1 oz. onions chopped
1″ rampe
3 teaspoons chillie powder
1 teaspoon cummin powder
½ teaspoon sweet cummin
1 teaspoon salt
1 oz. 2nd extract of coconut milk
1″ cinnamon

Method

1. Peel and cut potatoes into convenient pieces. Chop the onions.

2. Mix all the ingredients with the 2nd & 3rd extracts of coconut milk and cook till potatoes are done.

3. Add the 1st extract of coconut milk. Stir for a few minutes. Bring to boil and take off fire.

242. POTATO DRY CURRY

Ingredients for 8 *portions.*

1 lb. potatoes	2 oz. Bombay onions chopped
1″ piece rampe	½″ sera
a sprig of curry leaves	a thin slice green ginger
1-2 cloves garlic sliced	½ teaspoon chillie powder
1 teaspoon coriander powder	2 green chillies
½ teaspoon mustard	½ teaspoon sweer cummin powder
½ teaspoon turmeric powder	
8 oz. 2nd & 3rd extracts of coconut milk	1 teaspoon salt
½ teaspoon fenugreek	2 dessertspoons oil
4oz. 1st extract of coconut milk	

Method

1. Peel and cut potatoes into even pieces.
2. Add all the ingredients and half of the onions and curry leaves, sera, rampe and 2nd & 3rd extracts of coconut milk and cook till done, but not too soft.
3. Temper with rest of the onions, curry leaves in oil. Add mustard when onions are almist browned.
4. Add 1st extract of coconut milk and cook till quite dry.

243. POTATO CUTLETS

Ingredients for 8 *portions 8 or 16 (cutlets)*

1 lb. potatoes	½ oz. green chillies
a sprig of curry leaves	1 clove garlic chopped

4 ½ oz. Bombay onions chopped
½ teaspoon chillie powder
batter
oil for frying
1 - 1 ½ teaspoons salt
1 teaspoon pepper powder
1 dessertspoon oil
2 dessertspoon maldive fish
bread crumbs

Method

1. Boil and mash potatoes.
2. Temper onions, reen chillies, curry leaves, garlic for a few minutes in 1 dessertspoon oil.
3. Add mashed potatoes.
4. Season with pepper, salt chillie powder.
5. Form into cutlets. Coat in batter, crumb and deep fry.

Note:-This may be served plain or added to a gravy (Recipe Nos. 149, 150 or 160).

244. POTATO AND BEAN CURRY (WHITE)

Ingredients for 8 *portions.*

¼ lb. potatoes peeled and cut into small pieces
½ lb. beans cut lengthwise
a pinch of turmeric
1 ½ teaspoons fenugreek
a sprig curry leaves
8 oz. 1st extract of coconut milk
2 oz. onions chopped
4-6 green chillies chopped
8 oz. 2nd & 3rd extracts of coconut milk
½′ cinnamon
1 teaspoon salt
2 teaspoons maldive fish or dry prawn powder

Method

1. Soak fenugreek for about 10 minutes in the 2nd & 3rd extracts of coconut milk. Drain coconut milk.
2. Add all ingredients except 1st extract of coconut milk and bring to boil. Allow to simmer until potatoes are done.
3. Add 1st extract of cocout milk, bring to boil stirring all the while, remove from fire.

245. PLANTAIN FLOWER WITH JAK SEEDS

Ingredients for 8 *portions.*

¾ lb. plantain flower (tender portion) after removing outer leaves

¼ lb. jak seeds	2 green chillies
2 teaspoons chillie powder	1 oz. onions
1 ½ teaspoons cummin powder	1 ¼ teaspoons salt
	1 teaspoon coriander powder
12 oz. 1st & 2nd extracts of coconut milk	½ teaspoon sweet cummin
	¼ teaspoon turmeric

Method

1. Cut the plantain flower into ½″ slices and then into ½″ pieces. Crush the jak seeds into 2-3 pieces.
2. Wash plantain flower pieces and jak seeds well.
3. Chop the onions and green chillies.
4. Add all the ingredients together. Bring to boil and simmer till jak seeds are tender.

246. PLANTAIN FLOWER TEMPERED

Ingredients for 8 *portions.*

1 lb. plantain flower	¼ - ½ lb. Bombay onions (sliced fine)
a sprig curry leaves	2 dessertspoons chillie powder
¼ teaspoon turmeric	3-4 dessertspoons oil
1-2 dessertspoons maldive fish	
1 teaspoon salt	

Method

1. Cut the tender portion of the flower into even sized pieces. Add salt, curry leaves, chillie powder and mix well.
2. Heat oil and when it is very hot add the curry leaves and sliced onions. Fry till golden brown.
3. Add the plantain flower and keep tossing with the onions for a few minutes till done.

247. POLOS AMBUL

Ingredients for 8 *portions.*

1 medium sized polos	1 dessertspoon coriander
2 teaspoons cummin powder	2 teaspoons sweet cummin powder
8 pepper corns	10-15 dry chillies or
a sprig of curry leaves	2-3 dessertspoons chillie powder
2-3 cardamoms and cloves	6 pieces of goraka
¼ teaspoon turmeric powder	4 teaspoon salt
3 teaspoons maldive fish	¼ oz. garlic

1 ½ pints 2nd extract of coconut milk

½ teaspoon fenugreek

2 oz. red onions

½ pint 1st extract of coconut milk

Method

1. Peel polos and cut into convenient pieces. Score deep on skin side of pieces and put into water.

2. Chop onions, and roast the spices, pepper, fenugreek and curry powders except chillie powder till golden brown.

3. Put the polos with all the other ingredients, and the 2nd & 3rd extracts of coconut milk into a pan. Bring to boil and simmer until the gravy has reduced and the polos soft.

4. Add the 1st extract of coconut milk, bring to boil and simmer till gravy is reduced. Remove the goraka.

Note:-Use a small pan so that coconut milk covers polos. The 1st extract of coconut milk may also be added with other ingredients.

248. POLOS CURRY

Ingredients for 8 *portions.*

1 lb. polos

4 teaspoons salt

a thin slice of ginger

4 teaspoons coriander powder

2 teaspoons sweet cummin powder

¼ teaspoon turmeric powder

2 ½ oz. onions

2 ½ dessertspoons chillie powder

2 teaspoons cummin powder

2 teaspoons fenugreek

2 pieces goraka

4 cardamoms

½ oz. garlic
2 cloves
1″ cinnamon
coconut milk
(extract of one coconut)

Method

1. Peel polos and cut into big pieces. Chop the onions.
2. Add all the ingredients together with the coconut milk, mix well. Bring to boil and simmer till polos is soft and gravy is thick.

249. POLOS CUTLIETS

Ingredients for 8 *portions (16cutlets of 2″ diameter)*

1 lb. polos
1 oz. green chillies
1-2 dessertspoons maldive fish
¼ teaspoon cummin powder
a pinch of turmeric
Bread crumbs, flour and water batter
4 oz. onions
a sprig of curry leaves
1 teaspoon chillie powder
¼ teaspoon pepper powder
2 billings or 3-4 teaspoons lime juice
oil for deep frying
1 teaspoon salt

Method

1. Peel and cut polos into small pieces, cover with water and 1 teaspoon salt and boil till tender. Mince fine.
2. Chop the onions and green chillies. Heat 1 dessertspoon oil and fry onions and curry leaves. Add maldive fish, curry powder, chillies, salt and pepper and minced polos and fry for a few minutes mixing well. Form into cutlets, dip in a medium batter, crumb and deep fry until golden brown.

250. PINEAPPLE CURRIED

Ingredients for 8 *portions.*

1 lb. pineapple (unripe)	2 oz. onions
2 green chillies	2 teaspoons chillie powder
1 teaspoon coriander powder	1 teaspoon cummin powder
	1 ½ teaspoons ground mustard
1″ cinnamon	10 oz. 1st & 2nd extracts of coconut milk
1 teaspoon salt	

Method

1. Peel and cut pineapple into ¾″ pieces. Chop the onions and green chillies.
2. Mix all the ingredients together. Bring to boil and simmer till done.

251. RED PUMPKIN CURRIED

Ingredients for 8 *portions.*

1 lb. red pumpkin	1 oz. red onions
2-3 green chillies	a sprig of curry leaves
1 dessertspoon of maldive fish	1 teaspoon salt
a pinch of turmeric powder	½ pint 2nd & 3rd extract of coconut milk
1/4 pint 1st extract of coconut milk	

2-4 dessertspoons coconut 1 teaspoon mustard 3-5 cloves garlic	this thickening mixture may be raw or roasted and ground

Method

1. Wash and cut the pumpkin into 16 pieces. Chop onions and green chillies.
2. Grind the coconut mustard and garlic raw or after roasting.
3. Add all the ingredients except thickening mixture, with the 2nd and 3rd extracts of coconut milk and cook till done.
4. Dissolve the thickening mixture with the 1st extract of coconut milk and add to pumpkin. Bring to boil and simmer for a few munutes only.

252. PUMPKIN RED-WHITE CURRY

Ingredients for 8 *portions.*

1 lb. pumpkin	1 oz. Bombay onions
4 green chillies	1 teaspoon maldive fish
a sprig of curry leaves	a pinch of turmeric powder
1 teaspoon mustard ground	2 cloves garlic
1 teaspoon salt	8 oz. 2nd and 3rd extracts
1 teaspoon fenugreek	of coconut milk

4 oz. 1st extract of coconut milk

Method

1. Cut pumpkin into convenient sizes. Chop green chillies, onions and garlic.
2. Add all the ingredients with the 2nd and 3rd extracts of coconut milk and bring to boil, and cook till done. Add the mustard, dissolved in 1st extract of coconut milk. Bring to boil and simmer.

253. PUMPKIN RED TEMPERED

Ingredients for 8 *portions.*

1 1/2 lbs.pumpkin	2 dessertspoons oil
2 oz. onions	1/2 teaspoon turmeric
a sprig of curry leaves	1 clove garlic
2 teaspoon chillie powder	1 teaspoon salt
16 oz. water	

Method

1. Boil pumpkin with salt and a pinch of turmeric and water till tender but not soft.
2. Chop onions and garlic.
3. Heat oil in a pan, add onions and curry leaves and when light brown add chillie powder, garlic and salt. Toss for a few minutes.
4. Add the boiled pumpkin and toss for a few minutes.

254. PUMPKIN RED MEAT CURRY TYPE

Ingredients for 8 *portions*

1 lb. pumpkin	2 teaspoon chillie powder
2 teaspoons coriander powder	1 teaspoon cummin powder
1 piece cinnamon	2 oz. coconut lightly roasted and ground
1" rampe	12 oz. 1st & 2nd extracts of coconut milk
a sprig of curry leaves	
3 cloves garlic	1 teaspoon salt

Method

1. Cut pumpkin into convenient size pieces.
2. Chop onions, garlic.
3. Roast lightly, cinnamon, cummin, coriander and chillie powder.
4. Lightly roast coconut and grind.
5. Add all the ingredients to pumpkin together with the coconut milk and cook till tender.
6. Fast boil to reduce gravy to required amount.

255. ASH PUMPKIN MEAT CURRY TYPE

Ingredients for 8 *portions*

1 lb. pumpkin	2 oz. onions
1/4 teaspoon turmeric powder	1 teaspoon chillie powder
1 teaspoon coriander powder	1/2 teaspoon cummin powder
a pinch of sweet cummin powder	a small piece of cinnamon
	a sprig of curry leaves
1 teaspoon salt	1 dessertspoon oil
8 oz. 1st & 2nd extracts of coconut milk	1/4 teaspoon mustard seeds

Method

1. Cut pumpkin into large pieces.
2. Chop onions. Mix all the ingredients together with the coconut milk, half the onions and curry leaves and cook till tender.

3. Heat oil in a pan, add the remaining onions and curry leaves. Toss for a few minutes, add the mustard and then the cooked ash pumpkin. Bring to boil and take off fire.

256. ASH PUMPKIN WHITE CURRY

Ingredients for 8 *portions.*

1 lb. pumpkin
2 oz. onions
1 teaspoon maldive fish
a pinch of turmeric
2 oz. 1st extract of coconut milk
1 dessertspoon mustard
coconut, cadju or rice ground for thickening
2 green chillies
a sprig of curry leaves
1″ cinnamon
4 oz. 2nd extract of coconut milk
1 teaspoon salt

Method

1. Peel wash and cut pumpkin into convenient sizes.
2. Chop onions, green chillies. Grind thickening agents into a fine paste.
3. Mix all the ingredients together except the paste and 1st extract of coconut milk. Cook until tender.
4. Add 1st extract of coconut milk, mixed with the thickening paste. Bring to boil and take off fire.

257. ASH PUMPKIN (KALU POL) (BLACK CURRY)

Ingredients for 8 *portions*

1 lb. pumpkin	2 green chillies	
a spring of curry leaves	1″ rampe	
a teaspoon turmeric powder	1 teaspoon salt	
1 oz. onions	3 red onions	
1/2 teaspoon chillie powder	2 dessertspoons coconut	roasted and ground
2 oz. 1st extract of coconut milk	1 dessertspoon rice	
4 oz. 2nd & 3rd extracts coconut milk		

Method

1. Peel wash and cut pumpkin into convenient sizes.
2. Chop onions, chillies and put into a pan with pumpkin. Add the 2nd & 3rd extracts of coconut milk, turmeric, chillie, curry leaves, salt and bring to the boil and simmer till tender.
3. Dissolve the ground ingredients in the 1st extract of coconut milk. Add to the pumpkin. Bring to boil and simmer till gravy is thick.

258 RADISH (TEMPERED)

Ingredients for 8 *portions.*

1 lb. radish (roots)	1 sprig curry leaves
1/4 lb. onions	2 teaspoons chillie powder
1/2 oz. green chillies	2 teaspoons maldive fish (optional)
1 teaspoon lime juice	1 teaspoon salt
1/4 teaspoon turmeric powder	
4 dessertspoons oil	

Method

1. Peel radish, grate, cover with water and add 1 dessertspoon salt. Allow to soak for 1/2 an hour. Slice onions and green chillies.
2. Heat oil, add sliced onions, curry leaves, green chillies, fry until light golden brown.
3. Add radish well squeezed and mixed with lime juice, chillie powder, turmeric, salt and maldive fish if used.
4. Fry 2-3 minutes on high heat. Reduce and cook for 1/2 an hour or until tender.

259. RADISH WHITE CURRY

Ingredients for 8 *portions*

1 lb. radish (roots only)
2 oz. Bombay onions chopped
a sprig of curry leaves
10 oz. 2nd & 3rd extracts of coconut milk
1 teaspoon maldive fish
4 green chillies
1/2 teaspoon fenugreek
1/4 teaspoon turmeric
2 oz. 1st extract of coconut milk
1 teaspoon salt
1/2″ cinnamon

Method

1. Cut radish or grate radish with coarse side of grater. Chop the onions and green chillies.
2. Cook with all the ingredients except 1st extract of coconut milk until tender.
3. Add 1st extract of coconut milk, bring to boil stirring all the time.

260. RADISH TEMPERED

Ingredients for 8 *portions*

1 lb. radish (roots only)
1 teaspoon coriander powder
1/2 teaspoon sweet cummin powder
1 teaspoon maldive fish
3 dessertspoons oil
2 teaspoon chillie powder
1/2 teaspoon cummin powder
1/2 teaspoon turmericpowder
2 oz. red onions chopped
1 teaspoon salt
a sprig of curry leaves
8 oz. 1st extract of coconut milk

Method

1. Cut or grate radish with coarse side of grater.
2. Heat oil, add curry leaves, onions. Fry for a few minutes.
3. Add all the ingredients except the coconut milk.
4. Fry for a few minutes. Add the coconut milk and simmer until tender.

261. RIDGED GOURD SKINS (TEMPERED)

Ingredients for 8 *portions.*

10 oz. skins (from 2 lbs. ridged gourd).
2 green chillies
a sprig of curry leaves
2 dessertspoons maldive fish or kuni
4 dessertspoons oil
2 oz. onions
2 teaspoons coarse chillie powder
1 teaspoon salt
1/4 teaspoon turmeric powder

Method

1. Wash and shred skins fine. Chop the onions and chillies.

2. Add the chillie, turmeric, maldive fish, kuni, salt, green chillies, to the skins and mix well.

3. Heat the oil in a pan, and when very hot add the curry leaves and onions and fry till light brown. Add the skins and cook till tender.

262. RIDGED GOURD WHITE CURRY

Ingredients for 8 *portions.*

1 lb. ridged gourd	2 green chillies
2 oz. Bombay onions	1/2 teaspoon fenugreek
1/4 teaspoon turmeric powder	a sprig of curry leaves
3 oz. 2nd extract of coconut milk	1 teaspoon maldive fish (optional)
1 oz. 1st extract of coconut milk	1/2″ cinnamon
	1 1/2 teaspoons salt

Method

1. Peel off the ridged gourd and cut into 3/4″ pieces on the slant. Chop the onions and chillies.

2. Add all the ingredients together, except the 1st extract of coconut milk. Bring to boil and cook till tender and gravy has reduced.

3. Add the 1st extract of coconut milk, bring to boil and take off fire.

263. RIDGED GOURD CURRIED (WETAKOLU) - 1

Ingredients for 8 *portions.*

1 lb. ridged gourd	2 oz. onions
2 green chillies	1 1/2 teaspoon chillie powder
1/2 teaspoon coriander powder	1/2 teaspoon cummin powder
	a pinch of turmeric
1/2 teaspoon sweet cummin powder	1/2 pint 1st & 2nd extracts of coconut milk
a sprig of curry leaves	1 teaspoon salt
2 dessertspoons oil	

Method

1. Peel the gourd and cut into 1 1/4″ pieces on the slant. Chop the onions and chillies.
2. Add all the curry powders and salt to the gourd and mix well.
3. Heat the oil in a pan and when very hot add the onions and curry leaves. When the onions are light brown add the gourd. Fry for a few minutes. Add the coconut milk. Bring to boil and simmer till tender.

264. RIDGED GOURD SKINS (WETAKOLU) -2

Ingredients for 8 *portions.*

skins from 1 lb. ridged gourd

2 oz. onions	2 teaspoons chillie powder
1 small tomato	a sprig of curry leaves
a pinch of turmeric powder	4 dessertspoons oil
1 teaspoon salt	1 1/2 oz. dry sprats

Method

1. Wash and shred skins very fine. Chop onions and tomato.
2. Heat oil in a pan and when very hot, add the skins mixed well with all the other ingredients. Cook till tender.

265. RIDGED GOURD (WETAKOLU) -3 (WHITE TEMPERED).

Ingredients for 8 *portions.*

1 lb. ridged gourd	2 oz. onions
2 green chillies	1-2 teaspoons maldive fish
1/4 teaspoon turmeric powder	a sprig of curry leaves
1 teaspoon salt	2 dessertspoons oil

4 oz. 1st extracts of coconut milk

Method

1. Peel the outer skin of gourd. Wash and cut 1/4″ thick pieces on the slant. Chop the onions and chillies.
2. Heat oil in a pan and when very hot, add the curry leaves and onions and the rest of the ingredients, except coconut milk. Cook till tender.
3. Add the coconut milk. Bring to boil and simmer for 5 minutes.

266. SNAKE GOURD WHITE CURRY

Ingredients for 8 *portions.*

1 lb. snake gourd	2 green chillies

2 oz. red onions
a pinch of turmeric
2 oz. 1st extract of coconut milk
1 teaspoon fenugreek
1/2 teaspoon maldive fish
1 teaspoon salt
4 oz. 2nd & 3rd extracts of coconut milk.
1/2″ piece cinnamon

Method

1. Scrape skins remove seeds wash and cut snake gourd into slices. Chop green chillies and onions.
2. Mix all the ingredients with the snake gourd. Add the 2nd & 3rd extracts of coconut milk, and cook till tender.
3. Add the 1st extract of coconut milk. Bring to boil and take off fire.

267. SNAKE GOURD (TEMPERED)

Ingredients for 8 *portions.*

1 lb. snake gourd
1 teaspoon coriander powder
a pinch of turmeric
2 green chillies
6 oz. 1st extract of coconut milk
2 teaspoons chillie powder
1/2 teaspoon cummin powder
1 oz. onions
a sprig of curry leaves
1 teaspoon maldive fish
1 teaspoon salt
2 dessertspoons oil

Method

1. Cut snake gourd into slices. Chop green chillies and onions.
2. Heat oil, then add the green chillies, onions, curry leaves, fry until light brown.

3. Mix all the other ingredients with the snake gourd. Add to browned onions. Add the coconut milk and bring to boil, cook till tender.

268. SNAKE GOURD - STUFFED AND CURRIED

Ingredients for 8 *portions.*

1 lb. snake gourd (1 1/4″ in diameter)

1/4 lb. minced beef	4 oz. Bombay onions
1 clove garlic	1/2 teaspoon pepper powder
1 1/4 teaspoon salt	a sprig of curry leaves
2 dessertspoon oil	batter, crumbs, oil for frying

Method

1. Cut snake gourd into 1 1/4" lengths and remove seeds. Put into boiling water and cook for 2-3 minutes.
2. Chop chillies, onions and garlic.
3. Heat oil in a pan and when very hot add curry leaves and onions and fry till light golden brown. Add chillies, garlic, minced beef and salt and cook till tender.
4. Stuff boiled snake gourd. Dip stuffed pieces in a thick batter, crumb and deep fry. May be served with a gravy, Recipe Nos. 147 or 149, 150.

269. THALANA BATU - CURRIED

Ingredients for 8 *portions.*

1 lb. batu	2 oz. onions
1/4 oz. green chillies	a sprig of curry leaves

4 cloves garlic	2 teaspoon maldive fish
2 teaspoons chillie powder	3 teaspoons coriander powder
1 teaspoon cummin powder	1 teaspoon salt

1/2 pint 2nd & 3rd extracts of coconut milk

2 oz. 1st extracts of coconut milk

Method

1. Crush the batu with a hammer and remove seeds. Wash well and place in a pan.
2. Chop onions, green chillies, garlic and add to the batu. Add the curry leaves, and all the other ingredients except the 1st extract of coconut milk, and bring to boil and simmer till tender.
3. Add the 1st extract of coconut milk, bring to boil, simmer for a few minutes and take off fire.

270. THIBBATU - CURRIED

Ingredients for 8 *portions.*

1 lb. Thibbatu	4 oz. 1st extract of coconut milk
2 teaspoons chillie powder	2 oz. oil
1 oz. Bombay onions (sliced)	1 teaspoon salt
a pinch of turmeric	a sprig of curry leaves

Method

1. Wash well and boil thibbatu with just enough water to cover and boil till tender. Crush fruits with spoon.
2. Heat oil and add curry leaves, sliced onions and fry for a

few minutes. Add chillie powder, coconut milk and bring to boil. Add boiled thibbatu and simmer for about 5-10 minutes.

271. TOMATO AND ONION CURRY

Ingredients for 8 *portions.*

1 lb. green tomato	1/4 lb. onions
3-4 green chillies	1 1/2 teaspoons salt
1 teaspoon fenugreek	1/4 teaspoon turmeric powder
2 teaspoons coriander powder	1 1/2 teaspoons chillie powder
	a sprig of curry leaves
1/2 teaspoon cummin powder	6 oz. 1st & 2nd extracts of coconut milk

Method

1. Wash and slice the tomatoes, onions and green chillies.
2. Put in a pan with all the ingredients and bring to boil. Simmer till tender.

272. TOMATO (GREEN) CURRIED

Ingredients for 8 *portions.*

1 lb. tomato	2 green chillies
1/2 teaspoon cummin powder	a pinch of turmeric
1 teaspoon maldive fish	a sprig of curry leaves
1 oz. onions	2 teaspoons chillie powder
1 1/2 teaspoons salt	6 oz. 1st & 2nd extracts of coconut milk
1/4 teaspoon fenugreek	
2 dessertspoons oil	

Method

1. Wash and cut the tomato into 4 or 6, according to size. Chop onions and green chillies.

2. Heat the oil in a pan and when very hot add the onions and curry leaves, and fry till light brown.

3. Add the tomato mixed well with all the other ingredients except the coconut milk, and cook for a few minutes till tender.

4. Add the coconut milk, bring to boil and simmer till gravy has thickened.

273. THUMBA KARAWILA - CURRIED

Ingredients for 8 *portions.*

1 lb. thumba karawila	2 oz. onions
2 teaspoons chillie powder	2 teaspoons maldive fish
1 teaspoon cummin	2 teaspoons fenugreek
1″ cinnamon	2 cardamoms
1 clove garlic	2 teaspoons coriander powder
1 piece goraka	curry leaves
2 teaspoons salt	2 dessertspoons oil
1 oz. 2nd extract of coconut milk	6 oz. 1st extract of coconut milk

Method

1. Slit thumba karawila into four but keep intact, and boil with 2 teaspoons salt and goraka for 10 minutes. Separate into 4 and remove seeds.

2. Chop onions and garlic.

3. Heat oil. Add curry leaves and onions and fry until onions are brown. Mix together the boiled thumba karawila and the rest of the ingredients. Fry for a few minutes.

4. Add coconut milk and cook until gravy is reduced.

274. VEGETABLE CUTLETS

Ingredients for 8 *portions (8-10 cutlets)*

4 oz. carrots	4 oz. potatoes
6 oz. onions	6 oz. spinach
2 1/2 oz. dhal	1 1/2 teaspoons salt
1-1 1/2 teaspoons pepper	1/4 teaspoon chillie powder
a sprig of curry leaves	batter and crumbs
oil for deep frying	1 dessertspoon oil

Method

1. Boil, mash the vegetables and dhal. Chop onions and green chillies fine.

2. Heat oil in a pan and when very hot add the onions and curry leaves and toss till light brown. Add the vegetables and pepper, salt, and chillie powder and cook till quite dry.

3. Form into 8 or 16 cutlets. Dip in batter and crumb.Deep fry until golden brown.

275. YAMS (KIRIALA, MANIOC ETC.)(CURRIED)

1 lb. kiriala	2 green chillies
11/2 teaspoon fenugreek	1/2 teaspoon turmeric powder

a sprig of curry leaves
6 oz. 1st extracts of coconut milk
1 oz. onions
10 oz. 2nd & 3rd extracts of coconut milk
1 teaspoon salt

Method

1. Scrub the yams to remove outer skin, wash well. Chop onions and green chillies.
2. Add all the ingredients together with the 2nd and 3rd extracts of coconut milk. Bring to boil and cook till done.
3. Add the 1st extract of coconut milk. Bring to boil and simmer till gravy has reduced to the amount required.

Note:- When cooking manioc, the coconut milk must cover the yams completely and the lid left open so that the prussic acid will pass off with the steam.

MALLUM PREPARATIONS

276. ASH PLANTAIN MALLUM

Ingredients for 8 *portions.*

5 oz. skins (from 1 lb.)	1 oz. onions
1 green chillie	1/4 teaspoon turmeric powder
1 teaspoon salt	3 oz. coconut

a sprig of curry leaves

Method

1. Shred the skins very fine, and leave to boil with 2 oz. water and 1 teaspoon salt, till soft and all water has almost evaporated.
2. Chop onions, green chillies fine. Mix with coconut, salt, turmeric and curry leaves. Add to the boiled skins and keep tossing till coconut is cooked.

277. BEAN MALLUM

Ingredients for 8 *portions.*

3/4 lb. beans	4 oz. finely grated coconut
1/4 teaspoon turmeric powder	2 oz. onions
4-6 green chillies	3 teaspoons maldive fish or prawn powder
2 1/2 teaspoons salt	

Method

1. Wash beans, remove strings and shred vey fine.
2. Chop the onions and green chillies.

3. Add all the ingredients except the finely grated coconut and cook until beans are tender but not dry.

4. Add the coconut and cook for about 5 minutes over low heat. Coconut may be ground if desired before adding to beans.

278. CABBAGE MALLUM

Ingredients for 8 *portions.*

1/2 lb. cabbage	1 oz. onions
1/4 teaspoon turmeric	2 red chillies, dry
4 oz. coconut	1 teaspoon mustard ground
1/2 teaspoon pepper	1 teaspoon salt
a sprig of curry leaves	1 1/4 - 2 oz. water

Method

1. Wash and shred cabbage and stalks finely.

2. Chop onions and chillies, add to cabbage, with curry leaves, salt, water and cook till done, Stir from time to time.

3. Mix coconut, ground mustard, pepper and turmeric. Add to cabbage. Stir for a few minutes and take off fire.

279. DHAL MALLUM

Ingredients for 8 *portions.*

1/2 lb. dhal	1 oz. onions
2 sprigs of curry leaves	1/4 teaspoon turmeric powder

chillie powder	2-3 green chillies	ground
1 teaspoon salt	1/2 coconut	
	1 teaspoon mustard	
	4 cloves garlic	

Method

1. Wash and cook dhal with chillie powder and turmeric until soft.
2. Add ground ingredients, stir well, cook for a few minutes and take off fire.

Note:-This may be garnished with fried onions or with fragrant curry mixture.

280. JAK MALLUM

Ingredients for 8 portions.

1 lb. jak	2 oz. onions
1/2 oz. green chillies	1/2 teaspoon turmeric
2 1/2 teaspoons salt	3/4 pint water
a sprig of curry leaves	

4 oz. coconut	ground
3 teaspoons mustard	
2 teaspoons pepper corns	
6 - 7 cloves garlic.	

Method

1. Shred the jak very fine, wash it well, put into pan.
2. Chop onions, chillies, add to jak with salt, turmeric, water and curry leaves. Bring to the boil and lower heat till jak is cooked and all water has been absorbed.

3. Grind the garlic, coconut, mustard and pepper together. Add to the boiled jak, toss for a few minutes and take off fire.

281. KATHURUMURUNGA MALLUM - 1

Ingredients for 8 *portions.*

1 bundle kathurumurunga (1/2 lb.)

2-3 green chillies	1 medium size onion
a pinch of turmeric	3-4 oz. coconut
salt	2 oz. water.

Method

1. Wash and drain kathurumurunga sprigs.
2. Form a bundle and very carefully shred leaves very fine.
3. Add coconut, chillies, turmeric and water and cook until onions are done.
4. Add finely shredded kathurumurunga leaves. Mix well and cook for just a few minutes.

282. KATHURUMURUNGA MALLUM - 2

Ingredients for 8 *portions.*

Same as method 1

1. Add 2 oz. water to kathurumurunga leaves, with onions and chillies. Cook uncovered till leaves are done for about 5 minutes.
2. Add coconut mixed with turmeric and salt. Stir. Take off the fire.

283. KATHURUMURUNGA MALLUM - 3

Ingredients for 8 *portions.*

1. Follow steps 1 & 2, as stated in No.281 recipe.
2. Mix coconut, turmeric and shredded leaves together.
3. Heat 2 teaspoons oil, fry onions and green chillies, add coconut and shredded leaves mixed. Stir for a few minutes.

284. KOHILA YAMS - MALLUM

Ingredients for 8 *portions.*

1/2 lb. kohila yams	1/2 teaspoon turmeric
3-4 green chillies chopped	1 1/2 teaspoons salt
4 oz. coconut scraped fine	2 oz. onions chopped
1 oz. mustard ground	

Method

1. Peel and shred yams fine. Wash and remove threads with handle of spoon.
2. Cover with water, add salt, chopped onions, green chillies and boil till tender.
3. Mix the coconut, mustard, turmeric well and add to the kohila. Cook for a few minutes and take off fire.

285. MALLUM

1. Wathabanga leaves	6. Kuringnan leaves
2. Manioc leaves	7. Anguna leaves
3. Passion Fruit leaves	8. Thora leaves

4. Kankun leaves
5. Wattakka leaves
9. Diyaberaliya leaves
10. Diyahabarala leaves

Method

1. The above mentioned leaves, and many other edible leaves, may be cooked in the same manner as kathurumurunga leaves, recipe Nos. 281, 282 and 283.
2. Leaves must always be washed under running water several times.
3. Leaves must be shredded only after washing has been done.
4. The pan must never be covered when preparing allums if green colour is to be retained.
5. The cooked mallum must be covered only after it has cooled.

286. MUKUNUWENNA MALLUM

Ingredients for 8 *portions.*

1/2 lb. mukunuwenna (1 bundle)

a sprig of curry leaves
2-3 green chillies
8 oz. water
2 oz. onions
1/2 teaspoon turmeric
1 1/2 teaspoons salt

4 oz. coconut scraped fine

Method

1. Wash and shred mukunuwenna leaves.
2. Mix the coconut with the curry leaves, sliced onions,

green chilles, turmeric and salt and put into a pan with the water and cook till the onions are done.

3. Add the mukunuwenna and keep tossing for a few minutes.

Note:- It should not be over-cooked. Green colour should be retained.

287. PAPAW MALLUM

Ingredients for 8 *portions.*

1/2 lb. well seasoned papaw	1 1/2 teaspoons salt
1/4 teaspoon turmeric	4-6 oz. coconut
3-4 green chillies chopped	5 pepper corns bruised lightly

Method

1. Peel, wash and grate papaw or cut into fine shreds. Wash again to remove any papain.

2. Add turmeric, sufficient water to cover the papaw, salt, pepper corns, green chillies and cook until papaw is done.

3. Add finely scraped or ground coconut. Cook for a few minutes longer. Remove from fire.

288. WATTAKKA MALLUM

Ingredients for 8 *portions.*

Method

1. May be made in the same way as papaw mallum.

SAMBOL PREPARATIONS

289. ASH PLANTAIN SKINS - 1

Ingredients for 8 *portions.*

Skins from 1 lb. plantains
2 teaspoons mustard
10 pepper corns
1 teaspoon salt.
2 cloves garlic
3 teaspoons lime juice

Method

1. Cut skins into small pieces, cover with water and salt and boil. Drain off water.
2. Grind with the rest of the ingredients, add salt and lime and mix well.

290. ASH PLANTAIN SKINS - 2

Ingredients for 8 portions.

2 teaspoons mustard
10 pepper corns
1 teaspoon salt
2 cloves garlic
3 teaspoons lime juice
2 oz. coconut

Method

1. Cut skins into small pieces, cover with water, add salt, and boil till soft. Drain off the water.
2. Roast the coconut to a golden brown. Grind coconut, plantain skins with the rest of the ingredients, add salt and lime, mix well.

291. ASH PUMPKIN SKINS

Ingredients for 8 *portions.*

1/2 lb. ash pumpkin skins	3-4 dry chillies
2 cloves of garlic	3-4 pepper corns
salt to taste	3-4 red onions
lime juice	

Method

1. Wash ash pumpkin skins and boil until tender.
2. Grind the boiled ash pumpkin skins with the dry chillies, garlic, pepper corns and red onions.
3. Add lime juice and salt.

292. BANDAKKA SAMBOL

Ingredients for 8 *portions.*

1/2 lb. bandakka	1/4 teaspoon pepper
1/2 teaspoon salt	3 oz. Bombay onions
lime to taste	1 teaspoon maldive fish

Method

1. Boil or steam bandakka till cooked but firm. Cut into pieces.
2. Chop onions fine.
3. Mix all the ingredients, add to the boiled bandakka.

293. BILLING SAMBOL

Ingredients for 8 *portions.*

1 lb. billing (sliced fine and soaked in salt and squeezed out)
3 cloves
1 1/2 dessertspoons chillie powder
4 dessertspoons oil
2 Bombay onions
3-4 green chillies
1 1/2″ cinnamon
3 cardamoms
2 cloves garlic
2 pieces rampe
2 sprigs of curry leaves

Method

1. Slice billing fine and soak in salt water for a few hours. Chop the onions, green chillies and garlic.
2. Heat oil, and when very hot add the curry leaves, rampe and onions. Fry for a few minutes. Add the rest of the ingredients and fry till billing is cooked and almost dry.

294. BLACHAN (PRAWN) - 1

Ingredients for 8 *portions.*

1/4 lb. dried prawns
1 bulb garlic (15-20 cloves)
2 oz. dry chillies
3 oz. red onions
6 oz. 1st & 2nd extracts of coconut milk
1-4 teaspoons sugar
1″ rampe
1/2″ sera
1 oz. maldive fish
3 slices ginger
1 dessertspoon tamarind juice squeezed in 3rd extract of coconut milk
lime juice
2 sprigs of curry leaves
4-6 dessertspoons oil

Method

1. Wash and dry prawns, roast well and pound very fine. Pound the maldive fish very fine. Roast and pound the chillies fine. Sieve if possible.
2. Chop the garlic, ginger and red onions very fine.
3. Heat the oil and fry the garlic, ginger, red onions, rampe, curry leaves and sera till the onions are brown.
4. Mix the tamarind, prawns, maldive fish, chillie powder and the rest of the ingredienst well, except the lime juice and sugar. Add to the fried ingredients and simmer till gravy has reduced but blachan is moist.
5. Add the lime and sugar before taking off fire.

295. BLACHAN (PRAWN) - 2

Ingredients for 8 *portions.*

1/4 lb. of roasted dried prawns
1-2 dessertspoons chillie powder
2-4 cloves garlic
3-4 slices of ginger
salt and lime juice to taste

Method

1. Pound the prawns very fine. Grind the garlic and ginger.
2. Mix all the ingredients together well.
3. Season with lime juice and salt.
4. Make into small balls marble size if desired.

296. BOILED PRAWN SAMBOL

Ingredients for 8 *portions.*

1 lb. medium sized prawns boiled and shelled

1 dessertspoon finely ground mustard in vinegar

2-3 oz. finely sliced red onions or Bombay onions chopped

4-6 capsicum chillies sliced

1 medium size tomato chopped (optional)

Salt, lime juice and vinegar to taste

Method

1. Mix all the ingredients except tomato. Add prawns toss well Just before serving add tomatoes.

2. This sambol shoud be made at least 1 to 1/2 hour before required to give the prawns a good flavour. A dash of chillie pawder may be added for a better colour.

297. BRINJAL SAMBOL

Ingredients for 8 *portions.*

1/2 lb. brinjal

1/2 oz. green chillies

4 teaspoons vinegar

3 oz. Bombay onions

1 teaspoon salt

1/2 teaspoon ground mustard

1/4 teaspoon turmeric powder

Method

1. Wash and slice brinjal in rounds. Rub turmeric and fry till crisp.

2. Chop the onions, green chillies. Add salt, vinegar and mustard and mix well.

3. Add the fried brinjal and mix well.

298. CARROT SAMBOL

Ingredients for 8 *portions.*

6 oz. carrot
2 oz. onions
4 green chillies
1 1/2 oz. grated coconut
1/2 teaspoon salt
1/2 teaspoon pepper
1/2 teaspoon lime

Method

1. Peel, wash and dry carrot. Grate finely. Chop onions and green chillies fine.
2. Add all the ingredients to the grated coconut and mix well.

299. CUCUMBER SAMBOL - 1

Ingrredients for 8 *portions*

1/4 lb. cucumber
salt
2-3 oz. Bombay onion
2-3 green chillies
lime juice

Method

1. Slice cucumber fine. Put into salt water, leave for 1/2 hour. Chop the green chillies and onions. Add lime juice, 1/2 teaspoon salt and set aside.
2. Wrap cucumber in clean cloth and squeeze to remove moisture. Mix with onion-chillie mixture. Add salt and lime.

300. CUCUMBER SAMBOL - 2

Ingredients for 8 *portions*

3/4-1/2 cucumber
2 oz. Bombay onions sliced
1/2 dessertspoon maldive fish
salt
2 green chillies chopped
2 dessertspoons 1st extract of coconut milk
lime to taste

Method

1. Grate cucumber and place in salted water for 1/2 an hour.
2. Mix green chillies, onions, maldive fish, salt and lime juice
3. Wrap grated cucumber in clean cloth and squeeze to remove moisture.
4. Add to onion mixture. Add milk and mix lightly.

301. CUCUMBER SAMBOL - 3

Ingredients for 8 *portions.*

1 lb. small tender cucumber
4 capsicum chillies sliced
1 oz. red onions sliced or 1 Bombay onion
2 teaspoons maldive fish
salt to taste
a dash of lemon juice
4 oz. 1st extract of coconut milk.

Method

1. Cut a thin piece from the stem end of the cucumber. Rub it a number of times (only if the cucumber is not very tender). Peel cucumber cut into four lengthwise. Remove seeds and slice as thinly as possible.

2. Mix onions, maldive fish and anit chillies and salt with sliced cucumber. Add coconut milk and a dash juice.

Variation - 1-2 medium sized ripe tomatoes may be chopped and added to the above mixtur.

*302 EGG, TOMATO AND ONION SAMBOL WITH GREEN CHILLIES

Ingredients for 8 *portions.*

1/2 lb. tomatoes	2 oz. green chillies
juice of 1 lime	4 oz. Bombay onions
3 teaspoons salt	8 eggs boiled and shelled and cut into halves

Method

1. Slice onions, tomatoes and chillies.
2. Sprinkle lime juice and salt over onions and leave for 15-20 minutes.
3. Mix in the chillies. Add tomatoes just before serving and arrange eggs on sambol and pour gravy on cut egg.

* 303. EGG, ONION AND CHILLIE SAMBOL HOT

Ingredients for 8 p*ortions.*

8 boiled eggs	1 oz. green chillies
2-3 teaspoons coarse dry chillie powder	1/2 lb. onions
	salt and lime to taste

* *Half an egg may be used per portion depending on the menu.*

Method

1. Slice onions fine. Add the chillie, salt and lime and mix well.

2. Put into a flat dish. Arrange on top boiled eggs whole or cut in halves. Pour a teaspoon of the gravy on each egg.

304. FRIED LEAF SAMBOL (KATHURUMURUNGA)

Ingredients for 8 *portions.*

1/2 lb. kathurumurunga leaves	3 oz. Bombay onions
8 dry chillies	1 teaspoon salt

juice of 1 lime or vinegar

Method

1. Slice Bombay onion. Break up dry chillies.

2. Deep fry onions till light golden brown. Fry chillies for a second or two.

3. Mix salt and lime juice with the fried onions and chillies and toss for a few minutes.

4. Deep fry kathurumurunga leaves. Just before serving mix with onions, chillies, salt and vinegar or lime juice.

305. GOTUKOLA SAMBOL

Ingredients for 8 *portions.*

9 oz. gotukola (3 1/2 oz. cleaned)

1/2 oz. green chillies	3 oz. onions
1 dessertspoon maldive fish (optional)	4 oz. scraped coconut
	1 teaspoon salt

1 1/2 dessertspoons lime juice

Method

1. Pick wash and shred the leaves finely, slice onions and green chillies fine.
2. Add all the ingredients together and mix well.

306. KARAWILA SAMBOL

Ingredients for 8 *portions.*

1/2 lb. karawila
1 teaspoon maldive fish (optional)
1 teaspoon salt
3 green chillies
4 oz. Bombay onions
2 teaspoons vinegar or lime juice
1/2 teaspoon turmeric

Method

1. Slice karawila and rub turmeric. Slice onions and chillies.
2. Fry karawila till crisp. Mix all the other ingredients together.Add the fried karawila, mix well.

307.KOHILA SAMBOL

Ingredients for 8 *portions.*

1/2 lb. kohila
1/2 oz. green chillies
2 teaspoons lime juice
2 oz. onions
2 oz. coconut
1 teaspoon salt

Method

1. Cut the kohila in 1/4″ cubes and wash well and remove fibre with handle of spoon.

2. Add boiling water over kohila. Squeeze out all moisture.

3. Chop the onions and green chillies. Add to kohila with the other ingredients, mix well.

308. KUNI SAMBOL

Ingredients for 8 *portions.*

8 oz. coconut grated
1 1/2 oz. onions chopped
1/2 oz. green chillies chopped
2-3 teaspoons lime juice or chopped tomato
6 oz. 2nd & 3rd extract of coconut milk or water
1 teaspoon salt
1 teaspoon fenugreek
1-1/2 oz. kuni
1/4 teaspoon turmeric powder
1/2 oz. onions sliced
1/2 sprig of curry leaves - for tempering
2 dessertspoons oil
3 dry chillies

Method

1. Add chopped onions, green chillies, fenugreek, well washed kuni, turmeric, coconut milk or water, salt and cook until onions are soft.

2. Add the coconut and keep tossing till coconut is cooked.

3. Heat oil in a pan and when very hot add curry leaves, 1/2 oz. sliced onions, dry chillies and fry till onions are golden brown. Add the coconut mixture, Keep tossing for a few minutes and take off fire. Add the lime juice.

Note- Dried prawns or maldive fish may be broken into bits and used in place of dried kuni. Billing may be used in place of lime juice. If billing is used cook with onions and chillies from step 1.

309. LADY'S FINGERS FRIED SAMBOL

Ingredients for 8 *portions.*

3/4 lb. lady's fingers	1/4 lb. big onions
1/2 oz. green chillies	1 1/2 teaspoons lime juice
1 teaspoon salt	oil for frying

1 dessertspoon maldive fish (optional)

Method

1. Cut lady's fingers in slices and deep fry. Chop the onions and green chillies fine.
2. Mix onions, green chillies, maldive fish, lime and salt. Add the fried bandakka and mix.

Note:- This can be made with mature bandakka that cannot be cooked as a curry.

310. LIME PICKLE SAMBOL

Ingredients for 8 *portions.*

2 pickled limes	3 oz. red onions

2-3 teaspoons coarse dry chillie powder or 1 oz. green chillies

Method

1. Slice onions. Cut pickled lime into small pieces.
2. Mix sliced onions with chillie powder or green chillies and lime pickle.
3. Add salt and lime juice only if necessary according to the acidity and saltiness of the lime pickle.

311. LUNUMIRIS (CHILLIE)

Ingredients for 8 *portions.*

2 oz. dry chillies
1/2 oz. maldive fish
lime juice
2 oz. onions
salt to taste

Method

1. Grind all the ingredients well to a coarse or smooth paste as desired. Add salt and lime to taste.

312. MEAT SEENI SAMBOL

Ingredients for *1x1 lb. jar.*

1.lb. big onions
1/4 oz. garlic
2 cardamoms
1 clove, 1″ cinnamon
1 sprig of curry leaves
a thin slice ginger
3 dessertspoons tamarind dissolved
a piece of rampe
1 oz. maldive fish
1/2 lb. minced meat (may be increased to 3/4 lb.)
1 oz. chillie powder
8 dessertspoons oil
2 teaspoons lime juice
2 dessertspoons salt

Method

1. Cut the onions fine, chop the garlic and ginger.
2. Heat fat until very hot. Add all the ingredients except chillie powder, tamarind, lime juice, maldive fish and meat. Fry stirring all the while until onions become light brown.
3. Add meat and fry for about 5 minutes, until meat is cooked. Drain extra oil leaving very little, about 1 dessertspoon.

4. Add chillie powder, lime juice, tamarind, maldive fish and cook over low heat for about 15-20 minutes. Add 1 teaspoon sugar, allow to cool. Bottle and use in place of seeni sambol. If the meat is well cooked it may be kept for a few days off the refrigerator.

313. MINT SAMBOL -1

Ingredients for 8 *portions.*

2 oz. mint leaves	3-4 cloves garlic
3-10 pepper corns	2 dessertspoons coconut
1 oz. onions	salt and lime juice

Method

1. Wash and drain mint leaves. Roast the coconut, garlic and onions lightly.
2. Grind all the ingredients to a paste. Season with lime and salt. Make into 16-1/2″ diameter balls or serve plain in dish with a sprinkling of fresh coconut ground.

314. MINT SAMBOL -2

Ingredients for 8 *portions.*

2 oz. mint leaves	3-4 cloves garlic
2-3 pepper corns	salt
lime juice	1-2 green chillies
sugar	

Method

1. Pick, wash and drain mint leaves. Grind with all the ingredients to a fine paste. Add salt and lime to taste with a pinch of sugar.

315. ONION SAMBOL

Ingredients for 8 *portions.*

1/2 lb. big onions	1 oz. green chillies
salt and pepper	lime juice

Method

1. Slice onions and chop chillies fine. Add salt, pepper and and lime juice to taste. Mix well.

316. POL SAMBOL - 1

Ingredients for 8 *portions.*

6 oz. coconut scraped fine	2 oz. onions
1 dessertspoon maldive fish	1 teaspoon pepper corns ground
4 teaspoons chillie powder	
1 1/2 dessertspoons lime juice	1 1/2 teaspoons salt

Method

1. Grind the red onions and pepper together.
2. Mix well all the ingredients, season with lime juice, so that lime flavour is predominant.

317. POL SAMBOL - 2

Ingredients for 8 *portions.*

6 oz. scraped coconut

3-4 teaspoons chillie powder

1-2 teaspoons maldive fish (optional)

11/2-2 Bombay onions (chopped)

2 teaspoons salt

2-3 teaspoons lime juice

Method

1. Mix well all ingredients except coconut and lime juice.
2. Add coconut, mix well, add lime juice to be predominant in flavour.

318. POL SAMBOL - 3

Ingredietns for 8 *portions.*

Method

1. Follow step No.1 in recipe No.316.
2. Grind or pound grated coconut very lightly, add to the rest of the ingredients.
3. Mix well, add lime juice.

319. POL SAMBOL - 4

Ingredients for 8 *portions.*

6 oz. scraped coconut

2 oz. red onions (whole)

6-8 dry chillies whole
or 1 - 1 1/2 dessertspoons
of coarse chillie powder
1 clove garlic

3-4 teaspoons lime juice
2 teaspoons salt
4-6 pepper corns

Method

1. Pound preferably in a stone mortar all ingredients except coconut and lime juice.
2. Add coconut and pound until all ingredients are mixed well.
3. Add lime juice.

320. POL SAMBOL - 5

Ingredients for 8 *portions.*

Method

1. Use same ingredients as in recipe 2 or 3.
2. Mix all ingredients together. Mix well, add lime juice.

321. RAW MIXED VEGETABLE SAMBOL

Ingredients for 8 *portions.*

1 1/2-2 oz. each of raw cabbage
carrot or ripe papaw
3 dessertspoons ground mustard
2 teaspoons salt

2 oz. onions
2 teaspoons chillie powder
2 dessertspoons vinegar

Method

1. Chop onions.
2. Mix ground mustard and chillie powder.
3. Add the grated vegetables, ripe papaw and onions with the mustard and chillie powder. Then add the salt and vinegar. Prepare this at least one hour ahead.

322. SEENI SAMBOL - 1

Ingredients for 1 x 1 *lb. jar.*

1 lb. red onions (2 1/2 oz. of waste)	5 oz. maldive fish
2 dessertspoons chillie powder	6 cloves garlic
3 oz. tamarind squeezed in 4 oz. 2nd extract of coconut milk	4 oz. 1st extract of coconut milk
1/4 bottle oil	4 cloves
4 cardamoms	2″ cinnamon
a sprig of curry leaves	2 teaspoons sugar
juice of lime, or to taste	2 slices ginger
	2 teaspoons salt

Method

1. Peel wash and slice the onions, very fine.
2. Chop the garlic and ginger, bruise the cardamoms.
3. Heat oil in a pan and when smoking hot, add the onions, garlic and ginger and fry until golden brown, Keep stirring all the while to prevent unevern browning. Drain extra oil and leave only about 2 dessertspoons in a pan.

4. Mix chillie, tamarind, maldive fish, and rest of the ingredients and add to fried onions. Mix well, reduce flame and cook over very low heat, 1/2 - 3/4 hour. Add sugar just before taking off fire. Add salt to taste.

323. SEENI SAMBOL - 2

Ingredients for 1 x 1 lb. *jar.*

3-4 teaspoons chillie powder	1 clove
2 oz. maldive fish or dried prawn powder	1 cardamom
	a slice of ginger
1/2 lb. big onions	1-2 green chillies
2-3 sprigs of curry leaves	8 oz. 1st and 2nd extracts of coconut milk
2 teaspoons sugar	
a small piece rampe	salt and lime

Method

1. Chop the onions and green chillies, garlic and ginger.
2. Mix all the ingredients together with the coconut milk. Bring to boil and simmer till done. Add lime and sugar just before taking off.

324. SEENI SAMBOL - 3

Ingredients for 1 x 1 lb. *jar.*

1/2 lb. maldive fish	2 oz. dry chillies
1 lb. red onions	4 cloves, cardamoms. crushed
lime juice	1″ piece cinnamon

8-10 cloves garlic crushed	salt, 2 teaspoons sugar
a few slices of ginger finely	rampe
chopped	1/2 bottle oil

Method

1. Fry sliced onions separately until light golden brown in oil. Set aside.
2. To remaining oil, add the maldive rish and fry till half done. Add the rest of the ingredients except the lime juice.
3. When lightly fried add the fried onions. Remove from fire add lime juice and salt.

325. SEENI SAMBOL - 4 (Economical and on a large scale)

Ingredients for 75-100 *portions or 10 x 1 lb. jars.*

10 lb. red onions	1 lb. maldive fish
6 oz. chillie powder	2 oz. salt
10 large limes	3-4 bottles coconut oil
2 oz. sugar	

Method

1. Deep fry sliced onions until light golden brown, in samll batches. Set aside.
2. Add the pounded maldive fish, chillie powder with the rest of the ingredients except sugar. Mix well and cook until reduced to almost half on a very slow fire.
3. Add fried onions, mix well and cook on very slow fire for 40-60 minutes stirring from time to time to prevent burning.

4. Add sugar, take off fire and set at an angle to drain extra oil.

5. Cool and store.

326. SEENI SAMBOL WITH CAPSICUM CHILLIES

Ingredietns for *1 x 1 lb. jar.*

1/2 lb. capsicum chillies	1 lb. red onions
3-4 oz. maldive fish or dried prawns	4 cardamoms and cloves each
	1/2″ - 3/4″ cinnamon
curry leaves	2 oz. tamarind
3 oz. vinegar (or tomatoes)	1/4 oz. ginger
1/2 oz. garlic (chopped)	4 dessertspoons oil
2 teaspoons salt	

Method

1. Slice the capsicum and onions, chop garlic and ginger. Blanch tomato and chop if used, dissolve the tamarind in 4 oz. water.

2. Fry the sliced onions and capsicum till golden brown and crisp and set aside.

3. Heat oil in a pan and when very hot add the curry leaves. ginger, garlic, maldive fish, cardamoms, cloves and cinnamon and mix together. fry for a few minutes.

4. Add the tamarind juice and fry for a few minutes.

5. Add the fried ingredients vinegar and salt and keep tossing for 10 minutes, take off fire.

327. SPROUTED MOONG SAMBOL

Ingredients for 8 *portions.*

4 oz. moong gram sprouted	2 oz. finely chopped onions
3-4 capsicum chillies	
1 dessertspoon coconut milk	1 teaspoon salt
2 oz. fresh coconut	3 teaspoons lime juice

Method

1. Mix all ingredients except moong. Add sprouted moong gram after washing well to remover outer skin (green). Season with salt and lemon juice.

How to Sprout Moong -

Soak green gram overnight. Drain wrap in either a plantain leaf, or damp gunny sack, weight and let it stay for a day or two undisturbed. The number of days will depend on the length of the sprout required. The parcel ust be kept moist.

328. TOMATO - ONION SAMBOL WITH CURD

Ingredients for 8 *portions.*

1/2 lb. tomatos	4 oz. onions
2 oz. capsicum chillies	3 teaspoons salt
juice of 1 lime	6 oz. curd

Method

1. Slice onions, sprinkle lime juice and salt and allow to remain for about 1/2 an hour.
2. Slice capsicum chillies, add to above mixture.

3. Just before serving, add tomatoes cut into cubes 1/2″ -3/4″ mix tomato and curd with the rest of the ingredients.

4. Sprinkle chillie powder if desired.

329. TOMATO ONION SAMBOL

Ingredients for 8 *portions.*

1/2 lb tomatoes	4 oz. onions
2 oz. capsicum chillies	3 teaspoons salt

juice of 1 lime

Method

1. Slice onions, sprinkle lime juice and salt and allow to remain for about 1/2 an hour.

2. Slice capsicum chillies before serving, add tomatoes cut into cubes about 1/2- 3/4″. Mix well.

CHUTNEY, MOJU, PICKLE PREPARATIONS

*330. BILLING CHUTNEY

Ingredients for 1 1/2 x 1 *lb. jars.*

1 lb. billing

1/4 bottle vinegar	8 oz. sugar
1 dessetrtspoon salt	1/2 oz. garlic
1/4 oz. ginger	1 oz. chillie powder

salt

Method

1. Slice the billing fine, and soak in salt for a few hours and squeeze out. Wash well to remove salt.
2. Mix all the ingredients together and cook on a slow fire till cooked and syrup thick.

*331. DATE CHUTNEY SWEET

Ingredients for 2 x 1 *lb. jars.*

1 lb. dates, stoned and finely chopped.

1/2 oz. chillie powder	1/4 lb. sultanas
1 lb. sugar	2 teaspoons salt
4 teaspoons ground garlic	2 teaspoons ground ginger
1/4 bottle vinegar	2 teaspoons ground mustard

1 teaspoon powdered spices (cloves, cardamoms, cinnamon)

---

* *All chutneys should be taken off the fire when the consistency is a little thinner than what is required as it thickkens on cooling.*

Method

1. Dissolve over low heat sugar with vinegar. Add all ingredients except sultanas and salt, cook on low heat until syrup is thick, but dates not pulpy.

2. Just before removing from fire add sultanas add lastly the salt.

332. DATE CHUTNEY HOT

Ingredients for 2 x 1 *lb. jars.*

1 lb. dates	1 lb. sugar
1 oz. dry chillies or	3/4 bottle vinegar
2 dessertspoooons chillie powder	3/4 oz. garlic
1 oz. ginger	salt

Method

1. Stone and grind or chop the dates and boil in 1/2 bottle of vinegar until soft.

2. Grind all other ingredients in vinegar and add to the balance vinegar and strain to remove any fibrous parts in ginger.

3. Boil spices and sugar with the cooked dates. Cook until desired consistency is obtained.

*333. MANGO CHUTNEY SWEET

Ingredients for 2 x 1 *lb. jars.*

1 lb. mango	1 lb. sugar

* *All chutneys should be taken off the fire when the consistency is a little thinner than what is required as it thickkens on cooling.*

3/4 - 1/2 oz. chillie powder	1/4 oz. crushed mustard seeds
4 oz. vinegar	3 cloves } crushed in a gauze bag
1/2 oz. garlic	3 cardamoms } crushed in a gauze bag
1/2 oz. ginger	1″ cinnamon } crushed in a gauze bag
salt	

Method

1. Mix half the sugar and chopped mango and set aside for 3-4 hours.

2. Add all ingredients and balance sugar and cook on a steady fire until done but not pulpy.

*334. MANGO CHUTNEY HOT

Ingredients for 2 x 1 *lb. jars.*

1 lb. mango slices that have been peeled and kept in the sun for a few days, with a sprinkling of salt.

1 - 1 1/2 oz. dry chillies	1 lb. sugar
3/4 oz. garlic ground	1/2 - 1/4 lb. sultanas (optional)
1/2 oz. ginger ground	1/2 - 1/4 pint vinegar
2 teaspoons salt	1dessertspoon mustard ground

Method

1. Boil all ingredients with vinegar except sultanas if being used till the mangoes are well cooked, and the chutney thick.

2. Add the sultanas just before taking off the fire.

---

* *All chutneys should be taken off the fire when the consistency is a little thinner than what is required as it thickkens on cooling.*

335. DRY FISH MOJU

Ingredients for 2 x 1 *lb. jars.*

1/2 lb. dry fish
1 lb. green chillies
2-3 oz. mustard
1/3 bottle vinegar
salt
1 lb. red onions
2 oz. garlic
2 oz. ginger
4 dessertspoons coriander powder

Method

1. Deep fry dry fish cut into small pieces.
2. Deep fry onions and chillies for a few seconds. Grind mustard, ginger and garlic. Mix with the vinegar. Temper with a little oil and a piece of rampe.
3. Add the fried ingredients to the tempered mixture, bring to boil simmer, cool and store in bottles.

336. FISH MOJU

Ingredients for 2 x 1 *lb. jars.*

1 lb. seer or prawns shelled
1/2 lb. red onions
1/4 lb. capsicum chillies
12 oz. vinegar
1 sprig of curry leaves
1 desertspoon oil
oil for deep frying prawns or seer fish
1 1/2 dessertspoons salt
4 desertspoons coriander
1 teaspoon cummin powder
1 teaspoon chillie powder (optional)
1/2 oz. garlic ground
1/4 oz. ginger ground
2 oz. finely ground mustard
1 dessertspoon sugar
salt

Method

1. Shell prawns if used, wash seer fish and cut into thin slices. Deep fry until prawns or fish resembles dry fish.
2. Grind mustard, garlic and ginger with vinegar.
3. Heat the vinegar with 1 1/2 dessertspoons of salt and boil onion and chillies for just a few munutes only, so that the green and pink colour of the chillies and onions will not be lost due to over boiling.
4. Heat oil, add curry leaves, and all the powdered ingredients and fry for just a few seconds.
5. Add the mustard dissolved in the vinegar left over after boiling the onions and chillies. Bring to boil.
6. Add the fried prawns or fish and onions and chillies.Simmer for a few minutes. Stir well, cool and bottle. Can be kept for some time.

337. PRAWN MOJU

Ingredients for 2 x 1 *lb. jars.*

1 lb. prawns shelled
1 lb. onions sliced
8-9 dry chillies
3 dessertspoons coriander
1 dessertspoon cummin
} roasted well and ground fine.

1/2 lb. capsicum chillies sliced
2-4 cloves garlic ground
a few slices of ginger ground
1/2 bottle of vinegar
salt

Method

1. Boil vinegar, ground ingredients and salt.
2. Deep fry shelled prawns. Set aside. When vinegar mixture boils add sliced capsicum chillies and onions.
3. Bring to boil again, add the fried prawns. If gravy is too much remove prawns and reduce gravy. Cool and bottle.

338. SEER FISH MOJU

Ingredients for 2 x 1 *lb. jars.*

1 lb. fresh seer fish slices	4 oz. ground mustard
4 dessertspoons coriander powder	2 dessertspoons chillie powder
	1/4 oz. ginger
1 oz. garlic	curry leaves, rampe
2 oz. finely sliced red onions	1" cinnamon
2 teaspoons mustard seeds	8 oz. vinegar
2 cloves	a pinch of turmeric
2 cardamoms crushed	2 dessertspoons sugar
4 desertspoons oil	oil for deep frying
2 1/2 dessertspoons salt	salt

Method

1. Wash and cut fish slices into half if large. Dry well. Rub with turmeric and salt and shallow fry.
2. Grind the ginger, garlic and mustard to a fine paste with a little vinegar. Add the chillie, turmeric, coriander, salt and sugar and mix well. Slice the onions.

3. Heat oil in a shallow pan and when very hot add the curry leaves and rampe. Then the cliced onions and fry until onions are golden brown and crisp. Add the mustard seeds, then immediately the ground mustard mixture with the vinegar.

4. Bring to boil. Add the fried fish and simmer for 1/2 an hour. Cool and store in an earthenware jar.

339. SPRATS MOJU

Ingredients for 1 x 1 *lb. jar*

1 lb. sprats	1/2 lb. green chillies
1/4 lb. onions	1 dessertspoon salt
1/4 bottle vinegar	1 dessertspoon mustard
1/4 bottle oil	

Method

1. Fry sprats well.

2. Slice chillies into two and fry a few munutes.

3. Grind finely mustard with vinegar. Add sprats and the rest of the ingredients and mix well.

340. TAMARIND FISH MOJU

Ingredients

15 lb. seer fish	2 1/2 lb. of sugar
2 1/2 lb. of salt	4 bottles vinegar
4-5 lb.tamarind	

Method

1. Clean the fish well (no water to be used) and cut into thick slices. (use only fresh fish)
2. Sprinkle slices with salt, set aside, turn slices occasionally to let the juice drain off. After four hours wipe slices perfectly dry with a clean cloth.
3. Make a pulp of the tamarind with three bottles of vinegar and strain. Mix the sugar and salt.
4. Place the fish in layers in stone jar or bujama or earthenware jar. Cover with the tamarind mixture and lastly add the remaining bottle of vinegar. Cork down slightly.
5. It will be ready for use in a month. When required scrape off the tararind juice from fish. Fry fish and serve with tamarind sauce from salted fish heated to boiling point poured over fried fish.

341. DRY FISH PACHADI

Ingredients for 2 x 1 *lb. jars.*

1 lb. dry fish (seer)
1/2 lb. green chillies
2 dessertspoons mustard seeds
2 dessertspoons cummin powder
1/2 dessertspoons chillie powder
2 dessertspoons sugar
1/2 lb. red onions
1/4 oz. ginger chopped fine
1/2 oz. garlic chopped fine
2 dessertspoons sweet cummin powder
16 oz. vinegar
2 dessertspoons salt
rampe, curry leaves
sera

4 desseertspoons oil	salt
15 dry chillies	

Method

1. Wash the dry fish well, free of sand, dry and cut into 1/2″ cubes.
2. Wash the chillies and slit the ends. Peel and wash onions. Chop the garlic and ginger fine.
3. Roast the mustard. Roast the chillie and cummin till light golden brown. Grind fine with vinegar.
4. Fry the dry fish until crisp. Fry the onions and chillie for a few minutes. Leave all to drain well.
5. Put 4 dessertspoons oil in a pan and when very hot fry the curry leaves, rampe, garlic and ginger until garlic is light brown. Add the vinegar, sugar, ground ingredients and allow to cook for a few minutes.
6. Add the fried fish, onions and chillies. Bring to boil and take off fire. Allow to cool and store in dry jars or if vacuum packed, seal hot.

342. BRINJAL PAHIE - 1

Ingredients for 2 x 1 *lb. jars.*

1 lb. brinjal	1 teaspoon fenugreek
1 1/2 oz. onions	2 dessertspoons ground mustard
1 sprig of curry leaves	1/2 dessertspoon cummin
10-15 green chillies	1/2 dessertspoon sweet cummin
6 cloves garlic	1 dessertspoon chillie powder
2 cloves	2 dessertspoons coriander powder
2 cardamoms	

2″ cinnamon
4-5 dessertspoons tamarind dissolved in 2nd & 3rd extracts of coconut milk
8 oz. 1st extract of coconut milk
a thin slice ginger
1 dessertspoon vinegar
2 dessertspoons sugar
1/4 teaspoon turmeric
salt

Method

1. Wash and cut the brinjal into cubes, mix with 1 teaspoon salt and 1/4 teaspoon turmeric and deep fry to a golden brown.
2. Chop onions, chillies, garlic, ginger.
3. Put all the ingredients except fried brinjals into a pan with the milk. Bring to boil and allow to simmer till reduced to about half the quantity, stir occasionally.
4. Add the brinjal, sugar and vinegar. Simmer for a few minutes and take off fire. Store in bottles.

343.BRINJAL PAHIE - 2

Ingredients for 2 x 1 *lb. jars.*

1 lb. brinjals
1/4 lb. red onions
1/4 oz. ground ginger
rampe and curry leaves
8 oz. of vinegar
1 dessertspoon salt
1/4 teaspoon turmeric powder
1/4 lb. ripe green chillies
3/4 oz. ground garlic
1 dessertspoon chillie powder
1/2 teaspoon fenugreek
2 dessertspoons sugar
oil for frying brinjals

Method

1. Wash and cut brinjals into finger lengths about 2″. Rub turmeric and deep fry until golden brown, but do not over fry.
2. Slice red onions into two or three if large, cut chillies in two if large or slit if small.
3. Grind garlic and ginger.
4. Heat oil and temper onions, chillies, rampe, curry leaves, fenugreek. Do not fry till crispy.
5. Mix fried brinjals with chillie powder, garlic, ginger, sugar, vinegar and salt and add to tempered onions etc. Bring to boil and simmer for a few minutes. Cool and store in jars.

344.BRINJAL PAHIE - 3

Ingredients for 2 x 1 *lb. jars.*

1 lb. brinjals	1/4 lb. ripe green chillies
1/4 lb. red onions	1/2 oz. garlic
1/4 oz. ground ginger	4 teaspoons sugar
4 dessertspoons ground mustard	2 teaspoons chillie powder
	8 oz. vinegar
2 dessertspoons salt	curry leaves
1 dessertspoon oil	2 desertspoons slightly roasted coriander powder

Method

1. Wash and cut brinjals into cubes 1/2″ deep fry until golden brown.

2. Slit the ends of the chillie. Deep fry chillies and onions for just a few minutes only. Drain well.

3. Grind the ginger and garlic fine.

4. Heat one dessertspoon of oil until very hot. Add curry leaves and fry until crisp. Mix all ground ingredients with vinegar, sugar and add to oil, cook untio it comes to boiling point.

5. Mix in the fried ingredients. Add salt. Store in air tight bottles. Can be kept for some time.

Variation

1/2 lb. of good dry fish cut into small pieces and deep fried may be added to this mixture.

345. AMBARELLA PICKLE

Ingredients for 2 x 1 *lb. jars.*

16 ambarellas
1/2 bottle vinegar
salt

1 1/2 oz. mustard seeds
3/4 oz. each, dry chillies, ground garlic and ginger
1/2 botle vinegar

Method

1. Choose well seasoned fruits. Cut each fruit into four lengthwise and peel off the skin. Remove seed.

2. Then boil in 1/2 bottle vinegar for about 15 minutes. After the fruits are cooked put them into the mustard mixture.

Mustard Mixture

1. To half the bottle of vinegar add all the ground ingredients and mix well. Then add the cooked ambarella. Store in bottles, can be kept for some time.

346. CHILLIE PICKLE - 1 (STUFFED)

Ingredienyts for 1 x 1 *lb. jars.*

	Mustard Mixture	
8 capsicum chillies	1 1/2 oz. mustard	ground to a smooth paste
1/2 oz. mustard seeds	1/2 oz. ginger	
1/4 oz. green papaw	1/2 oz. garlic	
1/4 oz. garlic (grated)	1/4-1/2 oz. dry chillies	
1/4 oz. ginger	1/2 bottle vinegar	
8 oz. vinegar	salt	
1/4-1/2 oz. chille powder		

Method

1. Make a small slit in the chillies, lengthwise. remove seeds boil in vinegar until partly done, grind the ginger with vinegar.

2. Grate the papaw finely, add a little vinegar and salt and boil. Take it off the fire and mix with the other ground ingredients.

3. Stuff the chillies with the prepared mixture. Grind the remaining ingredients. Mix with vinegar and ground mustard to a smooth paste. Add stuffed chillies to the prepapred mustard mixture. Mix in the rest of the vinegar

347. FRIED SEER FISH PICKLE - 1

Ingredients for 2 x 1 *lb. jars.*

1 lb. seer fish (slices)
2 dessertspoons chillie powder
8 oz. vinegar
a pinch of turmeric
oil for deep frying
3 oz. tamarind
1 dessertspoon coriander powder
2 dessertspoons sugar
2 dessertspoons salt

Method

1. Cut fish into slices wash well, rub with turmeric and salt and deep fry.
2. Soak tamarind in vinegar and extract pulp. Mix all powdered ingredients with tamarind pulp, sugar and bring to boil.
3. Add fried pieces of fish and take off fire. Cool and store in earthenware jars.

348. FRIED SEER FISH PICKLE - 2

Ingredients for 2 x 1 *lb. jars.*

1 lb. seer fish (slices)
2 dessertspoons chillie powder
6 oz. vinegar
2 dessertspoons salt
oil for deep frying
1 teaspoon mixed spices powdered, cloves, cardamoms, cinnamon
salt
1/2 lb. tamarind
1 dessertspoon coriander powder
2 teaspoons cummin powder
pinch of turmeric powder
2 dessertspoons sugar
2-4 cloves garlic ground
2-3 slices ginger ground

Method

1. Cut fish into slices, wash well rub with turmeric and salt. Deep fry till golden brown.
2. Soak tamarind in vinegar and extract pulp. Mix all ground and powdered ingredients with tamarind pulp and sugar and bring to boil.
3. Add fried pieces of fish and take off the fire. Cool and store in earthenware jars.

349. LIME PICKLE

Ingredients for 3-4 x 1 *lb. jars.*

1/4 bottle vinegar	1/4 lb. salt
1 lb. sugar	25 limes or 20 lemons

Method

1. Prick the limes with a fork and set aside
2. Boil the vinegar and sugar to boiling point, add the limes. When the limes turn yellow in colour, remove the pan fromthe fire and allow to cool.
3. Pour into air tight bottle and leave for 2 weeks.

350. MALAY PICKLE

Ingredients for 2 x 1 *lb. jars.*

6 oz. Bombay onions cut into 4	1 oz. sugar
1 pickled lime cut into small pieces	1/2 oz. mustard
	2 cloves garlic

	chillie according to taste
4 oz. capsicum chillies cut into 3/4″ - 1″ pieces	a thin slice of ginger
1 oz. dried billing cut	3 oz. dates, each date cut into 8 pieces
2 oz. dried mango 1/4″- 1/3″ pieces	vinegar
	salt

Method

1. Grind chillies, ginger and mustard in vinegar.
2. Dilute this mixture to a thick paste and a dropping consistency with more vinegar.
3. Mix with all the other ingredients, add salt and sugar to taste.
4. Pack bottles without air bubbles.

351. MIXED PICKLE

Ingredients for 2 x 1 *lb. jars.*

2 oz. green chillies	4 oz. onions
2 oz. mustard	2 oz. each of carrots, beans, unripe papaw if available
2-4 cloves garlic	
1/2 oz. ginger	1 dessertspoon chillie powder
2 1/2 teaspoons salt	2 teaspoons sugar
1/2 pint vinegar	

Method

1. Wash and slit the chillies half way. Peel and wash the onions. Peel, wash and cut the carrots into slices. String, wash and cut the beans into strips. Peel wash and cut papaw into strips.

2. Grind the garlic, ginger, mustard, with a little of the vinegar.

3. Bring the vinegar to boil with 1 teaspoon salt and add chillies, when vinegar comes to boil remove chillies.Repeat same procedure with onions, carrots beans and papaw separately.

4. Mix ground ingredients with balance vinegar, add more vinegar if necessary. Add onions, chillies etc. Mix well and season.

352. PINEAPPLE PICKLE

Ingredients for 1 1/2 x 1 *lb. jars.*

1/2 lb. pineapple	2 dessertspoons ground mustard
6 dessertspoons vinegar	3-4 teaspoons chillie powder
2 teaspoons lime juice	1/2 teaspoon garlic ground
1/4 - 1/2 teaspoon ginger ground	1 teaspoon sugar
	salt

Method

1. Cut the pineapple into 3/4″ cubes. Grind the mustard, garlic and ginger with a little vinegar to a fine paste.

2. Mix all the ingredients with the vinegar. Add the well drained pineapple pieces and mix well. Keep in a china or glass bowl. Use same day.

353. PLANTAIN FLOWER PICKLE (Kehel Muwa)

Ingredients for 2 x 1 *lb. jars.*

6-8 oz. kehel muwa (about 2 plantain flowers)

4 oz. dried sprats

12 oz. small red onions

4 oz. mustard

1/2 oz. fenugreek

2 oz. dry billing cut into small bits

1 oz. coriander powder

2 sprigs of curry leaves

2 dessertspoons oil

4 oz. brinjal

3 oz. green chillies

1/2 oz. cummin

1/2 oz. sweet cummin

1/2 oz. chillie powder

salt to taste (preferably jardi salt water)

1/2 oz. ginger

1/2 oz. garlic

Method

1. Remove the outer petals of the plantain flower till only the centre and yellow part is left. Shred into very fine rings.

2. Wash with a little water and lime skin to remove the stickiness and prevent it from discolouring. Squeeze well to remove all traces of water, deep fry.

3. Wash sprats well and deep fry until crisp. Set aside.Cut brinjals into finger lengths deep fry until light golden brown. Deep fry red onions sliced or whole if small.

4. Grind mustard with vinegar. Heat oil add curry leaves with chillie powder, coriander, cummin, sweet cummin, ginger and garlic ground. Add mustard. Fry for a few seconds, add about 1/3-1/2 bottle vinegar., jardi water or salt, to make a thick paste.

5. Cook for 3-5 minutes. Bring to boil, add all fried igredients mix well. If necessary add a little more vinegar. Allow to cool, pack into jars.

354. POLOS PAHIE - 1

Ingredients for 1 x 1 *lb. jars.*

1 small tender jak (about 2 lbs.) (polos).

1/3 - 1/4 bottle vinegar	1 3/4 oz. mustard
2 slices ginger	10-15 dry chillies or 1-2 dessert spoons chillie powder
sugar	
1 teaspoon salt	1 clove garlic

Method

1. Boil polos until tender. Remove skins and chop centre very fine.
2. Grind mustard, garlic, ginger, dry chillies and salt with a little vinegar, to a fine paste.
3. Boil the rest of the vinegar with the ground ingredients. Add the chopped polos. Mix well. Add sugar and salt to taste.

355. POLOS PAHIE - 2

Ingredients for 1 x 1 *lb. jars.*

1 tender jak fruit (Polos).

Method

1. Wash and boil tender jak fruit until soft.
2. Remove the outer skin and grind the centre very fine with a little vinegar if necessary.
3. To every 1/2 lb. of ground polos add the following ingredients. Mix well.

   1 1/4 oz. ground mustard, 2-3 cloves garlic chopped fine.

   2-3 teaspoons chillie powder

   a few thin slices of ginger

   salt to taste

   4 oz. vinegar
4. Mix to a paste with vinegar. Mix in the boiled ground jak.
5. Store in jars. Can be kept for some time.

356. PRAWN PICKLE

Ingredients for 1 x 1 *lb. jars.*

2-3 Bombay onions
2-3 capsicum chillies
2-3 dates
1/2 lime pickle cut into small cubes
2 teaspoons sugar
chillie powder according to taste
16-20 medium sized prawns deep fried in oil
4 cloves garlic
2 slices ginger
1 teaspoon mustard
2 pieces dried mango
2 dried billings
salt to taste

Method

1. Grind chillies, garlic, ginger and mustard in vinegar and make a thick paste, add more vinegar. Add sugar and salt. Mix in the other ingredients.

357. QUICK MIXED PICKLE

Ingredients for 1 x 1 *lb. jars.*

2 oz. carrots	2 oz. cabbage
2 oz. half ripe papaw	4 oz. onions
2 oz. raw tender radish	4 oz. vinegar
2 dessertspoons salt	2 oz. finely ground mustard
2 cloves garlic	a thin slice ginger
3 teaspoons sugar	

Method

1. Grate the carrots and papaw. grate the radish and soak in salt water. Shred the cabbage finely, chop the onions.
2. Grind the mustard, garlic and ginger fine with a little vinegar.
3. Mix vinegar, ground ingredients, sugar and salt together well.
4. Squeeze out the radish from the salt water and mix all the vegetables together. Add the mustard mixture. Leave for a few hours before use.

358. SEER FISH PICKLE IN TAMARIND SAUCE

Ingredients for 2 x 1 *lb. jars.*

1 lb. seer fish slices
1/2 oz. chillie powder
1/4 oz. cummin seeds
1/4 pint vinegar
1/4 lb. tamarind
1/2 oz. coriander seeds
1/3 oz. sweet cummin seeds
salt, turmeric
4 dessertspoons oil

Method

1. Wash and dry the seer fish slices until all traces of moisture are removed. Rub with salt and a pinch of turmeric and shallow fry.
2. Grind the curry powder and chillie with a little vinegar.
3. Soak the tamarind in vinegar and extract pulp. Mix the ground ingredients with the tamarind pulp.
4. Mix the tamarind sauce with the pieces of fish. Simmer for a few minutes. Cool and store in an earthenware jar.

Note:- The sauce must cover the pieces completely.

359. JARDI - 1

Method

1. Take any type of fish that is fresh and not iced.
2. Wash with salt water or sea water. Arrange layers of fish in a chatty pot or an earthenware jar.
3. Sprinkle a little crushed kitcken salt on the layers of fish, add 1-2 pieces of goraka, 2-3 cloves, cardamoms, 1"piece cinnamon, with each layer of salt.

4. Repeat. Top layer must always be salt.
5. Press tight, allow it to remain in this manner for about a week. This may be sunned if necessary.
6. The fish may be used after a week. The brine, if used for gravies such as Kiri Hodhi, or in the preparation of Moju's in place of salt, gives a very fine flavour.

360. JARDI - 2

Method

1. Follow the same method as Jardi 1, but sun pieces of Jardi daily.
2. After 2-3 days dip fish in brine solution. More salt may have to be added to the brine solution.
3. This method is more suitable for slices of fish, that is to be made into Jardi.

SWEETMEAT PREPARATIONS

361. AGGALA WITH RICE FLOUR

Ingredients for 18 *aggalas.*

3/4 lb. parboiled rice washed and roasted in a pan until light golden brown.

1/2 lb. coconut finely grated and pounded

3/4 - 1 lb. kitul honey

10 pepper corns crushed (optional)

Method

1. Grind or pound the roasted rice and sieve.
2. Cook honey until it boils once. Remove about 4 oz. to be used later if necessary. Add coconut and cook until honey boils 2-3 times.
3. Allow to cook for 5-10 minutes. Add rice flour gradually. Mix well. Add more honey, if necessary. Mixture must be fairly stiff.
4. While it is hot make into balls 1 - 1 1/2″ in diameter and roll in a little bit of the roasted rice flour.

362. COCONUT ALUWA

Ingredients for 35 - 40 *pieces.*

1 lb. sugar
1 coconut grated (large) (1 lb.)

a few drops of colouring and rose water

2 oz. water

Method

1. Take 2 oz. coconut, add 2 oz. water, extract milk, add coconut milk and sugar and bring to boil.
2. When the sugar has reached boiling point add grated coconut and cook until the mixture begins to crystalize on sides of pan.
3. Pour on to greased baking sheet, flatten and smoothen top with a piece of grease proof paper.
4. Heat 4 oz. icing sugar with 2-3 dessertspoons of cocoa dissolved in 1 or 2 dessertspoons milk. Heat over low fire until mixture coats the back of the wooden spoon fairly thickly.
5. Pour over prepared coconut aluwa and cut into squares.

363. COCONUT ROCK

Ingredients for 35-40 *pieces.*

1 lb. coconut grated	8 oz. milk
2 lb. sugar	cadju

Method

1. Boil the sugar and the milk together.
2. Add the grated coconut, and cook until the mixture comes off the sides of the pan.
3. Then add the chopped cadjunuts. When done spread on a greased board or plate and cut into squares.

364. MILK ALUWA

Ingredients for 40-50 *pieces.*

1 bottle cow milk (any milk other than coconut milk)

1 1/2 lb. sugar

vanila

1/2 lb. cadjunuts, (chopped and lightly roasted)

1/4 lb. sultanas can be added (optional)

Method

1. Put the sugar and the milk into a pan, cook over a very low fire. If the fire is too hot the aluwa will not be white.
2. Keep stirring all the time. When half done add the chopped cadjunuts.
3. When it gets thick and almost dry put on a greased board. Flatten it out quickly and cut into desired shapes.

365. NEGOMBO ALUWA

Ingrredients for 20-25 *pieces.*

2 cups well roasted and sieved rice flour

3/4 - 1 bottle treacle or jaggery

25-30 cadjunuts, broken into large pieces

1 teaspoon ghee

a pinch of salt

extra roasted flour for dusting

Method

1. Put the treacle or jaggery into a pan and cook till thick.
2. Add the flour and stir well to prevent lumps. Mix in the coarsely chopped cadjunuts and the ghee.

3. Stir the mixture until it reaches non sticky pliable dough stage. Remove from fire, and put the mixture on to a board dusted with roasted flour.

4. Flatten the mixture to an inch thickness, dust the top with roasted flour and cut into diamond shaped pices.

366. POTATO ALUWA - 1

Ingredients for *35-40 pieces.*

1 lb. potatoes	1 1/2 lb. sugar
1 teaspoon coconut milk	2 oz. chopped cadjunuts

Method

1. Boil potatoes and pass through a sieve free of lumps. Boil sugar with cocnut milk, and cook until the sugar has slightly thickened.

2. Add boiled potatoes, 2-3 cardamoms powdered. Keep stirring all the time until setting point. (sugar will begin to crystallize on the sides of the pan).

3. Add chopped cadjunuts, turn out onto a greased baking sheet smoothen top and cut into squares.

367.POTATO ALUWA - 2

Ingredients for 35-40 *pieces.*

1 lb. potato, tapioca, sweet potato, red pumpkin or ash pumpkin may also be used for aluwa.

1 1/2 lb. sugar	1 dessertspoon butter
1 cup coconut milk or cow milk	roasted chopped cadjunuts.

Method

1. Boil potato or other yam used and pass through a sieve or blender.
2. Mix coconut milk or any other milk with the sugar and bring to boil.
3. Add the mashed potato or yam. Cook until the mixture comes off the sides of the pan.
4. Add the roasted chopped cadjunuts (if used) along with the buter.
5. Spread on a greased board or plate and cut into squares.

368. RULANG ALUWA

Ingredients for 35-40 pieces.

1 lb. rulang (roasted)	cadju
2 lb. jaggery	cardamoms
8 oz. milk	grated pineapple

a piece of cinnamon

Method

1. Roast rulang
2. Add jaggery gratede. Mix with milk and cook until it comes off the sides of the pan. Sugar may be substituted for this.
3. Add cadju, cardamoms and cinnamon. Cook until mixture comes off the sides of the pan.
4. Turn on to a greased board.Flatten on top and cut whilst still warm.

N.B. - 1/2 lb. rulang may be added with 1/2 lb. of grated pineapple. Procedure may be the same.

369. AASMI

Ingredients for 8-10 *asmes.*

1/2 lb. rice flour	1st & 2nd extracts of coconut
a handful of daul kurundu leaves	milk (1/2 coconut)

Method

1. Pound rice, and sieve through a very fine sieve.
2. Make a very stiff dough by mixing with coconut milk. Dough must be fairly stiff, add salt.
3. Grind the daul kurundu leaves and extract the juice. Add this to the coconut milk flour mixture so that a slimy consistency is obtained.
4. Dilute with a litle more coconut milk to get the consistency required for the batter. Dip fingers arched into this batter and with the fingers pour the batter into the heated oil.
5. Fold into two and set aside for a few days. Fry again to make aasmi light and crisp.
6. Pour very thick coloured sugar syrup over Aasmi to form a design.

370. ATHIRAHA

Ingredients for 35-40 *athiraha.*

1 lb. rice soaked and pounded and sieved well.

4-6 oz. of left over small pieces of rice roasted well. (kappi)

16 oz. thick sugar syrup.

Method

1. Heat sugar and keep on adding sufficient flour with all the kappi (broken bits of roasted rice) into the sugar until a stiff mixture is formed.

2. Continue to cook until the mixture forms a ball and leaves the sides of the bowl.

3. Place on a board and allow to cool.

4. Into the used pan add 1/2-1/4 of water and cook the left over mixture to be like stiff starch. With this liquid knead the stiff dough until very pliable and free from cracks.

5. Make marble size balls, dip in oil, flatten to be about 2″ in diameter. Deep fry.

Note:- A biscuit press may also be used for different shapes.

371. BIBIKKAN - 1

Ingredients for 1 *pan* 9″ x 12″

1 medium size coconut (1 - 1 1/2 lb)	1/4 lb. white wheat flour
2 lb. jaggery	1/2 lb. sugar
1/2 lb. cadjunuts	2 oz. ginger preserve
2 teaspoons mixed cloves cardamom and cinnamon	2 teaspoons grated rind of lime
	2-3 oz. sultanas (optional)

Method

1. Scrape coconut. Extract as much coconut milk as possible without adding water.

2. Pound coconut.

3. Dissolve jaggery and sugar with coconut milk. Add salt. Bring to boil.
4. Add pounded coconut and cook until mixture is sticky but not burnt or caramelized. Take off the fire.
5. Add flour. Mix well. Chop cadjunuts, ginger preserve,and spices. Mix well.
6. Add lime rind just before putting into pan 9 x 12″. Bake at 325^0 F, until done.

372. BIBIKKAN - 2

Ingredients for 1 *pan* **15″ x 18″** (a small round pan, 8-9″ diameter)

3 large coconuts (scraped)
(1 1/2 - 1 3/4 lbs)
1/2 lb. white wheat flour
a few cardamoms
1/2 lb. cadjunuts chopped
2 teaspoons vanilla
4 oz. coconut water
1 lb. rice flour
1 lb. treacle
1/2 lb. sultanas
1 teaspoon yeast
1/2 lb. dates

Note:

* 1 large coconut gives 1-1 1/4 lb. scraped coconut.

1 small coconut gives 3/4 - 1lb. scraped coconut

1 bundle jaggery - 2 lb.

Method

Dough

1. Roast the rice flour and white wheat flour slightly. Soak the yeast in 2 oz. water with 1/2 teaspoon sugar. Add the yeast and the coconut water to the flour.
2. Knead well. Leave to rise.
3. To make the pani pol, boil the treacle, add to the craped coconut, powdered cardamoms and vanilaessence.
4. Mix well. When the mixture is rather dry add the sultanas, cadjunuts and chopped dates.
5. Take off the fire and allow to cool and lastly add the dough. Pour into lined and greased baking trays and bake in a hot oven. 375 - 400 ^{0}F for 30-40 minutes.

373. COCKTAIL MIXTURE (SHORT-EATS)

Ingredients for 1 1 1/2 *lb.*

1/4 lb. gram flour

2 oz. peanuts

2 oz. cadjunuts

1 teaspoon salt

2 oz. gram dhal soaked in water for a few hours

sufficient coconut milk to make a stiff consistency like for string-hoppers

a sprig of curry leaves

5-6 green chillies finely cut

3 oz. habalapethi (pressed rice)

2 raw potatoes grated

1 teaspoon chillie powder.

Method

1. Mix gram flour with chillie powder, salt. Add sufficient coconut milk to make a stiff consistency as for string-hoppers.
2. Put it in the string-hopper mould and pipe into heated oil. Fry till light brown in colour. Set aside.
3. Fry peanuts, cadjunuts, gram dhal, curry leaves, green chillies, habalapethi (boiled pressed rice) and grated potatoes separately.
4. Break up the gram flour (fried) mixture into pieces. Add little chillie powder and salt and mix all the other fried ingredients. Bottle. This can be stored for any length of time.

374. COPPA PITTU

Ingredients for 25-30 *coppa pittu*

Pittu	**Pani Pol**
1 lb. rice flour	1/2 jaggery
1 lb. scraped coconut	1/2 lb. scraped coconut
salt	1 dessertspoon rice flour
water to mix	cinnamon and salt
4 oz. 1st extract of coconut milk	2 oz. water

Method

1. Put the flour and coconut and salt into a pan.
2. Mix the flour so that it forms into small grains. If necessary add water while forming the grains.

3. Fill 1/2 a cup with the pitu mixture. Make a hole in the centre and fill with panipol. Refil with pittu mixture. Turn on to string-hopper mats the moulded coppa pittu and steam.

4. Pour 1 teaspoon 1st extract of coconut milk over each coppa pittu.

Method - Pani Pol

1. Boil the honey. Add the grated coconut, powdered cinnamon and salt. Cook till the syrup thickens, add flour and stir for a few minutes longer.

375. HALAPE

Ingredients for 16-24 *halapes.*

1/2 lb. treacle	1 coconut scraped
1 lb. rice flour	a few cardamoms

Method

1. Make pani pol as stated in Recipe No.391 with coconut and treacle.

2. Mix in the flour to the pani pol mixture.

3. Flatten out on kenda leaves. Fold into two and place 2-3 halapes, on a steamer or on a string-hopper mat and steam.

376. KITHUL PITI HALAPE (KITHUL FLOUR)

Ingredients for 8 *portions.*

Blanc-mange	**Syrup**
1 lb. kithul piti cooked	16 oz. 1st & 2nd extracts
with 16-24 oz. of water	of coconut milk
till it reaches the	6 oz. grated jaggery
consistency of thick	2 cardamoms

blanc-mange, add 1 teaspoon salt

Method

1. Pour cooked kithul flour mixture into a flat dish and cut into 1″ squares. This should be done over night and kept.
2. Boil 16 oz. coconut milk with grated jaggery, add 2 cardamoms crushed.
3. Bring to boil, add kithul piti, blanc-mange prepared over night. Serve hot or cold.
4. There must be sufficient syrup for the pieces to stay in.

377. KURAKAN (TYPE OF MILLET) HALAPE

Ingredients for 16-24 halapes.

1/2 lb. treacle	1 coconut (scraped), (8-10 oz.)
(add more if necessary)	a few cardamoms powdered
1/4 lb. rice flour	1/4 lb. kurakkan flour

Method

1. Make pani-pol with the coconut and treacle.

2. Sieve the rice flour and kurakkan flour together. Add to the pani-pol mixture, mix well.

3. Flatten out on kanda leaves or plantain leaves. Fold into two and steam. Remove leaves and serve.

378. JALEBIS

Ingredients for 20-30 *jalebis.*

1 lb. flour	1 dessertspoon curd
8 oz. warm water	2 dessertspoons gram flour
1 dessertspoon ghee	1 dessertspoon hot fat

Method

1. Mix flour, ghee, curd with warm water to make a thick batter. Set aside for 24 hours to ferment.

2. Add gram flour, a pinch of yellow colouring and heated oil.

3. Fill batter into piping bag or coconut shell with hole. If necessary add a little water to batter so that the batter falls smoothly.

4. Heat sufficient oil to fill 2-3″ of a flat frying pan. Pipe the batter coil form into smoking hot oil. After a short while turn over. Fry crisp. Add to hot syrup, turn over jalebis in syrup. Drain on wire sieve.

Syrup

1 1/2 lb. sugar	12 oz water
rose essence	yellow colouring
2 bottles coconut oil	

Method

1. Boil sugar syrup a little. If syrup is not clean add 1 dessertspoon fresh milk to syrup. Bring to boil and skim or strain through a muslin and reboil till it reaches a thread consistency.

2. Take off fire, add essence and colouring and allow to cool a little till the steam goes off. The syrup should not be too thick as jalebis will not absorb the syrup. If too thin the crispness of the jalebis will be lost. It must be medium thick.

379. KAVUM (OIL CAKES)

Ingredients for 30-50 *kavum.*

1 lb. of rice soaked, pounded and sieved well.

16 oz. treacle or thick sugar syrup.

Method

1. Mix rice flour and treacle or thick sugar syrup well and allow mixture to stand for about 1/2 an hour.

2. Dilute with sugar syrup or more thin treacle, fry in deep frying pan (hoppers type) one at a time by pouring a little batter into the bottom of the pan and after a few minutes have passed, insert an ekel or wooden skewer into centre of the batter and keep turning ekel so that uncooked batter keeps coming up forming what is called a konde or a knot.

3. There must not be too much heat or else the outside will be browned and the inside uncooked. Drain.

Variation

As soon as the kavum is ready put into medium thick sugar syrup and drain, the porous texture of the kavum absorbs the syrup and gives a delicious flavour.

380. KALU DODOL - 1

Ingredients for 12-15 *lb. Kalu Dodol.*

3 lb. rice flour	3/4 lb. white wheat flour
9 lb. jaggery	15 coconuts large
1/4 lb. cadjunuts	10-16 cardamoms

1 teaspoon salt

Method

1. Grate the coconut, squeeze it a number of times to extract the maximum quantity of milk. Pound the refuse and extract the last extract of coconut milk. (Well dried seasoned coconuts are best for use).

2. Dissolve rice flour and wheat flour in a little coconut milk and set aside. Dissolve jaggery in balance milk and strain to remove grit in jaggery.

3. Bring to boil. Add coconut milk with flour dissolved. Cook until thick stirring all the while, until oil begins to come from mixture.

4. Remove oil from time to time, add cardamoms and cadjunuts and cook until mixture comes off the sides of the pan in a lump. Pour into flat pan, smooth top with plantain leaf or grease proof paper.

5. Leave pan at an angle for oil to drain. Use as required after 24 hours (rubber coagulating pan).

381. KALU DODOL - 2

Ingredients for 4-5 *lb. Kalu Dodol*

6 coconuts large	2 bundles jaggery (4 lbs.)
1 lb. rice flour	1/4 lb. cadjunuts.

Method

1. Scrape the coconut and extract the milk.
2. Coconut shoud be squeezed out three times. Put the coconut milk, scraped jaggery, flour into a preserving pan and leave on the fire.
3. Stir well, till the mixture thickens and is dark in colour. Remove oil as it oozes out. Add the chopped cadjunuts and take off fire when mixture forms into one mass and comes off the sides of the pan.
4. Flatten out on a board or pan and cut inti pieces. 15 x12″ size of pan.

382. KIRI DODOL

Ingredients for 20-25 *pieces.*

2-3 cups rice flour	a few cadjunuts (optional)
1 lb. jaggery or more	1″ piece of cinnamon powdered (optional)
1 pint coconut milk	
salt	

Method

1. Put the flour into a pan, add the milk gradually and mix until it is free from lumps.

2. Add the jaggery scraped, salt and cinnamon if used.

3. Stir over fire until the mixture thickens. Keep on stirring non stop to prevent burning at the bottom. Mix in the chopped cadjunuts if used before removing from fire.

4. When the mixture is non sticky and forms a lump remove from fire. Flatten the mixture on a greased board. Cut into desired pieces when cold.

383. KIRI KAKARUM

Ingredients for 20-25 *pieces.*

Same as kiri dodol

Syrup

12 oz. 1st & 2nd extracts of

coconut milk

jaggery

Method

1. Follow Recipe No.382 Kiri Dodol, but the mixture should be prepared in the night.

2. The following morning heat the coconut milk with the jaggery bring to boil and add the kiri dodol.

3. Cut into 1 1/2 - 2″ squares or diamond shaped pieces. The pieces must float in the jaggery milk mixture.

384. CADJU KORADIAL

Ingredients for 40-50 *pieces.*

1 bottle good treacle

3/4 - 1 lb. cadjunuts broken into pieces.

Method

1. Set aside 8 oz. of treacle and heat the rest until very thick. Add cadjunuts.

2. Stir well. Add more treacle if necessary. When the mixture comes off the sides of the pan, pour quickly on to a wooden board well greased and flatten very thin not more than 1/4 - 1/2″ in thickness. Cut into squares whilst hot.

385. GINGELLY KORADIAL

Ingredients for 40-50 *pieces.*

1 lb. washed and dried gingelly seeds

3/4 - 1 lb. cadjunuts broken into pieces

1 bottle good treacle.

Method

1. Set aside 4 oz. of treacle and heat the rest until very thick. Add cadjunuts and gingelly seeds.

2. Stir well. Add more treacle if necessary. When the mixture comes off the sides of the pan, pour quickly on to a wooden board well greased and flatten very thin not more than 1/4 -1/2″ in thickness. Cut into squares whilst hot.

386. KOKIS - 1

Ingredients for 75-100 *kokis.*

2 lb. raw rice

1 egg

salt to taste

milk of 2 coconuts

turmeric for colouring

Method

1. Soak rice only a few hours before it is to be pounded.
2. Sieve flour well, mix with coconut milk. add beaten egg, salt and turmeric.
3. Let it rest for about one hour. Heat oil, dip kokis or waffle mould in batter after dipping it in heated fat, fry until crisp, drain.

Variation

Chillie powder may be added 2-3 teaspoons for given proportion.

Cheese 2-3 oz. grated cheese may be added.

387. KOKIS - 2

1/4 lb. white wheat flour 8-12 oz. cow milk

1 egg.

Method

1. Beat egg, milk and add to flour to form a thin batter. Add 1/2 teaspoon salt. Heat oil.
2. Dip waffle or kokis mould in batter and fry as in kokis Recipe No.386-Kokis - 1.

388. LEVARIYA

Ingredients for 20-25 *lavariyas.*

	Pani Pol
1 lb. rice flour	8-12 oz. treacle
salt to taste	1/2 coconut grated
boiling water	2 cardamoms powdered
	a grating of nutmeg

Method

1. Roast the flour well and sieve into a bowl. Add enough boiling water to make a soft but not sticky consistency as for string-hoppers.
2. Squeeze through the mould on to plantain leaves or kanda leaves. Place a dessertspoon of pani-pol mixture in the centre and fold into two. Remove leaf and place 2-3 folded lavariyas on a string-hopper mat and steam.

Method for pani pol

1. Boil the treacle. Add the grated coconut, powdered cardamoms and nutmeg. Mix well. Allow to cool and use for levariya.

389. MASALAWADE

Ingredients for 30-35 *wades.*

1 lb. dhal	10 green chillies cut into pieces
10 dry chillies	salt to taste
1/2 lb. sliced red onions	1/2 oz. maldive fish (optional)
1/2 bottle oil for frying	

30-35 medium sized prawns cleaned and washed.

Method

1. Wash and soak the dhal for about three hours or overnight.
2. Grind 3/4 of the dhal coarsely and the other 1/4 is left whole. Add all other ingredients except prawns if used.
3. Make balls the size of limes, flatten into rounds, make a hole in centre. Place a prawn round the centre and deepfry. Temperature 340-350^{0}F. The oil must not be too hot as the dhal will not be cooked through.

390. MILK TOFFEE (COCONUT)

Ingredients for 35-40 *pieces.*

1 coconut scraped
3/4 lb. sugar
1/4 lb. cadjunuts (optional)
flavouring
colouring if desired.

Method

1. Add enough water to the scraped coconut to extract 16 oz. of thick coconut milk.
2. Add the sugar and stir over fire. When the mixture begins to thicken, stir non stop and cook until it leaves the sides of the pan.
3. Add the cadjunuts chopped.
4. Remove from fire and flatten on a greased board.
5. Cut whilst hot into even size pieces.

391. MUNG -GULI - 1 (GREEN GRAM SWEET BALLS)

Ingredients for 25-30 *mung-gulis.*

Pani-Pol

1 large coconut scraped
16-20 oz. treacle
a few cardamoms
oil for deep frying

Batter

1/2 lb. rice soaked and pounded and sieved
1/2 lb. mung washed, drained and roasted until crisp
coconut milk for mixing
a pinch of turmeric and salt.

Method

1. Boil the treacle. Add the scraped coconut, and powdered cardamoms, mix well. Allow to cool and make into balls about 1- 1 1/2″ in diameter. Dip in batter and deep fry.

Batter

1. Wash roast and grind rice and mung separately in a kurakkan grinding stone.Sieve well.
2. Mix the flour together. Add coconut milk, a pinch of turmeric and salt and mix to a batter consistency. Add more milk to get the correct consistency.
3. Dip the pani-pol balls in batter and deep fry. Drain.

Note:- White wheat flour batter may be used with or without an egg for convenience.

392. MUNG GULI - 2

Ingredients for 25-30 *mung gulis*

1/2 lb. roasted and ground rice flour and sieved.

1/2 lb. raw rice washed pounded and roasted and sieved.

1 3/4 bottle treacle or melted jaggery

3-4 oz. sugar candy coarsely pounded (optional)

oil for deep frying

Method

1. Heat treacle fairly thick. Do not over heat. Allow to cool slightly.
2. Mix the two flours well. Add the coarsely pounded sugar candy if used. Mix well.
3. Pour a spoonful of treacle or melted jaggery on a side of the mixed flour mixture. Whilst adding form into balls the size of a lime, adding treacle as needed until the whole flour mixture is used up to make mung guli.
4. Set aside. Prepare batter as in mung kavum recipe, dip the balls in batter, deep fry.
5. The above balls can be made and stored in an air tight tin for a few days before frying or it may be kept after frying.

Note:- Do not add the whole quantity of treacle to the entire quantity of mixed flour as the roasted flour absorbs the jaggery, making the mixture dry and brittle and the formation into balls is difficult.

393. MUNG KAVUM - 1

Ingredients for 35-40 *mung kavum*

1/2 lb. rice soaked and pounded and sieved

1/2 lb. mung washed, drained and roasted until crisp

1/2 - 3/4 bottle treacle.

Method

1. Grind mung well and set aside. Heat 1/2 - 3/4 bottle honey till fairly thick. Remove from fire, set 9 oz. aside, add rice flour and mung flour and mix well until fairly stiff.
2. Add more treacle if necessary to make mixture pliable.
3. Mixture must be stiff but pliable. Roll stiff mixture to be not more than 1/4″ the maximum. This may be cut into various shapes, dip in rice flour, coconut milk, batter with a little turmeric added. Dip the rolled out cut pieces in the batter and deep fry.
4. Egg may be added if necessary to the batter to get a richer batter.

394. MUNG KAVUM - 2

Ingredients for 15-20 *mung kavum*

6 oz. wheat flour

8 oz. mung flour (prepared as for mung kavum No.1)

1/2 - 3/4 bottle treacle

Method

1. Heat treacle until it has reached boiling point. Allow to boil for a few minutes. Set aside 4 ozs. of treacle to be added later if necessary.

2. Add the mung and wheat flour mixed, to the treacle whilst on the fire.

3. Cook for a few minutes. Take off the fire and keep on stirring until the mixture is stiff.

4. Flatten on a plate or board very lightly greased to be not more than 1/4″ in thickness. Cut into various shapes diamond, strip, rectangular or square.

5. Dip in the following batter. 2 oz. gram flour, 4 oz. 2nd or 3rd extracts of coconut milk, a pinch of salt. Deep fry as in mung kavum Recipe No.393.

395. MURUKKU

Ingredients for 8-16 *murukkus.*

1 cup gram flour

salt to taste

sufficient water to mix or preferably 1st and 2nd extracts of coconut milk

1 teaspoon chillie powder

oil for frying

Method

1. Mix all the ingredients together to a paste that could be passed through murukku mould.

2. This paste should be made and kept for an hour.

3. The same paste could be used for fine murukku. Use a fine mould.

4. Pipe through a murukku mould to form a spiral into the heated oil 340^0 F - 350^0 F. Turn over after murukku is fried and allow to fry a few seconds on other side.

396. MUSCAT - 1

Ingredients for 4-5 lbs. *muscat.*

2 pints water	2 lb. sugar
rose water	1/2 lb. flour

7 pints 1st, 2nd and 3rd extracts of coconut milk.

Method

1. Dissolve the flour in the water. Strain through a muslin to remove the gluten.
2. Put the coconut milk and the sugar into a pan and bring to the boil. Add the flour water mixture.
3. Cook stirring all the time over not too hot a flame. When mixture is thick and comes off the sides of the pan add cadjunuts if desired, rose water and the powdered cardamoms and mix well.
4. Pour on to a greased board or pan when mixture forms a mass.

397. MUSCAT - 2

Ingredients

3 coconuts (scraped) 3 -3 1/2 lb.	1/2 lb. good ghee
	1/2 a bottle rose essence
4 lb. sugar	1 lb. wheat flour
1/4 lb. cadjunuts	1 cup refined oil

5-7 pints water

Method

1. Using three pints water extract coconut milk. Using the other two pints water mix flour and allow to soak for at least 4-6 hours.

2. Drain all water from flour and add two more pints of water. Strain again to remove gluten. Heat coconut milk and sugar, add the strained flour water mixture that has been soaked for a while.

3. After 1/2 an hour add 1 cup good coconut oil and ghee. Keep stirring until mixture is quite thick and comes off sides of pan (about 2 hours). Add cadjunuts, rose assence and stire well.

4. Pour into flat pans. Allow to cool. This muscat should be made at least 3-4 days before it is required. Cut as required. A sugar crust forms on top.

398. PUMPKIN PRESERVE - 1

Ingredients for 2 - 2 1/2 lbs. *pumpkin cubes.*

1 lb. pumpkin (cut into cubes)	1 lb. sugar
4 oz. water	rose water
colouring	sugar for coating

Method

1. Prick the pumpkin cubes. Soak in water in which a teaspoon of chunam has been dissolved. Set aside for a few hours. Wash several times to remove all traces of chunam (Calcium Chloride).

2. Heat sufficient water to cover and bring to boil.

3. Add pumpkin and allow water to come to boiling point.
4. Remove at once and wash in several changes of water until cold. Drain.
5. Add sugar and water into pan and bring to boil. Add pumpkin pieces.
6. Flavour and colour and continue to cook, stirring all the while until sugar begins to crystalise on sides of pan.
7. Remove from pan and roll pumpkin in sugar.

399. PUMPKIN PRESERVE - 2

Ingredients for 2 lbs. *pumpkin preserve.*

1 lb. grated pumpkin	1 1/2 lb. sugar
4 oz. water	1 teaspoon rose water

Method

1. Grate pumpkin withcoconut scraper.
2. Put scraped pumpkin into a cloth bag and hang up to allow water to drain, fro about 1 - 1 1/2 hours.
3. Boil sugar and water until dissolved. Add pumpkin and cook until pumpkin is done and mixture comes off the sides of the pan.
4. Pour into a flat dish and smoothen top.
5. Cut into pieces as required.

400. PUMPKIN ROSES

Ingredients for 15-20 *roses.*

1 lb. pumpkin sliced fine	1 lb. sugar
4 oz. water	sugar for coating
rose water	colouring

Method

1. Prick the slices of pumpkin and place in water to which a teaspoon of chunam has been dissolved.
2. Leave for a few hours. Wash very well to remove chunam. Spread on a cloth to dry.
3. Put the sugar and water into a pan and bring to boil. Add the slices and see that they are placed flat in the pan. Add colouring and flavouring. Lower the heat slightly as syrup thickens. Spread some sugar on a board, take each slice and roll to form roses after sugar begins to crystalize on sides of pan.

401. PODI - KEMA

Ingredients

1/2 lb. well roasted sieved rice flour

1 teaspoon salt	6-10 oz coconut milk
1 egg yolk	

Method

1. Take 4 oz. coconut milk, beat up the egg yolk, add to flour and knead, adding more coconut milk until the mixture is smooth and free from cracks.

2. Form into different shapes and deep fry once. Mixture may also be piped through a murukku mould and cut into different lengths and shapes. A biscuit press too may be used for cutting out different shapes.

3. Store in air tight tins and deep fry a second time. After deep frying a second time coat with sugar syrup. 1/4 lb. sugar dissolved in 4 oz. water until sugar syrup is thick.

4. Put fried podi-kema into sugar syrup, drain and allow to dry.

402. SAGO TALAPHE (SAGO BLANC-MANGE)

Ingredients for 6-8 *portions.*

1/4 lb. sago	1/4 lb. jaggery or 6 oz. treacle
a pinch of salt	8 oz. 1st extract of coconut milk

16 oz. 2nd & 3rd extracts of coconut milk

Method

1. Wash sago to remove any surface dust, drain, add 2nd and 3rd extracts of coconut milk and soak for 30 to 40 minutes, if time permits. (This shortens cooking time).

2. Add jaggery and cook sago until grains are translucent or done.

3. Add half of the 1st extract of coconut milk and cook until mixture is of a thick consistency. Pour into a wetted mould, chill if desired, unmould, serve separately treacle and the balance 1st extract of coconut milk heated.

403. PITTU DODOL (SOU DODOL)

Ingredients for 10-15 *pieces.*

4 oz. raw rice flour or wheat flour, or steamed white wheat flour, (when wheat flour is steamed it is easier to handle)

1/4 teaspoon salt

3-5 pepper corns crushed

1/4 - 1/2 cup water or 2nd or 3rd extract of coconut milk (optional)

Method

1. Using coconut milk or water make small grains as for pittu. This is done by sprinkling the liquid on to the flour and tossing it to form small grains.
2. The granules formed shoud not be more than pepper corns. Steam either in a pittu bamboo or in a steamer with a muslin cloth at the bottom.
3. Allow to cool. Prepare a syrup with 6 ozs. of treacle or 4 oz. jaggery with 12 oz. of 1st, 2nd or 3rd extract of coconut milk. Bring to boil and simmer for 5 minutes.
4. Add ready-made pittu broken up. Stir until the mixture is thick and flatten out on a plate. Cut into diamond shapes, serve when cold.

404. STRING-HOPPER DODOL

Ingredients for 10-16 *pieces.*

15-20 string-hoppers

1/2 lb. jaggery

8 oz. 2nd or 3rd extract of coconut milk

4 oz. 1st extract of coconut milk

Method

1. Break string-hoppers into pieces and soak in 1st extract of coconut milk.
2. Boil jaggery with 2nd or 3rd extract of coconut milk till it reaches boiling point. Cook for 5 minutes.
3. Add broken string-hoppers soaked in coconut milk into the jaggery syrup and stir until the mixture comes off the sides of the pan.
4. Add cardamom or cinnamon powder or grated nutmeg, according to taste. Flatten on a greased plate. Cut into squares or diamond shaped pieces.

405. SWEET POTATO PRESERVE

Ingredients for 35-40 *pieces.*

1 lb. sweet potatoes　　1 1/2 lb sugar

8 oz. coconut milk

Method

1. Wash, boil and mash sweet potatoes, free of lumps.
2. Add the sugar and milk, bring to boil. Add sweet potatoes. Stir till it leaves the sides of the pan.
3. Spread on a well greased pan and cut into pieces.

406. THALAGULI

Ingredients for 20-25 thalagulis.

1/2 lb. gingelly seeds washed and dried

1/2 coconut dry (copra)

1 lb. jaggery

Method

1. Slice copra fine. Pound it well in the mortar with jaggery.
2. Add gingelly seeds and pound it till a certain amount of oil oozes.
3. Mix well. Make into balls.

407. UNDU WALALU

Ingredients for 36-48 *undu walalu.*

2 lb. undu gram or black gram (free of skins) soaked for 36 hours

3 1/2 lb. of rice flour

1 pint of sugar syrup, medium thickness

very thick coconut milk

oil for frying

Method

1. Wash and grind soaked undu gram and set aside for 12 hours to ferment.
2. Mix rice flour and ground undu with just sufficient thick coconut milk to form a very stiff piping batter. Set aside for 2-4 hours.
3. Heat oil in a flat frying pan. Pipe through a piping bag with 1/4 - 1/2 opening, in coil form, into deep fat (350 - 375^0 F).
4. When light golden colour, turn, fry for a minute or two

and add to syrup that must be hot but not boiling (see jalebis Recipe No.378 for syrup).

408. ULUNDU WADDE

Ingredients for 16-20 *waddes.*

8 oz. undu or black gram (free of skin)
4 oz. red onions
4-5 red chillies broken up
1 teaspoon mustard
2 oz. parboiled rice
6-8 green chillies
2-3 sprigs of curry leaves
2-3 thin slices of ginger chopped
1 dessertspoon oil

Method

1. Soak gram overnight. Wash rice and gram well and grind to a smooth paste and set aside for a few hours to ferment.
2. If wadde is to be made in a short period add 1/2 teaspoon yeast dissolved in 2-4 teaspoons water and allow to ferment.
3. Heat oil. When smoking add curry leaves, onions, green chillies and fry until golden brown.
4. Just before removing add mustard seeds and take off the fire immediately.
5. Fold this mixture into the fermented undu gram rice mixture. Season with salt, shape like doughnuts and deep fry in fat not too hot. Drain and serve with curd or plain.

409. WELITHALAPA

Ingredients for 15-20 *pieces.*

1 lb. rice flour unroasted
1 easpoon salt

1/2 - 3/4 cup of 2nd and 3rd extracts of coconut milk or water

1/2 bottle kithul treacle

Method

1. Using water or coconut milk make very fine granules out of the flour, like making pittu. The grain must be very fine. Do not use too much water at a time, only finger tips should be dipped into the water or milk, each time the water is added to prevent big grains from forming.

2. Steam this mixture and when done break into granules again, either by using a little coconut milk or a fork whilst still hot.

3. Heat 1/2 a bottle of kithul treacle, bring to boil. Remove about 4 oz. of treacle, to be added later if necessary. Add steamed pittu mixture and cook until the mixture is stiff. Set in a bowl or serving dish.

4. More kithul treacle may be added if necessary. Mixture must be soft but well saturated with treacle.

410. WANDU AAPPA

Ingredients for 10-12 *wandu aappa*

4 oz. rice flour
2 oz. jaggery

1/2 teaspoon yeast
coconut milk (sufficient to form a batter which is stiffer than a hopper batter).

Method

1. Prepare a batter as Recipe No.6 (jaggery hopper).
2. Heat an iddli pan with water and place a kanda leaf on each of the iddli pans.
3. Pour a spoonful of the batter on the kanda leaf.
4. Allow mixture to steam.
5. If an iddli pan is not available use a steamer or a wide mouth pot half filled with boiling water and a cloth tied round mouth. Place kanda leaf on the cloth and pour a spoonful of batter and steam. Cover with the string-hopper steamer and steam until done.

MISCELLANEOUS

A few popular Dutch, Portuguese and Chinese recipes:-

411. BOLO FIADO - 1

Ingredients for 16-20 *portions.*

Flaky pastry with 1 lb. flour (2 pies can be cut from this quantity).

2 1/2 lb. grated pumpkin with 1 1/4 lb. sugar

1/2 lb. cadjunuts with 1/2 lb. sugar and 8 oz. water

1/2 lb. sultanas with 1/2 lb. sugar and 8 oz. water

Almond Essence and Rose Essence

1 egg white for glazing

Pumpkin Preserve Filling

1. Grate pumpkin
2. Boil until pumpkin is cooked and most of the water has evaporated.
3. Add sugar and cook until thick and comes off the sides of the pan.
4. Add a few drops of pink colouring and rose essence. Set aside to cool.

Cadjunut Filling

1. Chop cadjunuts very fine, heat sugar with water until it reaches boiling point.

2. Add cadjunuts, cook until the mixture is thick but not dry.

Sultana Filling

1. Chop sultanas.

2. Heat sugar and water. Add sultanas.

3. Cook until the sugar is thick.

Note:- All fillings should be of a spreading consistency and should be taken down a little thinner than required as on cooling it thickens.

Method

1. Prepare pastry according to 'Flaky pastry instructions. Roll out the pastry and cut three 9″ diameter rounds, one 12″ diameter round (2 sets can be cut from 1 lb. pastry).

2. Place the 12″ diameter pastry round on a flat ungreased baking sheet and cover a 9″ diameter area with half of the pumpkin filling.

3. Place one of the 9″ diameter pastry rounds on the pumpkin filling and spread half of the cadjunut filling on pastry. Cover filling with the second of the 9″ diameter pastry round.

4. Spread half of the sultana filling on the pastry. Place the last and third 9″ diameter pastry round on sultana filling.

5. Damp the 12″ pastry round with white of egg and fold sides to meet top pastry with an overlap of at least 1/2 - 3/4″. Straighten up sides. Glaze with egg white. Decorate with 'pastry strips' and leaves to make an attractive design.

6. Bake at 425^{0}F for 1/2 an hour - 45 minutes. Reduce temperature after 1/2 an hour to 400^{0} F in case the pastry gets over browned. Allow to cool. Cut into wedges and serve.

Note:- The 12″ large pastry round should not be rolled too thin, it should be about 1/4″ in thickness. If the pastry is too thin it will crack and filling will ooze out. Use after 24 hours, after baking as keeping improves the flavour.

412. BOLO FIADO -2

Ingredients for 16-20 *portions.*

Prepare pumpkin preserve with 4 lb. grated pumpkin and 2 1/4 lb. sugar

4 oz. chopped cadjunts 2 oz. chopped raisins.

Method

1. Cook pumpkin preserve in the same manner as stated in Recipe No.411.

2. When the mixture is not very thick add sultanas and cadjunuts lightly toasted. Remove from fire when the mixture is on the soft side. The mixture should never be too thick.

3. Divide into 3, colour one portion with pink colour and add rose essence. Colour 2nd portion with a little yellow colour and add vanilla or cherry essence.

4. Proceed using half of each mixture for each Bolo Fiado in the same manner as in Recipe No.411. This is a cheaper Recipe and equally tasty,

Note;- Pineapple fillings may also be used. The preparation is done in the same manner as pumpkin preserve.

413. LOVE CAKE - 1

Ingredients.

3/4 lb. rulang	1/2 oz. rose water
1 1/4 lb. soft sugar	1 1/2 oz. bee's honey if available
6 oz. butter	1 teaspoon each of grated nutmeg
3/4 lb. cadjunuts	cinnamon powder, and
12 yolks of eggs	cardamoms
3 egg whites	1 1/4 teaspoons grated lemon rind
2 teaspoons vanilla	

Method

1. Mix rulang after it has been lightly roasted with butter and set aside in a warm place. Butter should not be oily.

2. Cream soft sugar with egg yolks until very light. Add all essences, spices, bee's honey. Mix well.

3. Add rulang, butter mixture, mix well. Add cadjunuts which should be toasted until crisp in a low oven and chopped fine.

4. Whisk egg whites until stiff. Fold in only the required quantity to give it a stiff dropping consistency.

5. Pour mixture into 2 flat cake tins 8 x 12″ lined with 3-4 layers of paper. Bake at 300^{0} F for about 1 - 1 1/2hours or until done.

6. If a crusted love cake is desired sieve very lightly a thin layer of icing sugar over the cake before placing in the oven.

7. This cake should be made a few days before it is required as keeping improves the flavour.

414. LOVE CAKE - 2

Ingredients

1 lb. cadjunuts	1/2 lb. rulang
1/4 lb. butter	1 1/2 lb of soft sugar
3-4 egg whites	12 egg yolks
1/2 teaspoon each of cardamom, cinnamon, nutmeg	1/4 teaspoon cloves
	1 oz. each of bee's honey, rum or brandy

Method

1. Follow the same method as Recipe No.413.

415. LOVE CAKE -3

Ingredients for 2-8 *or* **12** *pans.*

1 lb. cadjunuts	3/4 lb. rulang
10 egg yolks	1 lb. sugar
3-4 egg whites	4 oz. butter
1/2 teaspoon cardamom	1 teaspoon each of grated nutmeg, cinnamon powder, lemon rind
2 teaspoons almond essence	
1/2 lb. crystallized pumpkin preserve minced or cut into very small pieces.	

Method

1. Follow same method as for Recipe No.413. Add pumpkin preserve before egg whites are added.

416. FOUGETTI

Ingredients

1 lb. flour	1 oz. fat
3 egg yolks	2-4 oz. milk or liquid

Method

1. Crumb flour with fat, beat up egg yolks with milk, and add to flour kneading well until a soft dough is obtained.
2. Add more milk if necessary to make the dough pliable.
3. Cut bamboo 3/4″-1″ in diameter and 3″ in length 1/8 grease slightly. Roll pastry 1/2″ in thickness. Cover bamboo with strips of pastry sealing the edge very neatly with egg white or water 1/4″ of the bamboo to be free on either side.
4. Deep fry until golden brown. When cool push bamboo out of fried paastry. Fill with the pumpkin filling, dip in sugar syrup.
5. Can be stored in an air tight tin indefinitely.

Pumpkin Filling

Use the filling given in Bolo Fiado Recipe No.2 without sultanas.

Sugar Syrup - See syrup for jalebies. The sugar in the Fougetti should be allowed to crystallize before it is taken out.

417. BRUDHER - 1

Ingredients for 6 *brooders.*

3 lb. wheat flour dough	1 lb. butter
30 egg yolks	1 1/4 lb. sugar
1/4 lb. raisins	

Method

1. Knead the dough to a firm consistency, add the butter in pats. Kneading, add the yolks of the eggs, knead all the while the sugar being added in the same way.
2. It is important that the ingredients are added in gradually so as to keep the batter firm, beating up or clapping together the batter alternately as well as kneading it.
3. Put in brooder pans. Place pans in the sun for half an hour. Bake in a hot oven 375F - 400 F for 30-40 minutes.

418. BRUDHER - 2

Ingredients for 2 x 7" - 8" *pans*

Dough

2 teaspoons dry yeast	2 oz. fat
6 oz. liquid	1 oz. sugar
1 lb. flour	

Cream

10 egg yolks	10 oz. soft sugar or icing sugar
6 oz. butter	1/2 lb. sultanas.

Method

1. Prepare dough. Mix flour, knead and allow to rise until double in size.

2. Prepare cream mixture by adding the egg yolks to the icing sugar and creaming well. Add the butter.

3. Punch dough down, knead and mix in the creamed mixture well. Add 1 teaspoon bicarbonate of soda mixed with 2 dessertspoons milk.

4. Grease brudher mould. Sprinkle a few sultanas all round the mould. Add balance sultanas to dough. Very carefully spoon in the mixture half way into the brudher mould. Allow to rise until double. Bake at 375 F for about 45 minutes or until done.

419. BRUDHER - 3

Ingredients for 2 x 7" *or* **8"** *pans.*

Dough

2 teaspoons dry yeast	2 oz. water
1 lb. flour	8 oz. milk

Cream

8 oz. butter	4 oz. icing sugar or soft sugar
2-4 well beaten eggs	1/2 lb. sultanas.

Method

1. Dissolve yeast in water (temperature not to be more than 70^0F.) Add 1/4 lb. flour and stir. Add the balance 3/4 lb. flour over the yeast and allow yeast mixture to sponge through the dry flour.

2. Mix the milk with the sponge flour mixture.The dough should be smooth and elastic.

3. Cream well the butter, icing sugar and the eggs. Add this mixture into the dough. Add the sultanas.

4. Grease well 2 brudher pans. Pour in the mixture very carefully till pans are half full. Allow to rise until double.

5. Bake at 375 F. Unmould, allow to cool. Dust with icing sugar or coat with glazed icing on top to drop down the sides.

420. POFFERTJE

Ingredients

1 lb. dough (wheat flour)	6 eggs
6 desserspoons milk	1/4 lb. sultanas

Method

1. The dough should be throughly kneaded.

2. Add to it the yolks of eggs, one at a time, kneading all the while, then add the milk, making not too thin a batter. This may be set aside for half an hour.

3. Place the poffertje pan, over the fire.

4. Add 1 teaspoon fat into each receptacle.

5. When very hot take a dessertspoon of batter depending on the size of the round receptacle used, add 1/2 the batter, add a few raisins, and pour the balance batter.

6. When golden brown turn over quickly with a fork.

7. With a little experience one should be able to turn out the poffertje round with the raisins in the centre.

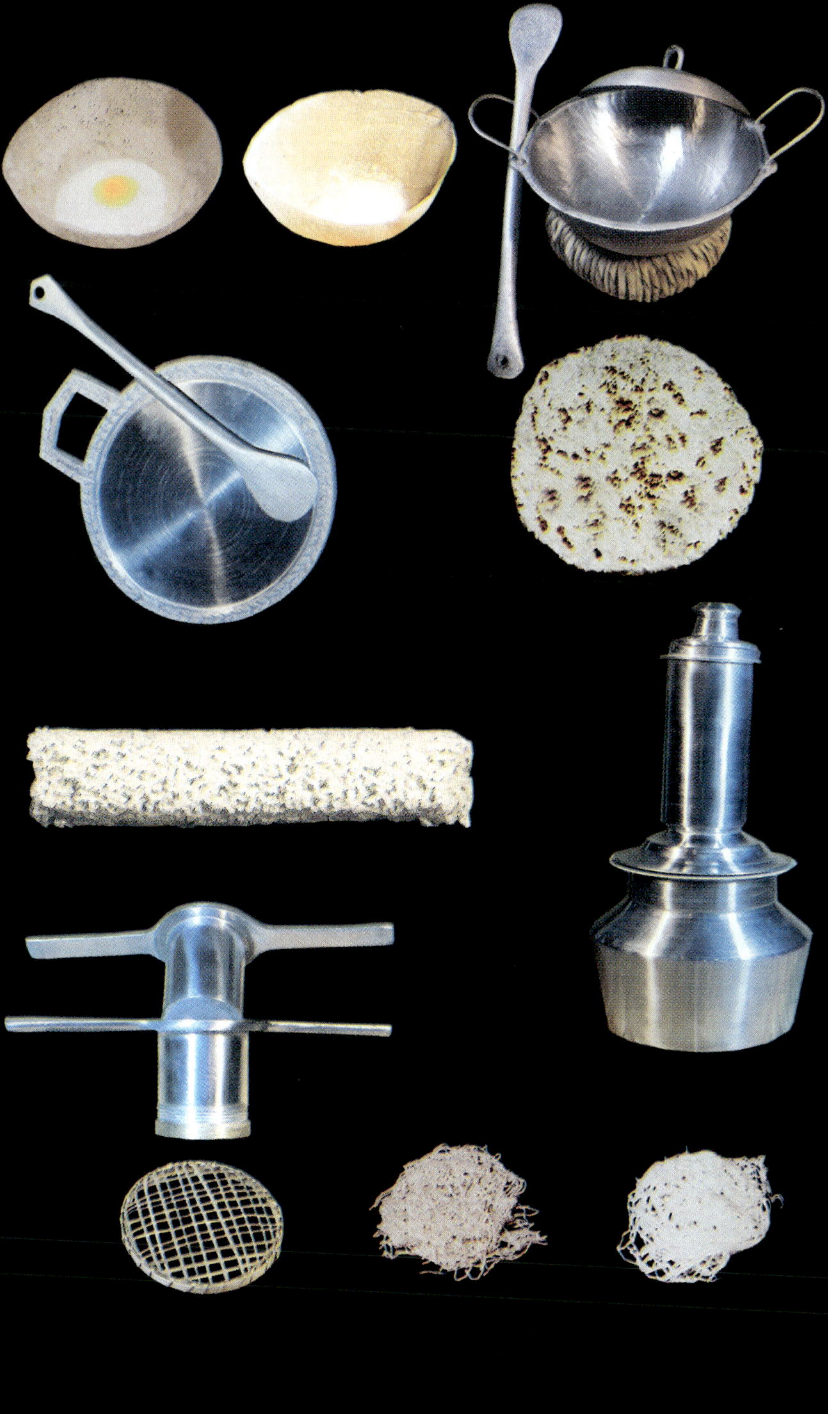

8. This should be served hot with a sugar syrup or honey, and sprinkled with nuts.

Dough for Poffertje

See bread dough recipe and use 1 lb. of the prepared dough.

421. CREAM OF CHICKEN SOUP (EGG OR CHICKEN)

Ingredients for 8 *portions.*

Stock 1

1 lb. bones
1 lb. of mixed meats (chicken,pork, mutton meat)
6-8 pints of water

Carrots, Onions, celery, moong } 1 lb.

salt to taste

1/4 cup boiled chopped chicken per portion
4 eggs
2-3 teaspoons corn flour
2 teaspoons Aji-no-moto

Method

1. Boil all ingredients for stock. Simmer for a few hours. Strain and set aside.
2. Chop boiled chicken. Whisk eggs. Dissolve cornflour with a little water.
3. Heat stock. Add cornflour and bring to boil. Reduce heat. Pour beaten egg in a steady stream stirring all the while.
4. Remove from fire, add chicken and aji-no-moto and serve at once.

422. MULLIGATAWNY (FISH)

Ingredients for *any required quantity.*

1 pint fish stock per 3 persons

2 oz. thick coconut milk per pint of fish stock

5 cadjunuts per pint of stock

1 clove garlic chopped per pint of stock

a thin slice of ginger chopped per pint of stock

1 - 1 1/2 teaspoons coriander powder per pint of stock

3/4 teaspoon cummin powder per pint of stock

2 cardamoms, 1 clove, a piece of cinnamon per pint of stock

1/2 teaspoon fenugreck per pint of stock

lemon juice or a small tomato

1 oz. boiled rice per person (if used as a soup, omit if using Mulligatawny for string-hoppers).

3 oz. boiled shelled prawns or boiled flaked fish per pint of stock

2 teaspoons fat per pint of stock

1 oz. onions per pint of stock

onions, fat and a sprig of curry leaves for tempering.

Method

1. Heat oil, add curry leaves, onions, garlic, ginger and fry until golden brown.

2. Add other spices, fry for a minutes or two. Add coconut milk and the rest of the ingredients along with stock.

3. Bring to boil, simmer for 5 minutes. Add shelled chopped prawns or boiled flaked fish. Serve hot ifserved as a soup. Add rice.

423. MULLIGATAWNY

Ingredients for 8 *portions.*

1 lb. meat with bones	1 1/2 pints water
8 oz. 1st extract of coconut milk	1/4 teaspoon sweet cummin
	1/4 teaspoon cummin
1/2 teaspoon fenugreek	a pinch of turmeric
1 large onion	4 cloves garlic cut
20 pepper corns	1/4 lb. tomato cut into pieces
1 carrot (optional)	salt to taste
1 oz. red onions sliced	1 dessertspoon fat
(for tempering)	1/2 teaspoon coriander powder

Method

1. Add all the ingredients together, except the coconut milk. Bring to boil and simmer to 3-4 cups stock.
2. Remove and cut the pieces of meat and strain the stock.
3. Heat fat and temper the red onions until crisp. Add the pieces of meat. Cook 5 minutes.
4. Add the stock and the coconut milk. Add a dash of lime juice before serving.

N.B. - If the coriander taste is not enough, add a little of the coriander powder when tempering onions.

424. FRIED FISH IN SWEET SAUCE

Ingredients for 8 *portions.*

1 fish (about 2-3 lb.)	2 dessertspoons soya sauce
2 tomatoes (cut into 8)	1 1/2 dessertspoons flour

1 small cucumber cut into cubes	1 dessertspoon vinegar
	1 dessertspoon lemon juice

Method

1. Remove fish head. Make a cut lengthwise on side and remove bones. Keep fish intact as much as possible. Wash and dry.
2. Rub salt and pepper and cover with flour.
3. Heat oil until it is very hot. Add fish and fry on both sides for about 5 minutes on each side.
4. Remove fat, add sugar, cucumber, soya sauce,tomatoes, lemon juice and vinegar. Cook for another 5-10 minutes, on low heat making sure that the fish does not get stuck to the pan.
5. Slightly thicken sauce with a teaspoon of cornflour and serve fish with sauce.

425. SWEET AND SOUR PRAWNS

Ingredients for 8 *portions.*

1 teaspoon Aji-no-moto	1/2 teaspoon of fresh ginger
1 1/2 lbs. of prawns cleaned	2 oz. flour
1 egg	8 oz. water
1 dessertspoon cornflour	1 teaspoon soya sauce
6 oz. sugar	6 oz. vinegar
1 tomato cut into 8 or 10 pieces	4 oz. each of carrots, leeks, onions, capsicum chillies, cut rather big
4 oz. pineapple chunks	
4 oz. sliced ginger preserve	salt

Method

1. Mix water, egg and flour together to form a batter.
2. Season prawns and dip in batter and fry until golden brown.
3. Mix soya souce, cornflour and water with vinegar and sugar. Add to the heated pan and allow to boil.
4. Add mixed vegetables, chillies, tomatoes, pineapple and cook for 2 minutes until gravy thickens.
5. Either pour prepared sauce over fried prawns, or put fried prawns into the gravy just before serving.

Note:- Sugar may be reduced if a lesser sweet sauce is required.

426. CHOPSUEY

Ingredients for 8 *portions.*

2 dessertspoons fat
1 clove garlic crushed
1/2 teaspoon ginger finely chopped
4 oz. cabbage sliced
4 oz. tomatoes
1 dessertspoon cornflour
1 teaspoon sugar
8 oz. of stock
1 dessertspoon of Aji-no-moto
8 oz. raw meat very finely cut (chicken, beaf etc)
2 oz. mushrooms sliced (thin)
4 oz. bamboo shoots
1 dessertspoon rice wine, rum or brandy
1 oz. capsicum chillies chopped fine
4 oz. of water

Method

1. Heat fat until very hot. Add garlic and meat and fry for a minute or two.

2. Add sauces, Aji-no-moto and ginger. Fry for a minute or two. Add all the other vegetalbles fry for a minute or two.

3. Add stock, cover and cook for 2-5 minutes. Add water mixed with cornflour. Cook until it thickens for a few minutes. Serve hot on noodles or plain rice.

427. DEVILLED CHICKEN OR CHICKEN WITH CHILLIE

Ingredietns for 8 *portions.*

1/4 lb. capsicum chillies red or green

1 lb. boned chicken,broiler	1 dessertspoon cornflour
1 egg white	2 dessertspoons oil
2 dessertspoons soya sauce	1 teaspoon sugar

1 dessertspoon rice wine.

Method

1. Remove seeds from capsicum chillies and cut into 1"cubes.

2. Cut boned chicken into 1/2" cubes. Dip in beaten egg white. Roll in cornflour.

3. Heat oil until very hot, add the chicken and fry for 2-3 minutes on a hot flame.

4. Add soya sauce, rice wine, sugar and stir for about 5 minutes until chicken is almost done. Add diced chillie and cook for not more than 3-4 minutes. Chillies must remain green in colour.

428. PAPER WRAPPED CHICKEN

Ingredients for 8 *portions.*

1 1/2 lb. chicken	4 dessertspoons soya sauce
1 teaspoon Aji-no-moto	1/2 teaspoon garlic
2 teaspoons rice wine	1/2 teaspoon mustard

Method

1. Cut chicken into 1″ cubes.
2. Mix in the soya sauce. Aji-no-moto, rice wine, garlic and mustard.
3. Leave the mixture soaking for 1 - 1 1/2 hours.
4. Take pieces of paper 4″ square.Place a few pieces of chicken on each piece of paper, fold and deep fry for 10-15 minutes. Serve on a bed of lettuce or plain.

429. WATALAPPAN

Ingredients for 8 *portions.*

1 cup coconut milk (thick)	3 eggs
1/2 bundle jaggery (1/2 lb)	a good pinch spices
cadju	(cinnamon, cardamoms,cloves nutmeg)

Method

1. Dissolve the jaggery in the coconut milk and strain into the lightly beaten eggs, strain.
2. Add spices, pour into a mould. Cover with greased paper and steam 40-45 minutes.

430. WOODAPPLE MOUSSE

Ingredients

1 tin Woodapple Puree

1/2 tin Condensed Milk

1 cup ideal milk chilled

3 measuring tablespoons of gelatine dissolved in 6 dessertspoons of water

1 cup Kitul treacle.

Method

1. Chill evaporated milk and woodapple puree separately. Dissolve gelatine over hot water, add to treacle.
2. Whip evaporated milk until very stiff, add condensed milk to chilled woodapple puree. Add treacle towhipped evaporated milk and continue to whip.
3. Fold in woodapple into milk, chill. Unmould, sprinkle with grated jaggery and sliced cadjunuts (to be lightly toasted) it may also be served in a glass bowl and decorate on top.

431. WOODAPPLE CREAM

Ingredients for 8 *portions.*

4 ripe woodapples 3″ - 4″ diameter

1 pint 2nd and 3rd extracts of coconut milk

1 pint 1st extract of coconut milk

1 lb. jaggery grated or 8 oz. thick kithul treacle.

Method

1. Crack and scoop woodapples.

2. Mash. Add 2nd and 3rd extracts of coconut milk. Mix well.

3. Strain through soup strainer, or wire strainer, or a piece of mosquito netting.

4. Dissolve jaggery in 1st extract of coconut milk. Strain. Add to woodapple mixture. Mixture should not be too watery.

5. Chill very slightly If chilled too much the fat in coconut milk will congeal.

6. Serve with boiled rice or grated jaggery or plain.

BEVERAGES

432. TEA

Ingredients for 4 *portions.*

5 teaspoons tea leaves	sugar
6 cups of water	cream, milk or slices of lemon

Method

1. Fill kettle with fresh water. Bring to boil
2. Heat teapot with half a cup of water just before water reaches boiling point.
3. Add tea leaves, (1 teaspoon per person and one for the pot).
4. As water comes to boiling point take tea pot to kettle and pour 4 1/2 cups of water. Stir, cover, brew for 3-5 minutes.
5. Rinse cups in hot water and strain tea into cups. Serve with cream, lemon and sugar.

N.B. - Milk may be added first to the heated cup before tea is poured.

433. COFFEE

Ingredients

1 heaped teaspoon of coffee powder per cup,

or 1 1/2 teaspoons coffee powder if coffee is to be very strong.

Method

1. Bring water to boiling point. Either add coffee to boiling water or add boiling water to heated coffee pot to which coffee powder is being added.
2. Stir. Allow to stand for 5 minutes. Strain and serve with cream milk and sugar.

434. SHERBERT

Ingredients for 2 *drinks.*

1/4 cup sherbert syrup	1 dessertspoon condensed milk
1/2 cup crushed ice	1/2 cup water
1 dessertspoon faluda	1 teaspoon kas kasa seeds (soaked over night)
	2-3 sliced roasted almonds or cadjunuts.

Method

1. Add to a tumbler 1/4 cup sherbert syrup and crushed ice.
2. Pour water and condensed milk mixed. Stir well. Add kasa kasa and faluda.

435. FALUDA

Ingredients

2 oz. cornflour	1/2 cup water

Method

1. Dissolve cornflour in water and cook till thick.

2. Put paste into a string-hopper mould and pipe into boiling water, cook until the mixture becomes translucent.

3. Strain, rinse faluda in cold water. Cut into 1/4″ pieces.

436. ICED COFFEE

Ingredients for 25-30 *drinks.*

1/4 lb. coffee powder
6 bottles water (26 gs:)
1 lb. sugar
2 tins condensed milk
1 bottle vanilla

Method

1. Boil water. Add coffee and allow to boil for 1 minute.

2. Remove from fire. Allow to stand for 5 minutes. Strain.

3. Add sugar and milk. When cold add vanilla and chill.

437. CORIANDER WATER

Ingredients for 2 *cups.*

2 oz. coriander seeds
1″ cinnamon (optional)
2-3 cups water
2 slices of green ginger (optional)

Method

1. Heat a pan and add washed coriander seeds and toss seeds in pan until seeds are lightly roasted.

2. Add cinnamon and green ginger if used just before water is added.

3. Add water, bring to boil and simmer for 10-115 minutes.

4. If a very light coriander is desired remover after allowing mixture to boil for 5 minutes.

5. Strain, serve hot with or without sugar.

438. CANJEE WATER

Ingredients for 1 - 1 1/2 *cups.*

1/4 lb. parboiled rice

1 - 1 1/2 teaspoons salt

4-5 cups water

Method

1. Wash rice, add salt water and bring to boil

2. Simmer until rice is over boiled and liquid reduced to 1 - 1 1/2 cups.

3. Strain if clear canjee is desired and only liquid is required or crush rice in the nambiliya lightly and serve with the boiled rice.

439. SAGO CANJEE (SWEET) - 1

Ingredients for 2 *cups.*

2 oz. sago

3-4 cups water

2-3 oz. jaggery or sugar

1/2″ cinnamon (optional)

Method

1. Wash and soak sago in water if time permits.
2. Add water, sugar or jaggery and cinnamon if used and cook until sago is translucent. Reduce liquid to 2 cups. Stir constantly to prevent lumping.
3. Serve hot or cold with grating of nutmeg if desired.

440. SAGO CANJEE (SWEET) - 2

Ingredients for 2 *cups.*

Method

1. Follow Recipe No.1, but add 4 oz. 1st & 2nd extracts of coconut milk or cow's milk just before removing from flame and bring to boil.

441. SAGO CANJEE PLAIN

Ingredients for 1 - 1 1/2 *cups.*

2 oz. sago — 2-3 cups water

1/2 teaspoon salt

Method

1. Wash sago. Soak in water to be used if time permits and bring to boil.
2. Simmer until sago is translucent and liquid has reduced to 1- 1 1/2 cups.
3. Serve hot or cold.
4. If desired grated jaggery or sugar may be served separately.

442. BARLEY WATER

Ingredients for 1 - 1 1/2 *cups*

1- 1 1/2 oz. barley seeds
4-5 cups of water
a pinch of salt
lemon, orange juice, sugar(optional)

Method

1. Wash and soak barley if time permits.
2. Bring water and barley to boil and simmer until liquid is reduced to 1 - 11/2 cups.
3. Strain and serve hot or cold with salt or sugar.
4. If served with fresh lime juice about 1/2 lime, 1/2 orange juice to a cup, always serve cold.
5. Add lime juice to cold barley water. Sweeten with sugar if desired. (The boiled barley seeds may be utilised in a stew).

443. GINGER TEA

Ingredients for 1 *cup*

1 teaspoon tea leaves
4-5 slices of thin fresh ginger
sugar to taste
1 1/4 cups boiling water

Method

1. Heat tea pot. Add 2 slices of ginger and tea leaves.
2. Pour 1 1/4 cups water
3. Allow to stand for 3-5 minutes.
4. Strain into heated cup.

5. Add ginger and serve hot with or without sugar.

Note:- If a stroner ginger tea is desired boil water for tea with ginger or add ginger slices crushed into tea.

444. CINNAMON TEA

Ingredients for 1 *cup.*

1 teaspoons tea leaves

1/2″ cinnamon piece or

1/4 teaspoon cinnamon powder.

Method

1. Brew tea as stated in Recipe No.432.
2. Strain tea into heated cup with cinnamon powder or crushed cinnamon.
3. Serve hot with or without sugar.

445. LEMON TEA

Ingredients for 1 *cup.*

2-3 slices lemon or lime with rind.

Method

1. Brew tea as stated in Recipe No.432.
2. Strain tea into a heated cup with lemon slices.
3. Serve hot or cold with or without sugar.

446. PORI KENDA (Pop Rice Water)

Ingredients for 1 *cup*

4 oz. paddy
1-2 cups water
1/4 teaspoon salt

Method

1. Heat a heavy bottom pan with a well fitting lid.
2. Add 1/2 paddy, close pan and shake the pan when the paddy begins to 'pop' to prevent burning of 'pop paddy'.
3. Remove pan from fire and empty 'pop paddy' on to a tray or kitchen paper.
4. Repeat in same manner with balance paddy.
5. Sort out pop paddy.
6. Add water, salt and bring to boil and simmer until reduced to required quantity.
7. Strain and serve hot or cold with or without sugar or with the addition of salt.

447. HAAL BEDI KENDA (Roasted Rice Water)

Ingredients for 1 - 1 1/2 *cups*

3-4 par-boiled rice
1 teaspoon salt
4-5 cups hot water

Method

1. Wash rice free of stones.
2. Heat pan and add washed rice and toss pan with rice until it is light brown in colour or well roasted.

3. Add water, bring to boil.

448. THAMBUN HODHI

(See Recipe No.156 or 157)

449. MIRIS HODHI

(See Recipe No.158)

WESTERN DISHES

Only a limited number of dishes that are inexpensive and easy to prepare have been included since there is a wide selection of International Cook Books available to those who need greater variety.

SOUPS

Dhal Soup

Leek and Onion Soup

Minestrone Soup

Spinach Soup

Tomato Soup

Vegetable Soup

FISH DISHES

Cream Fish or Prawn

Fish Menuire with Parsley

Fish Puddings

Fish Rolls.

Lobster in Tomato Puree

Macaroni and Cheese

Stuffed Fish

MEAT DISHES

Beef Olives

Brown Stew

Chicken Fried Steak

Goulash

Liver and Bacon

Meat Balls with Spaghetti

Meat Pie

Meat Loaf

Mixed Grill

Roast Chicken

Steak and Kidney Pie

Steak with Onions

PUDDINGS

Baked Custard
Bread Pudding
Caramel Custard
Chocolate Mousse
Fruit Salad
Italian Cream
Lemon Chiffon Pie
Lemon Cups
Lemon Meringue Pie
Triffle
Upside down Pudding

PASTRY & BREADS

Breads
Choux Pastry
Cinnamon Rolls
Doughnuts
Flaky Pastry
Pancake Batter
Patty Pastry
Pineapple Muffin
Pizza Pie
Prawn filling Pastry
Meat filling Pastry
Fish filling Pastry
Short Crust Pastry

SALAD

Boiled Vegetable Salad
Cabbage Salad
French Dressing
Hot Potato Salad
Mayonnaise
Tossed Salad
Fresh Mixed Vegetable Salad

SOUPS

450.DHAL SOUP

Ingredients for 8 *portions.*

1/4 lb. dhal	4 oz. onions
4 oz. carrots	3 oz tomato juice

4 pints white stock

Method

1. Wash the dhal well and drain. Place in a clean pan, add stock and bring to the boil, removing all scum as it rises.

2. Add the peeled, chopped, carrot and onion and tomato juice, Allow to simmer steadily for 1-1 1/2 hours, stirring occasionally.

3. Remove the carrot and onion. Pass the soup through a sieve with pressure, reboil.

451. LEEK AND ONION SOUP

Ingredients for 8 *portions.*

1/4 lb. leeks	2 big onions (chopped)
2 tablespoons fat	2 dessertspoons flour

2 cups chicken or beef stock

1/2 cup light cream or top milk
or undiluted milk

1/2 teaspoon salt	1/4 teaspoon pepper

1/4 teaspoon nutmeg

Method

1. Clean and slice leeks, cook with onion in butter for 5 minutes.
2. Add flour and blend, add stock. Cook till it slightly thickens.
3. Cool slightly, add cream. Season with salt, pepper and a dash of grated nutmeg. Heat and serve immediately.

452. MINESTRONE SOUP

Ingredients for 8 *portions.*

1 medium tomato	2 pints stock
4 oz. carrots	salt and pepper
1/2 small turnip	1 tablespoon broken spaghetti
1 stalk celery	chopped parsley
1 onion	2 oz. finely grated
1/2 small cabbage heart	Parmesan cheese
2 oz. bacon rind	1 tablespoon oil

Method

1. Blanch the tomatoes and cut all vegetables. Saute them with the bacon rind in hot oil for 5 minutes.

2 Add stock and seasonings and simmer in covered pan for about 1/2 an hour. Add spaghetti and cook 20 minutes longer. Remove rind and serve sprinkled with chopped parsley. Serve cheese separately. 2 oz. Ma bean seeds may be added.

453. SPINACH SOUP

Ingredients for 8 *portions.*

1 lb. fresh and tender spinach	1/4 cup of water
1 medium size onion	3 dessertspoons of fat
2 dessertspoons of flour	1 pint milk
salt, pepper, dash of nutmeg	1 pint stock
grated cheese	

Method

1. Wash the spinach and remove thick stems. Drain.Add1/4 cup water and place the leaves in a pan. Cook for about 5 minutes, and turn the leaves and cook for a few more minutes, until the leaves are cooked but still green in colour.

2. Drain the liquid, if any, and pass the leaves through a food blender. Fry one mediium size onion chopped, in the fat until light brown, add the flour and blend until the flour is cooked.

3. Add the milk, stock and the sieved spinach and cook until it comes to boil. Add salt and pepper and a dash of nutmeg. Serve hot with grated cheese sprinkled on top.

454. TOMATO SOUP

Ingredients for 8 *portions.*

2 oz. fat	2 oz. flour
4 oz. onions	4 oz. carrots
2 oz. ham bones	2 pints white beef stock (heated)
1/2 pint milk	4 oz. tomato puree or
seasoning salt and pepper	16 oz. tomato juice.

Method

1. Heat in a sauce-pan. Add bacon and the chopped carrots and onions.
2. Cook until light golden brown. Stir in the flour and cook for a few minutes.
3. Add the tomato puree and the heated stock.
4. Simmer for a few minutes. Pass through a sieve, reboil and season to taste. Add boiled strained milk just before serving.

455. VEGETABLE SOUP

1 1/2 pints of rice stock
1 small cabbage heart
2 large onions chopped fine
3 medium blanched tomatoes chopped fine
1 1/2 oz. fat
1 sprig of parsley
2 oz. spaghetti or rice.
2 large carots cut very fine
3 cloves garlic, pepper salt
cheese
2 dessertspoons tomato puree if available

Method

1. Add all of the vegetables and fry for a few minutes. Add the stock and cook until tender.
2. Once the mixture comes to boil add the spaghetti broken into small pieces. Cook until spaghetti is done.
3. Rice may be added instead of the spaghetti. Serve with cheese.

FISH DISHES

456. CREAMED FISH OR PRAWNS WITH CHEESE SAUCE

Ingredients for 8 *portions.*

1 1/2 oz. butter	1 1/2 oz. flour
16-20 oz. milk	4 oz. grated cheese
1 1/2 lb. boiled fish or prawns	16 oz. creamed potatoes

Method

1. Melt the fat and add the flour. Stir over low flame until the roux is cooked. Avoid browning.
2. Take off the fire, add the milk gradually to avoid lumps. Stir all the time.
3. Return to fire and cook until the sauce is thick. Remove from fire, add the grated cheese.
4. Cook 2 dessertspoons each of chopped onions and capsicum chillies in fat added to the sauce. Mix with the boiled flaked fish. Pipe a border on the serving dish with mashed potatoes and pile the creamed fish mixture in the centre.
5. Bake or grill if desired.

457. FISH MENUIRE

Ingredients for 8 *portions.*

8 portions of prepared fish (fillets or slice)	3 oz. oil
	2 lemons

2 oz. butter
flour for coating
4 dessertspoons chopped parsely.

Method

1. Heat the oil in a clean frying pan, season fish with a little salt and pepper, coat the fish in seasoned flour. Shake off extra flour.

2. Place the floured fish in the smoking hot oil, presentation side first. Fry quickly until golden brown. Turn the fish over, and fry till golden brown on the other side.

3. Place the cooked fish on a heated dish. On each portion of fish place a slice of lemon. Sprinkle the top of fish with the chopped parsley then with the strained juice of the second lemon.

4. Heat the butter in a clean frying pan, allow to froth and when beginning to turn light nut brown, pour over the fish.

458. FISH PUDDING

Ingredients for 8 *portions.*

To every 1 lb. of boiled fish allow one cup of cleaned and boiled small prawns.

1/2 cup chopped onions
1/2 cup capsicum chillies
1/4 cup chopped parsely
4 dessertspoons of fat
2 dessertspoons of flour
1 1/2 cups of fish stock or milk
1 egg

(1 1/2 lb. boiled fish for 8 portions).

Method

1. Heat fat. Add the onions, chillies and parsely, saute for a few minutes and add the flour.

2. Cook for a minute or two and add the stock gradually. Cook until thick and remove from fire.

3. Add the boiled fish and the prawn and the beaten egg. Season with pepper and salt and lemon juice. Grease well a mould and sprinkle dry bread crumbs, pack mixture into mould and bake for about 15 minutes. Unmould and serve hot or cold with boiled vegetables or salad.

459. FISH ROLLS

Ingredients for 24 *rolls.*

1 lb. fish	1/4 lb. prawns
1 lb. big onions	a sprig of parsely
2 capsicum chillies	1 dessertspoon tomato sauce
2 teaspoons salt	2 dessertspoons fat

2 portions pancake mixture Recipe No.491.

Method

1. Boil and flake fish, chop prawns.

2. Heat fat. Add the chopped onions, capsicum chillies, parsely and cook until light brown.

3. Mix in the flaked fish and prawns. Add the tomato sauce.

4. Spread a little of the mixture very thinly on the prepared pancake leaving a half inch border and roll.

5. Dip in batter and crumb. Heat oil and fry rolls until light brown in colour. (Allow 10-15 minutes time to lapse after crumbing before frying).

460. LOBSTER IN TOMATO PUREE

Ingredients for *2 portions.*

1 lobster	3/4 lb. tomatoes
1 - 1 1/2 oz. butter	chopped parsely
2 cloves garlic	pepper, salt
1-2 dessertspoons olive oil	1 onion finely chopped
stock for cooking	1/2 cup brandy

Method

1. Cook lobster in stock.
2. Cut lengthwise, remove intestine and simmer for a few minutes in melted fat and brandy, with the cut sides down.
3. To this add the chopped onions, tomatoes, peeled and chopped garlic, pepper and salt.
4. Cook until tomatoes are very tender.
5. Arrange lobster in serving dish, cut sides up and cover with cooked tomato sauce. Serve with any type of buttered, or parsley or egg rice.

461. MACARONI AND CHEESE

Ingredients for 8 *portions.*

12 oz. macaroni	3/4 portion white sauce (Recipe No.456)
	use 4 oz. extra cheese for sauce.

Method

1. Prepare white sauce as given in Recipe No.456.
2. Mix boiled and drained macaroni with cheese sauce. Season. Put into greased baking dish.
3. Sprinkle bread crumbs with sauce. Dot with fat and bake at 375^0 - 400^0 F for about 25-30 minutes.

462. STUFFED FISH

Ingredients for 8 *portions.*

8 full kumbalawos.

Filling

8 oz. chopped onions	1 sprig parsley
1 capsicum chillie	1/2 cup bread crumbs.
1-2 dessertspoons fat	10-15 boiled cadjunuts
salt and pepper	1-2 dessertspoons fat

Method

1. Clean and bone fish without cutting. Remove intestines. Press fish with thumb right along centre to loosen centre bone. Snap at head and tail to break off bone. Very carefully draw out centre bone from opening near intestine-gills. Fish should be intact with no cuts except with opening just below gills.
2. Cook all the ingredients used for the filling, in fat, and lightly fold in bread crmbs. pack into fish.
3. Wrap streaky bacon round fish in diagonal manner. Bake 10-15 minutes at 350^0 - 400^0 F.

Sauce

1. Prepare 1 portion Mayonnaise sauce. Blend 1 cup medium thick white sauce. Pour this on to a serving dish.
2. Place baked fish and decorate with chopped parsley.

Mayonnaise Sauce

2 egg yolks	1/4 teaspoon salt
1/8 teaspoon pepper	4 oz. olive oil
1/2 teaspoon mustard	1 teaspoon vinegar.

Method

1. Beat in a bowl rinsed with hot water, 2 egg yolks, add 1/4 teaspoon salt, 1/8 teaspoon pepper and 1/2 teaspoon mustard and 1 teaspoon vinegar.
2. Mix well and add 4 oz. olive oil, drop by drop, at first and continue beating without stopping.
3. Add extra 1/2 teaspoon of vinegar and continue to beat adding the rest of the oil. Lemon or lime juice may be added instead of vinegar.
4. Should the sauce curdle add an egg yolk into a fresh bowl and start adding the curdled mixture into the egg yolk a little at a time.
5. Season and flavour according to taste.

MEAT DISHES

463. BEEF OLIVES

Ingredients for 8 portions.

8 thin slices of beef
4 oz. each
8 oz. sausage meat
1 oz. bread crumbs
chopped parsley
4 oz. sliced carrots.
1 1/4 lbs. tomatoes
2 cloves garlic
3 dessertspoons oil
2 oz. sliced onions
1/2 - 3/4 pint stock

Method

1. Mix the sausage meat with chopped parsley, fresh bread crumbs and crushed garlic. Divide into 8 portions. Spread one portion on slice of beef.
2. Roll and tie each tightly. Brown rolls well in oil. Brown slices of onions and carrots and pour off excess oil. Add stock and tomatoes.
3. Place fried beef olives on bed of fried onions, carrots etc., and cook until meat is tender. Turn olives from time to time.
4. Sieve vegetables. Thicken gravy with flour if necessary, and pour sauce over beef olives. Sauce should be just sufficient to coat or glaze beef olives.

464. BROWN STEW

Ingredients for 8 *portions.*

2 lb. meat	1 1/2 oz. flour
2 teaspoons salt	1/4 - 1/2 teaspoon pepper according to taste.
2 oz. fat	

Method

1. Wash and dry meat. Cut meat into 1 1/2 - 2″ squares. Roll pieces of meat in seasoned flour. Add pepper according to taste.
2. Heat fat until very hot and add the pieces of meat and fry until very well browned on all sides.
3. Add hot water to cover the meat. Place a tight fitting lid and simmer till tender. 5-10 minutes before the stew is done, boiled potatoes and parboiled onions may be added. Garnish with chopped parsley.

465. CHICKEN FRIED STEAK

Ingredients for 8 *portions.*

1 1/2 lb. minced meat	1 cup chopped onions
1/2 cup milk	3 slices bread, soaked in milk
4 dessertspoons chopped celery	1 teaspoon salt
	1 chillie chopped
1 teaspoon pepper	flour and crumbs
2 eggs well beaten	oil for frying.

Method

1. Mix all the ingredients and shape into cutlets 1/2″-3/4″ thick. Dip in milk and eggs, or flour and water, and crumb or coat with flour.

2. Shallow fry on both sides turning well after each side is well browned.

466. GOULASH

Ingredients for 8 *portions.*

2 lb. meat cut into 2″ cubes or the smaller 1 1/4″ - 2″

2 dessertspoons fat	1/4 - 1/2 lb. big onions
2-4 teaspoons chillie powder	4 large tomatoes

2-4 capsicum chillies chopped or 1 large pepper

a piece of salt pork fat about 2″ x 4″.

Method

1. Heat pan and add fat, when the fat is very hot add the onions and the chillie powder. Add the meat and increase the heat and brown the meat until cubes are browned on all sides.

2. Stir to prevent meat sticking to pan. Add the tomatoes cut into four or eight and the chillies chopped.

3. Season with pepper and salt, add the piece of salt pork on top of the meat mixture. Cover with a well fitting lid.

4. Lower the flame and simmer until the pieces of meat are tender. Shake the pot from time to time to prevent sticking to pan, and avoid opening pan. Serve hot on a bed of buttered rice. Made 12 - 24 hours ahead improves the flavour.

467. LIVER AND BACON

Ingredients for 8 *portions.*

1 1/2 lb. liver	1/2 lb. bacon (streaky)
1/2 lb. onions sliced	8 small tomatoes
	salt, pepper

Method

1. Cut very thin strips of liver to be a little smaller than the size of the bacon, after washing and removing membrane and other blood vessels.

2. Sprinkle pepper and very little salt on the liver. Roll each strip of bacon with the liver and fastenwith a toothpick.

3. Put very little oil into a pan, add onions and fry lightly, set aside. Add bacon and liver and cook tossing from time to time for 7-10 minutes until liver is done. Towards the end of the cooking add a tomato cut into two and cook for a minute or two. Add onions to reheat.

468. MEAT BALLS WITH SPAGHETTI

Ingredients for 8 *portions (24-32 meat balls)*

Sauce

1/2 lb. chopped onions	3 dessertspoons fat
1 1/2 lb. tomatoes (cooked)	1 dessertspoons sugar
2 oz. tomato paste (optional)	2 teaspoons salt
2 cups water	1/2 teaspoon mixed herbs
2 oz. capsicum chillies	1 cardamom crushed
3 cloves garlic chopped	1 clove and 1 1/2" cinnamon.

Method

1. Cook onions and chillie in fat and add all the other ingredients and gently cook for 40-45 minutes on a slow fire.

2. Add meat balls and simmer for a further period of 30-45 minutes. Serve on hot spaghetti.

Meat Balls

4 1/2" thick slices dry bread	2 dessertspoons chopped parsley
1/2 cup grated cheese	1/2 teaspoon mixed herbs
1 1/2 lb. minced beef	4 cloves garlic chopped
2 eggs	6-8 dessertspoons oil

Method

1. Soak bread for a few minutes in water and squeeze the water and mix with all other ingredients except the oil. Make about 24-32 meat balls and fry in the oil. Add to the sauce. Simmer in sauce for 30-40 minutes.

Spaghetti

1. Add plenty of water to cook spaghetti. Add a teaspoon of oil to the water with salt. The oil prevents the spaghetti from sticking to the pan. When water boils, slide the spaghetti. Boil untill done in open pan.

2. Drain, add a pat of butter to the spaghetti. Serve with the sauce and meat balls.

469. MEAT PIE

Ingredients for 8 *portions.*

1 lb. meat cubes
3-4 teaspoons flour
1 teaspoon salt
1 teaspoon pepper
1 teaspoon vinegar
4-6 oz. stock

1/4 lb. each of diced carrots potatoes, onions and a sprig of parsley or celery.
1-2 teaspoons Worcestershire sauce or cooking sauce
6-8 oz. pastry.(short crust or puff)

Method

1. Roll out pastry. Line the pie dish. Roll pastry for top.
2. Mix all ingredients except the stock, season. Fill pastry lined dish. Filling must be 2″ - 3″ above edge of dish.Add stock.
3. Place an extra strip of pastry round edge of pie dish. Cover pie with pastry. Crimp and trim edge.
4. Make decorative cuts on pastry to allow steam to escape and prevent pastry cracking. Decorate if desired with pastry leaves and flowers.
5. Glaze with beaten egg and milk. Bake at 425^0 F until pastry sets. 15-20 minutes. Reduce heat to 350^0 F - 325^0F and bake 45 minutes to 1 hour, or until meat is done.

470. MEAT LOAF

Ingredients for 8 *portions.* - **1** *loaf*

1 1/2 lb. minced meat
2 eggs well beaten

4 oz. of fresh bread crmbs
4 oz. minced onions

8-12 oz. milk*

4 oz. tomato sauce

2 teaspoons salt

2oz. chopped capsicum chillies

1/2 teaspoon mixed herbs.

*Add greater amount of milk if tomato sauce is not added.

Method

1. Mix all the ingredients. Season, Pack into a loaf pan and bake at 350^0 F for 45 minutes to 1 hour.

471. MIXED GRILL

Ingredients

4 oz. steak of a chop

half mutton kidney

a slice or two of bacon

pepper and salt

a little cornflour

a piece of liver, 2-4 oz.

a tomato

a sausage

a little milk

Method

1. In a mixed grill a wide variety of items may be included but usually a small steak or a chop, a piece of liver, half a mutton kidney, a tomato, a slice or two of bacon and a sausage.

2. Season with pepper and salt the steak or chop, the liver, the kidney. Brush lightly with melted fat and place the steak first under the grill. Grill for a few minutes and then place liver, kidney and the sausage.

3. Turn over the chop, liver and kidney, place tomato seasoned with pepper and salt and brushed lightly with fat. When done place in a heated dish and use drippings in the drip pan to make sauce.

4. Add a little cornflour, a little milk and bring to boil. Pour over meats. Sauce should not be thick. Accompaniments: glaced potatoes. Boil potatoes of even size (small size). Add sugar in a frying pan and allow to caramalize lightly. Add a little melted fat and boiled potatoes. Toss until potatoes are well coated. Season with pepper and salt and just before serving add chopped parsley.

472. ROAST CHICKEN

Ingredients

Filling

1 oz. butter	1/2 cup bread crumbs
1/4 teaspoon salt	a dash of pepper
2 oz. cubed potatoes deep fried	1 egg hard boiled and chopped
	a dash of grated lemon rind
1 dessertspoon chopped onions	2 teaspoons chopped celery
	2-3 tablespoons chopped mushrooms or cadjunuts
1 oz. seedless raisins	
a dash of grated nutmeg	2-3 rashers of bacon chopped and fried
1 chicken 2 1/2 - 3 lb.	

Method

1. Heat fat and fry bacon, celery, onions and rest of the ingredients and mix well.

2. Add stock to get the desired moistness. Cool.Fill bird.

The Bird

1. Wash and wipe bird. Smear well with salt and pepper at the rate of 1 teaspoon of salt 1/4 teaspoon pepper and 1 dessertspoon fat, per 1 lb. weight of bird.

2. Place the chicken on its back and neck and away from you fill the cavity with filling taking care to fill very loosely.

3. Sew the opening or fix with skewers and tie the legs turn the wings. Place two strips of streaky bacon on the breast and coat the bird with seasoning.

4 Roast the chicken wrapped in 2-3 folds of grease proof paper if bird is large.

5. The bird is always roasted with its chest up.

6. During the last half hour remove the paper if used and allow to brown.

7. Allow 20-30 minutes per 1 lb. weight depending on type of bird used plus 15-30 minutes extra. Baste if chicken is roasted unwrapped.

473. STEAK AND KIDNEY PIE

Ingredients for 8 *portions.* 1 *pie* 8″ - 9″ *diameter.*

1 beef kidney (or 8 oz. other kidney)	3/4 lb. steak
	salt and pepper
about 1/4 pint stock or water	6-8 oz. rough puff pastry
flour	a little fat or 1/4 lb. bacon.

Method

1. Wash the kidney, remove the core and cut in thin pieces.
2. Cut the steak into thin slices.
3. Dust with seasoned flour. Place a piece of kidney on each slice of steak, a small piece of bacon or fat and roll steak.
4. Half fill unlined pie dish with the meat rolls. Add a little stock. Place the rest of the rolls.
5. Roll out the pastry to about one-third inch in thickness 2″ - 2 1/2″ larger than the pie dish to be covered.Cut a strip size of the pie rim. Set pastry round rim. Damp edge. Cover with rolled pastry round. Crimp and trim.
6. Follow steps 4 and 5 in Recipe No.469.

474. STEAK WITH ONION

Ingredients for 8 *portions.*

2 - 2 1/2 lb. steak, 1″ thick
4-5 dessertspoons fat
2 -2 1/2 teaspoons salt
3-4 cloves garlic finely chopped
2 oz. flour
1/2 lb. sliced onions
1/2 teaspoon ground mustard
1/4 teaspoon pepper
a thin slice of ginger
2 stalks celery chopped
1 cup tomatoes cooked or 1/2 cup tomato sauce and 1/2 cup water
1 capsicum chillie chopped.

Method

1. Mix the pepper and salt with the flour and pound well into the meat. Fry the onions in the fat until light brown, but not crisp.

2. Remove from oil and fry the steak until brown on both sides and add the rest of the ingredients and place the fried onions on top of the steak

3. Cook over low heat for about 2 hours or until fork tender or bake at 300 F for about 1 1/2 - 2 hours. Add more water if necessary.

PUDDINGS

475.BAKED CUSTARD

Ingredients for 8 *portions.*

2 pints milk (scalded)
4-6 eggs
6-8 oz. sugar
4 drops vanilla essence
1 small nutmeg, grated

Method

1. Beat the eggs and sugar add vanilla essence. Add all the milk. Strain into a greased pie dish. Sprinkle a little finely grated nutmeg over the top.
2. Place pie dish in a deep tray. Add hot water to come half way up the side of the pie dish.
3. Bake at 325^0 - 350^0 F for about 30-45 minutes until golden brown on top and the custard is just set. Clean around the pie dish and serve hot or cold. Never over bake a custard.

Note:- When baked custard is prepard as an invalid food, only 1 egg per pint of milk is used. The egg content is sufficient to just set the milk

476. BREAD PUDDING

Ingredients for 4 *portions.*

1. egg
8 oz. milk
1 dessertspoon sugar
1 dessertspoon coconut
4 slices of 1/2" thick bread spread with butter and jam
1 oz. dried fruits
1 oz. nuts

2-3 oz. fruits - pineapples
bananas or stewed pears.

Method

1. Cut bread into 1/2" - 3/4" rectangles or into squares.
2. Grease pie dish, put half the bread, then put some fruits either pineapple, plantain or stewed pears with nuts.
3. Put the balance bread on top, beat 1 egg with sugar and milk. Pour a little of this mixture on the bread and allow it to soak.
4. After 5 minutes or so pour the balance mixture. Sprinkle the top with finely grated coconut and sugar mixed.
5. Bake in a moderate 350^{0} F oven until set and golden brown.

477. CARAMEL CUSTARD

Ingredients for 8 *portions.*

8 dessertspoons sugar
5-6 egg yolks or 4 whole eggs
1 pint milk (scalded)

dessertspoons extra sugar for caramalizing

Method

1. Cream 2-8 dessertspoons sugar with egg yolks or whole eggs. Add milk and pour into bowl lined with caramel.

Caramel

2. Melt 2 dessertspoons sugar in a pan until light brown in colour. Pour caramalized sugar into pudding bowl. Pour milk and steam until custard is set or bake as for baked custard.

478. CHOCOLATE MOUSSE

Ingredients for 8 *portions.*

1/2 lb. sugar
3 eggs
3/4 pint ideal milk or full cream milk
2 level teaspoons cornflour.
2 dessertspoons gelatine dissolved over low heat in four dessertspoons of water.
3 oz. grated chocolate dissolved and melted in two dessertspoons of milk

Method

1. Beat the egg yolk with sugar, until very light and add the melted chocolate cooled, and beat well.
2. Mix in the cornflour and the milk, cook over low heat, until it thickens. Do not boil, cook very well. Whisk the egg whites stiff add dissolved gelatine to the egg whites. Fold the chilled mixture into egg whites.
3. Pour into a wetted mould and chill. Decorate with cherries and cream.

479. FRUIT SALAD

Ingredients for 8 *portions.*

2 cups pineapple pieces
2 plantains (optional)
1/2 - 3/4 cup sugar
1/2 lb. papaw
1 mango
1 orange

Method

1. Cut papaw and pineapple into 1/2 - 3/4" cubes. Slice plantains, remove pips from orange. Peel and cut mango into small pieces.

2. Mix all fruits. Boil 1/2 -3/4 cup sugar with 1/4 cup water, until sugar is dissolved for about 5 minutes.

3. Cool sugar and add to cut fruit. Serve with custard if required. (For custard see Trifle pudding, custard. Use 1/2 quantities of custard for fruit salad, omitting pineapple juice and pieces).

480. ITALIAN CREAM

Ingredients for 8 *portions.*

8 oz. sugar
8 oz. pineapple juice
3 1/2 teaspoons gelatine
3 teaspoons custard powder
2 eggs
16 oz. milk
a little milk to dissolve custard powder
1 tin pineapple pieces (12 oz.)
1 teaspoon vanilla
green & red colouring.

Method

1. Mix custard powder a little milk and sugar. Boil rest of sugar with milk. When mixture reaches boiling point add custard powder mixture. Cook until mixture thickens.

2. Add beaten eggs, after removing from fire. Add gelatine pineapple mixture to custard. Cool.

3. Divide mixture into 3 colours and set in a ring mould. Unmould and decorate with pineapple pieces.

481. LEMON CHIFFON PIE

Ingredients for 8 *portions.*

4 beaten egg yolks	1/2 cup sugar
1/2 cup lemon juice	1 dessertspoon gelatine
1/4 cup cold water	1 teaspoon grated lemon peel
1/2 cup sugar	4 stiffly beaten egg whites
1 pie shell (baked)	1/2 cup chilled whipped ideal milk

Method

1. Cream egg yolks, sugar, lemon juice and cook until thick, stirring constantly.
2. Add gelatine, softened in 1/4 cup water and stir until dissolved. Add lemon rind and cool until partially set.
3. Add 1/2 cup sugar to stiffly beaten egg whites whisk well and fold into cooled lemon mixture. Add the whipped chilled milk. Fill pastry shell and chill.

482. LEMON CUPS

Ingredients for 8 *portions.*

8 oz. sugar	1 oz. flour
2 dessertspoons butter	4-5 dessertspoons lemon juice and 1 tablespoon rind
3 well beaten egg yolks	
3 stiffly beaten egg whites	12 oz. milk, scalded

Method

1. Mix flour, sugar, egg yolks and butter, then lemon juice and rind, cream well.

2. Add scalded milk to flour sugar mixture.

3. Fold in egg whites and pour into a greased dish and bake in a pan with hot water for about 45 minutes at 325^0F.

483. LEMON MERINGUE PIE

Ingredients for 8 *portions.*

Cake Base	**Filling**
3 oz. butter	6 oz. sugar
1 1/2 oz. sugar	6 oz. water
1 egg	2-3 dessertspoons lemon juice
3 oz. flour	2 egg yolks
1/2 teaspoon baking powder	2 dessertspoons butter
	3-4 dessertspoons cornflour

Meringue

2 whites of egg

4 dessertspoons sugar

1 level teaspoon baking powder if meringue is to be baked and kept for sometime.

Method - Cake Base

1. Cream butter and sugar. Add egg and flour with the seived baking powder.

2. Grease a glass dish, round or rectangular. Spread mixture not more than 1/2″ in thickness. Bake at 350^0F until light brown for 10-15 minutes. Allow to cool.

Method - Filling

1. Bring water to boil. Mix sugar, cornflour and stir in boiling water.
2. Cook over low flame until mixture is translucent. Add lemon juice. Take off fire, add egg yolks. Cool.
3. Spread the mixture over cake base.

Method - Meringue

1. Whisk egg whites until very stiff. Fold in sugar gradually. Use baking powder if necessary.
2. Pile or pipe meringue in any attractive design over lemon filling. Place under grill to brown if desired.

484. TRIFLE

Ingredients for 8 *portions.*

Swiss Roll

3 eggs	4 oz. sugar
3 oz. flour	4-5 oz. jam
2 dessertspoons boiling water	1/2 sheet of grease proof paper
	extra sugar

Fillings

Custard	Fruit & Jelly	Meringue
1 egg	1/2 tin pineapple pieces	1 white of egg
8 oz. milk	1 cup pineapple juice	2 dessertspoons sugar
3-4 dessert-spoons sugar	2 teaspoons gelatine dissolved in 2 dessert-spoons water	
vanilla	1/4-1/2 teaspoon colouring	

Method - Swiss Roll

1. Whisk eggs until very light and lemon coloured with the sugar. The mixture should be ribbon stage.
2. Fold the flour and then add the boiling water and pour into a swiss pan and bake at 425 F for about 7-10 minutes, turn on to a paper that has sugar sprinkled on to it and trim the edges, make a shallow cut 1" away from edge narow side towards you.
3. Spread the jam and roll. Allow to cool. Slice.

Method - Custard

1. Cream sugar and eggs, heat milk and add to the beaten eggs strrring all the time.
2. Return to fire and cook on low heat until it begins to thicken. Cool.

Method -Jelly

1. Add the dissolved gelatine to the heated pineapple juice. Add red colouring. Mix well. Cool or chill stirring from time to time.

Method

1. Arrange swiss roll slices to form a pattern in a glass dish, covering the bottom and the sides.

2. Carefully pour chilled jelly over the arranged swiss roll slices to soak slices. Place the pineapple pieces in the centre. If there are any left over slices of swiss roll, arrange another layer on top of the pineapple pieces. Pour jelly enough to soak the second layer.

3. Chill for about 15 minutes. Pour prepared and cooled custard over the cake jelly layer.

4. Chill again for 15 minutes, or until set.

5. Whisk egg whites until very stiff. Fold in sugar gradually. Pipe on top to form a pattern.

6. Garnish with toasted chopped nuts, cherries. Chill, made 24 hours ahead of time, adds flavour. Meringue and garnishing should only be done just before serving.

485. UPSIDE DOWN PUDDING

Ingredients for 8 *portions.*

Cake	**Base**
4 oz. fat	2 oz. soft butter
1 egg	8 oz. brown sugar
8 oz. sugar	1/2 tin pineapple rings or pieces
5 oz. flour	5-6 imitation cherries
1 1/2 teaspoons baking powder	1/4 teaspoon orange rind grated
4 oz. orange juice or lemon juice or pineapple juice.	

Method

1. Spread 2 oz. of butter on bottom of 8″ pan and sprinkle brown sugar or jaggery.
2. Arrange the pineapple pieces in an attractive way, with cherries.
3. Cream fat and sugar add the egg and beat well.
4. Add flour and baking powder sieved well with the syrup alternately, commencing with flour and ending with flour.
5. Pour batter very carefully over the pineapple-sugar base. Bake at 350^0 F for 45-50 minutes.

Allow to cool for 5 minutes and invert on to a serving dish.

BREAD AND PASTRY

486. BREAD DOUGH

Ingredients for 12-16 *rolls* 1 x 1 1/2 *lb. loaf.*

1 lb. flour	2 teaspoons yeast dissolved in
2 oz. fat	1/4 cup water (luke warm)
6-8 oz. milk (lukewarm)	sugar and salt.

Method

1. Mix flour and fat as for short crust pastry. Mix in the yeast dissolved ub water with the milk and knead well. Allow to rise until double. Punch down and knead 5-10 minutes.

2. Shape into rolls or loaves, allow to rise until almost double. Brush with melted fat. Bake at 400^0 F for 40-45 minutes or until done. Rolls bake at 375^0 F.

3. Glaze with egg or milk 5-10 minutes before removing from oven.

487. CHOUX PASTRY

Ingredients for 24-30 *eclairs or* 40 *short-eats.*

3 large eggs	5 oz. water
2 oz. fat	4 oz. flour
1/2 teaspoon salt	

Method

1. Melt fat and water until it reaches boiling point. Add flour at once and stir only until the mixture comes off the sides of the pan, and forms a ball.

2. Remove from heat and allow to cool slightly. Add one egg at a time and beat until the mixture has come back to the original consistency.

3. Repeat until all eggs have been used. Shape as required and bake at 375^0 F or until double then reduce to 350^0 F and cook until done.

4. Use for cream buns, eclairs, short-eats or desserts.

488. CINNAMON ROLLS

Ingredients for *(2″ - 8″ round pans)*

2 teaspoons dry yeast	4 dessertspoons warm water
2 dessertspoons sugar	4 dessertspoons fat
1 teaspoon salt	8 oz. warm milk
3/4 - 1 lb. flour	1/2 cup cold water
2 oz. butter or margarine	1/2 cup sugar
	1 1/2 teaspoons cinnamon.

Method

1. Soften yeast in warm water. Mix sugar, shortening, salt and warm milk in a large mixing bowl. Add cold water. Cool mixture till lukewarm.

2. Mix in the softened yeast.

3. Make a stiff dough with the flour. Knead on a floured surface until smooth. Place in a greased bowl and cover. Allow to rise until double for about 1 hour. Punch, knead.

4. Roll out dough to 1/4″ in thickness. Cut with fluted 2″ round cutter. Dip each roll in the following syrup:-

Melt butter or margarine, then add 2/3 cup sugar and cinnamon.

5. Arrange rolls around edges of greased 8″ round pans overlapping slightly. Place 5 rolls in centre of each.

6. Allow to rise in a warm place until light for about 30-45 minutes. Bake at 375^0 F for 25-30 minutes. Frost with glace icing or vanilla glace if desired.

Vanilla Glace

Blend 1 cup sifted icing sugar with 1 1/2 oz. butter and 1/2 teaspoon vanilla. Beat until it reaches a spreading consistency.

489. DOUGHNUTS

Ingredients for 25-30 *doughnuts.*

2 teaspoons dry yeast	3/4 cup lukewarm milk
1/4 cup water	1 1/4 teaspoons salt
2 oz. sugar	2 oz. soft butter or margarine
1 egg	1 lb. flour

Method

1. Sieve flour with salt and add the yeast and leave for a few minutes. Melt fat and add milk and sugar.

2. Add beaten egg, milk and fat into the flour and knead well.

3. Place in greased bowl turning once to grease surface. Let rise until double in bulk. Punch down let rise until double again.

4. Roll out dough 1/4″ thick. Cut, with doughnut cutter. Let it rise till very light or almost double.
5. Leave uncoverdd for crust to form. Deep fry.
6. Glaze in sugar syrup if desired.

490. FLAKY PASTRY

Ingredients

6 oz. fat

8 oz. flour

1/2 teaspoon salt.

6-8 oz. ice water with juice of 1/2 a lemon

Method

1. Sieve flour with salt. Divide fat into four. Cut 1 portion into the flour knead it very well until a soft dough has formed adding sufficient water from time to time.
2. Allow it to rest for 15 minutes. Roll into a rectangle. Work the fat into a soft pliable consistency. Dot 2/3 of the pastry from the top to the bottom.
3. Fold the undotted 1/3 area over the centre. Fold the top dotted areas over the centre. Turn with the fold to your right let it rest 15 minutes.
4. Repeat this same process twice over until the fat has been used up. Rest 15 minutes between each rolling.
5. Use as required.

491. PANCAKES

Ingredients for 10-12 *pancakes.*

4 oz. flour	1/2 pint milk
1 egg	a pinch of salt

Method

1. Sieve the flour with the salt into a basin or pass it lightly through the fingers.
2. Make a well in the centre of the flour, add unbeaten egg into the flour with 2 dessertspoonsful of the milk and begin to mix the flour in, very smoothly from the sides with a wooden spoon.
3. Using half the quantity of the milk to make batter. If the batter is kept rather thick in the early stage of mixing there is less risk of lumps forming.
4. Beat thoroughly for about 5-10 minutes, until the batter is full of air bubbles on the surface, mix in the remainder of the milk, being careful not to expel the air, cover the basin and leave the batter to stand in a cool place for about half an hour. Use as required.

492. PATTY PASTRY

Ingredients for 45-50 *patties.*

1 lb. flour	3 egg yolks
2 oz. fat	3/4 teaspoons salt
dash of lemon juice	

Filling Recipe Nos. 495, 496 or 497.

Method

1. Bread crumb the fat into the flour after the salt has been mixed.

2. Beat the egg yolks with the water about 1/2 cup and make a well in the flour and knead well until the dough is soft and pliable, but not too soft. Add more water if necessary.

3. Set aside for a short time, before use. Roll pastry very thin. Cut rounds, place filling fold into two and crimp edges.

493. PINEAPPLE MUFFINS

Ingredients for 12 *muffins.*

1 egg	8 oz. pineapple juice
1/4 cup fat	8 oz. flour
4 teaspoons baking powder	1/4 cup sugar

extra sugar and lemon rind.

Method

1. Cream egg and sugar, add pineapple juice, and melted fat.

2. Fold in flour very lightly, Spoon into greased muffin pans and bake at 400^0 F for 15-20 minutes or until done.

3. Sprinkle sugar and lemon rind after 10 minutes have lapsed after baking on top of each muffin.

494. PIZZA PIE

Ingredients for *1 pizza pie* 8" -9" *diameter*

Dough	**Sauce**
2 1/2 cups flour	4 oz. chopped onions
1/2 cup milk	2 dessertspoons fat
1/2 oz. yeast	1/2 cup tomato paste
1/2 teaspoon salt	1/2 cup tomato puree
1/2 cup fat	1 dessertspoon sugar
	1/2 teaspoon salt
	1-2 cloves garlic chopped
	1/2 teaspoon oregano
	1 dessertspoon chopped parsley
	4 oz. cheese.

Method

1. Make dough and allow to rise until double. Punch, knead dough, spread, on pan and set aside. Prepare sauce.
2. Heat oil add the onions, tomato paste, tomato puree, sugar, salt, garlic, oregano and parsley. Simmer for 5-10 minutes. Cool.
3. Spread on dough, 1/2 the cheese pour sauce, top with any one of the fillings and sprinkle balance cheese.
4. Bake at 400^0 F for 15-20 minutes or until filling is cooked.

Fillings

(a) Sprinkle 1 cup cooked chopped prawns. 1 teblespoon parsley chopped.

(b) Slice 1 lb. pawkies and spread on top.

(c) Bone and separate 2 tins of sardines and spread on top.

(d) Egg Pizza. Hard boil 2 eggs and cut into two. Press into the dough before pouring the tomato sauce, top the egg halves with grated parmeasan cheese and chopped parsley.

495. PRAWN FILLING FOR PATTY PASTRY

Ingredients

1 lb. prawns boiled,shelled and chopped
2 oz. onions
1 hardboiled egg (optional)
1/2-1 teaspoon chillie powder
1 teaspoon curry powder
1/4 lb. boiled potatoes
3-4 green chillies
1 small tomato chopped
2 dessertspoons 1st extract of coconut milk (optional)

salt to taste.

Method

1. Heat oil. Add onions, chillies, curry leaves etc. and fry until light golden brown.

2. Add chopped prawns and potatoes chopped or mashed and fry for a minute or two. Add coconut milk according to the desired moistness.

3. Bring to boil. Remove from fire.

4. Add chopped hardboiled eggs. Mix well, cool and use for filling.

496. MEAT FILLING FOR PASTRY

Ingredients

3/4 lb. minced meat
3-4 billing finely chopped
1 clove
1 cardamom
1″ cinnamon
2 green chillies
a piece of rampe
2-3 dessertspoons oil
salt to taste
1/4 lb. potatoes boiled and chopped
1 teaspoon coriander
1 teaspoon chillie powder
1/2 teaspoon cummin
2 oz. onions
1 sprig of curry leaves
a piece of sera
6-8 oz. 1st, 2nd & 3rd extracts of coconut milk

Method

1. Heat oil. Add curry leaves, rampe, sera, onions and fry for a minute or two.
2. Add meat with all ingredients except coconut milk and boiled potatoes. Fry for 5-7 minutes.
3. Add coconut milk and potatoes.Bring to boil and simmer until mixture is almost dry, but has the required moistness. Stir from time to time. Cool and use as filling.

Note:-2 oz. chopped bacon fried and 2 oz. hardboiled eggs, chopped may be added to the meat mixture for a richer filling.

497. FISH FILLING FOR PATTY PASTRY

Ingredients

1 lb. fresh fish boiled flaked

4 oz. chopped onions	4 oz. boiled potatoes
2 oz. chopped green chillies	2 oz. tomato chopped
1 sprig of curry leaves	2 teaspoons chillie powder
1″ rampe	2-3 dessertspoons oil
1 teaspoon curry powder	1/4 teaspoon turmeric
2-3 oz. fish stock	lime juice and salt.

Method

1. Heat oil. Fry rampe, sera, curry leaves, onions, chillies until light golden brown.
2. Add all other ingredients and tomato except fish, potato and stock.
3. Add fish, fry for a few minutes. Add potatoes and fish stock. Cook for a few minutes until mixture is moist but not too dry.
4. Season with lime juice.

Note:-Hard boiled eggs, fried bacan may also be added for a richer filling.

Note:- Recipe Nos. 495, 496 and 497 may also be used for bread rolls, or pancake rolls.

498. SHORT CRUST PASTRY

Ingredients

4 oz. flour	2 oz. fat

a pinch of salt if for savoury pies.

Method

1. Cut fat into flour to resemble fine bread crumbs. Add water a little at a time, and toss moistened flour with a fork.

2. Press lightly into a little ball. Roll on a lightly floured board.

3. The pastry must be kept free from sticking on the board by lifting if from time to time, and dusting with flour. Roll to 1/8″ or any other required thickness.

How to line a Pie Pan

1. Roll pastry 1/8″ or to any other required thickness. Fold in two.

2. Lift and place pastry in pie pan. Open out to cover the other half of the pie and ease pastry to fit the pan without stretching. There should be no air bubbles under pastry.

3. Trim the edges holding the pie shell on your left palm and the knife in your right hand and cut the edge away from you. Trim the pastry round the pan away from you.

4. Roll out the scraps and cut 1/2″ strips and place on the edge of the pie pan.

5. Crimp the edge of the pie shell. Prick the base of the pie shell all over with a fork to allow steam to escape and place grease proof paper with rice and bake at 425^0 F for about 10 minutes and remove paper with rice. Cook for a further 4-5 minutes.

6. After the pie has browned evenly remove pie shell very carefully. Fill with any savoury or sweet filling.

SALADS

499. BOILED VEGETABLE SALAD

Ingredients for 8 *portions.*

4 oz. carrots
4 oz. potatoes
2 oz. green beans
2 oz. peas
4 tablespoons French dressing
1/2 pint Mayonnaise sauce
salt, pepper
1 teaspoon chopped parsley.

Method

1. Wash, peel and rewash the carrots and potatoes.
2. Cut into 1/4″ dice. Place each of the vegetables in a separate sauce pan, cover with cold water, bring to the boil and remove any scum. Add a little salt and boil gently until cooked. Drain well, place in a basin and sprinkle with the French Dressing.
3. Remove the ends from the beans and string. Cut into 1/4″ dice. Place the beans in boiling salt water, after 5 minutes add the peas and cook for a further 12-15 minutes. Drain well and add to the other vegetables.
4. Season the vegetables with a little salt and pepper, add the Mayonnaise sauce and mix well.

500. CABBAGE SALAD

Ingredients

1 clove garlic
a thin slice of ginger

Chillie powder a few drops of salad oil

Cabbage mustard, a little vinegar

Method

1. Grind mustard with vinegar, garlic and ginger into a fine paste. Add chillie powder, salt and a few drops of salad oil.

2. Mix well with finely shredded raw cabbage.

501. FRENCH DRESSING

Ingredients

1/4 cup of good vinegar
1 teaspoon salt
1/4 teaspoon pepper
1/2 teaspoon chillie powder
1-2 teaspoons lemon juice
1 teaspoon sugar
1 small clove garlic crushed
3/4 cup corn oil or olive oil

Method

1. Place all the ingredients in a bottle and shake well until well blended. Pour over salad and toss until all vegetables glisten. Serve at once and also prepare dressing just before use.

502. HOT POTATO SALAD

Ingredients for 8 *portions.*

1/2 lb. bacon
5 potatoes cooked in their jackets and diced (3 1/2 cups)
1 onion chopped
1/2 teaspoon salt
1/4 teaspoon pepper
1 teaspoon sugar
1/2 cup vinegar, 1 egg beaten

Method

1. Fry the bacon till crisp.
2. Combine potatoes, bacon and onions. Add remaining ingredients to bacon dripping.
3. Heat thoroughly, stirring constantly. Pour over potato mixture and mix well.

503. MAYONNAISE

Ingredients for 3/4 *cup.*

2 egg yolks	1/2 teaspoon mustard
1/2 teaspoon salt	1 teaspoon vinegar
1/8 teaspoon pepper	4 oz. olive oil

Method

1. Beat in a bowl, rinsed with hot water, 2 egg yolks, add 1/2 teaspoon salt, 1/8 teaspoon pepper and 1/2 teaspoon mustard and 1 teaspoon vinegar.
2. Mix well and add 4 oz. olive oil, drop by drop at first and continue to beat without stopping. Add extra 1/2 teaspoon vinegar and continue to beat adding the oil until required consistency is reached.
3. Lemon or lime juice may be added instead of vinegar.

504. TOSSED SALAD

Ingredients

Method

1. Use any type of fresh vegetable available. Wash well and chill well until required.
2. The following combination of vegetables make a very fine tossed salad.

   Lettuce leaves, celery 1-2 red and green capsicum chillies 1 large carrot grated with the coarse section of the cheese grater. 1 stalk of leeks (white section) sliced fine, 1/2-3/4 cup of finely shredded cabbage, 6-8 sprig onion stalks cup up into lengths not more than 1 1/2 - 2″, 1 medium tomato cut into wedges (to be added last).
3. Place all chilled vegetables in a salad bowl, or glass bowl add French dressing toss until the leaves glisten. Add the tomato wedges and toss once. Serve at once.

505. FRESH MIXED VEGETABLE SALAD

Ingredients for 8 *portions.*

1 cup fresh pineapple cut into cubes
1 cup cubed tomatoes
1/4 cup grated carrot
1/2 cup cucumber
1/4 cup chopped fresh onion leaves
Mayonnaise or salad cream
2-3 capsicum chillies chopped

Method

1. Cut all fruits into cubes.

2. Mix the fruits with Mayonnaise or salad cream, diluted with cream or a little milk.

3. Sprinkle chillie powder.

SRI LANKAN RECIPES WITH SUBSTITUTES

MENU PLANNING FOR THE FOREIGNER

For the Foreign visitor who wishes to have a typical Sri Lankan rice and curry meal, any Recipe may be used with substitutes so that the preparation may have more or less the same flavour but will be less pungent or piquant. Certain ingredients in a Recipe may be substituted as has been done in the sample menus.

Note on Rice

Different varieties of rice are available in other countries and it is always best to follow the instructions regarding the cooking of rice on the packet.

If however, the rice is raw rice, it is always advisable to cook the rice in water, until the water reaches boiling point. Strain the water and wash the rice to remove all traces of surplus starch. Thereafter, follow the procedure recommended in the Recipe. This preliminary step is very essential, whenever, packeted rice with a heavy starch content is used.

Substitutes for Ingredients

i. *Paprika or Cayenne Pepper (for chillie powder).*

ii. *Coriander, Cummin, Sweet Cummin.*

Instead of these, use curry powder or curry paste. In doing so always omit turmeric as the curry paste or curry powders sold abroad has an excess of turmeric, 1-2 dessertspoons of curry powder is generally sufficient for 1 lb. meat, fish or vegetable, depending on the strength in flavour.

2-4 dessertspooons of curry paste for 1 lb. meat, fish or vegetable should suffice depending on the flavour required.

iii. *Cloves, Cardamoms, Cinnamon.*

If not available or too expensive may be replaced with all spice powder, 1 teaspoon, or even dried all spice leaves, 1-2 leaves.

iv. *Coconut Milk*

Skimmed milk to which 1/2-1/3 cup of desiccated coconut has been added, and worked in a liquidizer or food blender will give you just as good results as fresh coconut milk. Remember to strain before use. Use hot milk or water to get the best extract of coconut milk, from the desiccated coconut.

Coconut for Sambol, Mallum.

Desiccated coconut can be reommended by adding 1-2 dessertspoons of boiling water before mallum is made. It may also be steamed.This is the nearest to fresh coconut which is so expensive, in other lands.

v. *Curry Leaves.*

May be replaced with bay leaves, though different in flavour, but it gives a good aroma.

vi. *Rampe.*

Can be omitted without much loss of flavour. Increase number of bay leaves.

vii. *Kithul treacle, Coconut treacle, Jaggery.*

These may all be replaced with Molasses.

LUNCHEON OR BUFFET EVENING DINNER MENUS

Menu 1

Yellow rice

Chicken curry

Egg plant curry

Tomato onions sambol

Tempered potatoes.

Accompaniments : (for special occasions) Fried prawns crumbed or in batter, salted nuts, chutney, Prawn crackers or pappadam or chips.

Dessert: Fresh fruit salad. Tea or Sherbert.

Menu 2

Buriyani

Mint or cucumber sambol or burnt coconut sambol

Malay pickle or Mixed pickle Recipe No.511

Chicken khorma

Fried bacon rashes.

Accompaniments: Chutney or pickle, nuts, fresh grated coconut or desiccated coconut.

Dessert: Watalappan, Tea or Sherbert.

Menu 3

Plain rice

Meat balls

Bean curry

Sauted leeks

Cabbage mustard salad.

Accompaniments: Chutney, pickle, fresh grated coconut or desiccated coconut. Sliced banana with lemon.

Dessert: Pineapple slices, Fresh fruit salad or Woodapple mousse, Tea.

Menu 4

Ghee rice, prawn or fish

Meat or pork curry

Tempered potatoes

Chutney

Brinjal pahie

Egg curry

Seeni sambol.

Accompaniments: Pineapple, tit bits, with a sprinkling of paprika and desiccated coconut, nuts, sauted sultanas, chutney.

Dessert: Yoghurt with golden syrup or molasses, Fresh fruit salad, or Fruits.

Note: It might be mentioned that unlike in a western recipe, when increasing or decreasing portions in a Sri Lankan curry recipe, the condiments and spices are never doubled or halved exactly. An addition or decrease up to 1/2 lb. of meat or fish or vegetable may be done with the same spices and condiments stated in the recipe. The liquid may be increased by 1/4 to 1/2 amount.

All portions in the recipe have been worked out on the basis that a meal consists of a rice preparation, a meat or fish curry, two vegetable curries and a fresh leafy sambol or mallum.

506. YELLOW RICE

Ingredients for 4 *portions.*

1 cup or 8 oz. rice (Uncle Ben's long grain)

2 cloves	1 large onion chopped
4 cardamoms	3-5 tablespoons fat, (spry, margarine, corn oil, or Wesson oil).
2-3 bay leaves	1 1/2-2 cups water or stock or 1/2 cup of desiccated coconut, blended with 1 1/2 cups of water until very fine, strained to remove residue
a pinch of turmeric or 1/2-1 teaspoon yellow food colouring	
1 teaspoon salt.	

Method

1. Wash and drain rice. Boil, drain and wash to remove excess starch if any.
2. Heat fat, add all ingredients except rice, turmeric, salt and liquid, fry until golden brown.
3. Add rice, turmeric and salt. Fry for a minute or two. Add liquid (stock, water or mixture of desiccated coconut and water, quantity 1 1/3 - 2 cups).
4. Cook until rice is cooked through. Reduce temperature and simmer or place in over until rice is fluffy, grainy and water absorbed.
5. Remove cloves, cardamoms, etc., on serving and garnish with any one of the following garnishings suggested for rice, mentioned on page 81.

507. CHICKEN CURRY

Ingredients for 4 *portions.*

1 chicken, 2 1/2 - 3 lb.cut into
10-8 pieces

1 1/2 teaspoons salt

3-5 cloves

1/2 teaspoon fennel powder

2 cardamom pods crushed

1" piece of cinnamon stick or

1 teaspoon cinnamon powder

3/4 - 1 teaspoon cummin powder

1/2 - 1 teaspoon chillie powder or

2 teaspoon paprika

1/4 teaspoon turmeric powder

2-3 tablespoons shortening

2-3 bay leaves

1/2 onion chopped or sliced

1-2 cloves of garlic 1/2 can (8 oz.) tomato puree 1/2 can tomato paste (optional) 5 oz. chopped nuts (cadju, almond, walnut)	to be put into a blender or liquidizer and worked to a fine paste.

4 oz. desiccated coconut

4-8 oz. skimmed milk, to almost cover chicken when all other ingredients have been added.

Method

1. Cut, clean and wash chicken.
2. Mix all ingredients except milk, bay leaves, and sliced onions with chicken and set aside for half an hour.
3. Heat fat, add bay leaves, sliced onions and fry until onions are light golden brown.
4. Add pieces of chicken free of any liquid and fry for 5-10 minutes.
5. Add liquid in which chicken was allowed to marinade with sufficient milk to just cover chicken.
6. Cook until tender.

508. EGG PLANT OR BRINJAL CURRY

Ingredients.

1 large egg plant (aubergine, brinjal)

1 medium sized onion chopped

2 peppers (red and green if possible)

1/4 teaspoon dill seeds	1/4 teaspoon fenugreek
1 teaspoon coriander powder	
2 cloves	2 cardamoms crushed
1/8 teaspoon fenugreek	2-3 tablespoons vinegar
1/2 teaspoon salt per1/2 lb. egg plant	
4 oz. milk	2 cloves garlic
1 bay leaf	2 teaspoons sugar

2 teaspoons mustard powder or

1 teaspoon Heins French mustard
(reduce 1 tablespoon vinegar if
French mustard is used).

oil for deep frying.

Method

1. Wash, dry and cut egg plants into 2 - 2 1/2 finger lengths. Cut peppers into 1″ squares.
2. Deep fry egg plant until light golden brown, and peppers for just a minute or so separately.
3. Cook all other ingredients except sugar, until onions are pulpy. Add more milk if necessary. Gravy or sauce must be medium thick.
4. Add fried ingredients. Simmer for 5 minutes. Add sugar and season if necessary.

509. BURNT COCONUT SAMBOL

Ingredients for 4 *portions.*

4 oz. desiccated or fresh coconut, oven roasted until golden brown.

2 cloves of garlic	lime juice
salt	1 teaspoon paprika or
2 pepper corns or	1/4 teaspoon chillie powder

a pinch of pepper powder.

Method

1. Mix all ingredients in a blender until a smooth paste is formed.
2. Add 1-2 teaspoons water or milk if necessary.
3. Season and form mixture into small marble size balls or place in serving dish, sprinkle chopped parsley.

510. MINT SAMBOL

Ingredients for 4 *portions.*

4 oz. mint leaves	2 tablespoons vinegar
1 teaspoon sugar	salt
1 slice ginger	1/4 chopped onion
1/8 teaspoon pepper powder	2 teaspoons desiccated coconut.

Method

1. Wash and clean mint leaves.
2. Place in blender, or liquidizer, all ingredients and blend until smooth.

3. Season. Place in a serving dish and sprinkle desiccated coconut.

511. MIXED PICKLE

Ingredients for 4 *portions.*

1/4 cup shallots, or pickle onions

1 pepper capsicum chillie cut into 1/2″ squares

1/3 cup cauliflower (flowerets) 1/3 cup grated carrots

2 teaspoons sugar 2 gherkins sliced

4-6 tablespoons mustard powder or French mustard

1 teaspoon chillie powder.

Method

1. Boil all ingredients for a minute or two in vinegar, separately. (Boil 1 cup vinegar, 1 tablespoon salt).

2. Mix other ingredients into a paste with some left over vinegar. Add salt if necessary. Add boiled vegetables.

512. CHICKEN KHORMA

Ingredients for *4 portions.*

1 chicken (2 1/2 - 3 1/2 lb) cut into 8 portions

1/4 cup desiccated coconut roasted until golden brown

1/4 cup nuts (cadju, almond, walnut)

2 teaspoons rice or 2 teaspoons rice flour (do not use flour) (omit if not available)

1 teaspoon chillie powder or 2 teaspoons paprika

1/2 teaspoon cinnamon powder	Cayenne pepper or 1 1/2
2 cloves	teaspoons all spice
2 cardamoms	powdered
1 teaspoon fenugreek	2 bay leaves
1/2 cup sliced onions	1 cup tomato chopped

1 cup curd or junket (without 2 teaspoons lime juice, sugar) or yoghurt

salt

Method

1. Cut, clean and wash chicken. Dry pieces well.
2. Mix curd or yoghurt, spices, chillie powder, salt, lime juice, and set aside for 1/2 an hour.
3. Heat fat, add bay leaves, onions and fry until golden brown.
4. Add chicken and fry for 5-10 minutes, after 5 minutes add tomatoes.
5. Add all other ingredients. Cook on slow fire until tender.
6. Garnish with chopped toasted nuts or sauted sultanas or finely chopped parsley.

   How to saute sultanas. Heat a little fat, add sultanas or raisins and toss in fat until raisins swell. Drain.

513. MEAT BALLS

Ingredients for 4 *portions.*

1 lb. minced beef	12-16 meat balls
1/2 teaspoon pepper powder	1 cup chopped onions
1 teaspoon salt	1 tablespoon chopped celery

1 teaspoon curry powder

Gravy

11/2 - 2 cups skimmed milk

1 bay leaf

1/2 teaspoon all spice powder

1/3 cup desiccated coconut blended with milk

3 teaspoons curry powder or

1 teaspoon coriander powder

1/4 teaspoon dill seed, 1/4 teaspoon cummin powder, 1/4 teaspoon turmeric

1/4 cup chopped onions

1/4 teaspoon paprika or

1/4 teaspoon chillie powder.

Method

1. Mix all ingredients well and make into 12-16 balls. Set in frigidaire.
2. Cook all ingredients for gravy until onions are pulpy and pass through sieve to make gravy smooth in texture.
3. Heat gravy to boiling point. Remove from heat, add meat balls. Return to heat after 5 minutes on low flame. simmer until meat balls are cooked through, 5-10 minutes depending on the size of meat balls.

514. BURIYANI CHICKEN

Ingredients for 4 *portions.*

Rice

8 oz. rice

1/4 cup chopped onion

1" cinnamon

2 bay leaves

Meat

1 chicken (cooking) cut into 8 portions

2-4 teaspoons curry paste or

1 teaspoon curry powder

2 cardamoms
2 cloves
pinch Spanish saffron or
1 teaspoon yellow colouring

stock 1 1/2 - 2 cups
2 tablespoons fat
1 1/2 teaspoons salt

1/4 cup sour milk or yoghurt or curd
1/4 cup chopped onions
2 chopped capsicum chillies
1/4 cup tomato puree
2 tablespoons fat
1 oz. finely chopped nuts
1 oz. desiccated coconut
salt, 1 teaspoon paprika
1 clove cardamom, cinnamon
bay leaf, salt 2 teaspoons

Method

Meat

1. Cut, wash dry meat.
2. Blend in liquidizer, tomato puree, curd or yoghurt, nuts, chillies and coconut.
3. Add blended ingredients and all other ingredients except, fat, cloves, cardamoms, bay leaves, cinnamon and chopped onions. Set aside for 10-15 minutes.
4. Heat fat add spices, onions, chillies, fry for 3 minutes. Add only pieces of chicken.
5. Fry further 5-10 minutes.
6. Add liquid in which chicken was minced with very little water.
7. Simmer until chicken is half done. Place in casserole.
8. Place partially pre-cooked rice and set in oven until rice grainy and free of moisture 25-30 minutes.

Rice

1. Wash, drain rice.
2. Heat fat, and onions add spices and fry until light brown.
3. Add rice and fry for a few minutes or until rice begins to crackle.
4. Add stock and cook until partially done and water level is well below rice level.
5. Cover partially cooked chicken placed in casserole with rice and yellow colouring or Spanish saffron to a part of the rice. Cover and cook in oven until free of moisture 25-30 minutes at 300^0 - 325^0F.

515. TEMPERED POTATOES

Ingredients for 4 *portions.*

1 1/3 cups boiled cubed potatoes
1 teaspoon paprika
1/4 teaspoon turmeric
1/2 cup sliced onions.
1/8 cup fat
2 bay leaves or
2 stalks chopped celery
1 teaspoon salt

Method

1. Heat fat, add onions bay leaves and fry until onions are light golden brown.
2. Add other ingredients and fry for 5-7 minutes or until the fat is absorbed by the potatoes.
3. Stir or shake pan from time to time.

516. CRAB CURRY

Ingredients - *3 crabs.*

1/2 crab per portion (3 crabs)

1 dessertspoon coriander powder	1 bundle coriander leaves (to be finely ground)
2 teaspoons fenugreek	1 bundle fenugreek leaves (to be finely ground)
1/2 teaspoon pepper powder	5-6 green chillies (to be finely ground)
2 oz. onions sliced	1 oz. onions (to be finely ground)
1/2 teaspoon turmeric powder	6-7 cloves of garlic (to be finely ground)
1 teaspoon chillie powder	ginger a thin slice
1 cup 1st extract coconut milk	2 dessertspoons roasted coconut ground (optional)
1 cup 2nd & 3rd extract of coconut milk	2 cardamoms, 2 cloves
curry leaves, rampe, sera	a sprig of drumstick leaves
salt	

Method

1. Wash and cut crabs by removing the shell from the main body. Remove gills, cut into 2 diagonally and vertically after taking off big claws.

2. Mix all the ground ingredients and dry powders with 1/2 cup 1st extract of coconut milk. Mix this mixture with the crabs and set aside for 10-15 minutes.

3. Heat oil add curry leaves, rampe, sera, fry until light golden brown, add crab claws and cut crab, toss and fry for a few minutes.

4. Add the balance coconut milk to the mixture, add the fried crabs, cover and bring to boil. There should be sufficient gravy just to cover the crab mixture only.

5. Cook for 10-15 minutes and during the last 5 minutes of cooking add the drumstick leaves and lime juice for acid.

N.B.:- If there is too much gravy remove piece of crab, boil gravy down, add the crab and serve hot. Drumstick leaves are only added during the last stage of boiling.

GLOSSARY

Ambarella A tropical big tree about 30-40 feet in height with oval shaped fruits, green in colour and muddy yellow when ripe. The size is no bigger than a very large egg. It is very acidic. It has a centre seed resembling a knot of fibrous roots. It is used for preserves, chutneys, curry etc. Supposed to do good for diabetic patients.

Ambul Thial A preparation usually made with different varieties of tuna fish or any blood fish with goraka added as acid, which acts as a preservative.This preparation if done well, can be kept for 3-4 months, over the hearth or near the hearth.

Anti-bilious This prevents biliousness or cures biliousness.

Anthelminities A substance that deadens worms in the intestines and helps their evacuation.

Aphrodisiac A substance that stimulates sex desires.

Blachan A preparation made of dried prawns with condiments and spices. This preparation is usually highly spiced and well seasoned.

Bolle curry A preparation made of raw minced meat or fish, shaped into small size balls. The balls are added to a gravy and allowed to simmer until the meat or fish is cooked. The meat or fish balls may be spiced but generally not fried.

Bran The dust which includes the husk of the paddy after it has been pounded. It is rich in Vitamin B and very often the husk is winnowed and the bran used for making sweetmeats.

Buriyani A very rich rice preparation with meat. The meat is cooked with condiments, spices and plentyof curd and added to the partially cooked rice. After the addition of the meat, the lid of the pan is sealed with a flour water dough and allowed to further cook until rice is fluffy, and grainy, over coals or dying embers with coals placed on the top of the lid. This may be said to be the richest rice preparation. Spanish saffron is added to a section of the rice to give the necessary flavour and colour. The scattered coloured grains of rice enhance the dish.

Carminatives A substance that helps digestion by increasing the secretion of the various digestive juice in the stomach and intestines and generally calms and settles the intestines. Some condiments that contain carminatives are: ginger, fenugreek, nutmeg, cardamom and coriander, cummins.

Chatty An earthenware vessel used for the preparation of curries. See picture, earthenware cooking utensils.

Condiments Ingredients with the exception of cloves, cardamoms cinnamon, nutmeg and mace, used in the preparation of curries are referred to in this book as condiments.

Chew of Betel Usually consists of 1-2 leaves of betel, a dash of chunam, shreds or wedges of betel nut or arecanut. A few strands of tobacco may be included. A special chew of betel served on festive occasions has cloves and cardamoms as spices, in addition aromatic ginger, sweet cummin and coloured shredded coconut. This is usually served after a meal as the ingredients have carminative, diuretic and stomachic properties.

Country Raw Rice	Paddy that has been milled or pounded to remove only the husks. It may be dark brown in colour or white where most of the bran is removed and it is then known as polished country raw rice or white raw rice.
Dress All Curries	This refers to the addition of spices and condiments to a curry with the necessary seasoning.
Diuretic	A substance that increases the output of urine. Some condiments are diuretic e.g. garlic, coriander, cardamom and fenugreek.
Fenugreek	A condiment used in the preparation of a curry. This seed is small and square shaped, dark golden brown in colour, with a very high mucilage content. When roasted it has a very strong smell. It is used by certain communities in Sri Lanka together with other ingredients in the preparation of hair oil for children. It is soaked over-night with sliced lime and boiled and used as a prophylactic against dandruff. This same preparation is also applied on the body for softening of the skin. Fenugreek contains carminatives and diuretic properties.
Fricadells	Meat or fish minced raw, made into small balls, coated in batter, crumbed and deep fried.
Goraka	A bright orange coloured segmented fruit when ripe sand has a very high acid content. The segments are broken up and sun dried. On drying they become black in colour and kidney shaped. It has certain tenderizing properties due to the presence of a particular acid. This acid is normally used for flavouring fish curries. If it is to be stored, it is usually mixed with kitchen

salt and stored in earthenware or glass jars.It should never be kept in any aluminium containers as the acid reacts very strongly with the metal.

Grainy (rice) Cooked rice that is fluffy and the grains of which are separate and do not cling together.

Hopper Pan A concave pan with two handles on either side made of cast iron. In the past the hopper pan had an earthenware concave lid to hold live coals. Few, now uses live coals on top of the hopper pan. A saucepan lid is normally used. It is suggested that the hopper pan be fitted with one heat proof handle to enable easy manipulation of the hopper batter in pan with one hand.

Iddli A steamed breakfast preparation commonly used by the Tamil community in Sri Lanka. The batter consists of a fermented mixture of rice and black gram with certain condiments and seasonings added. A special steamer is used for its preparation.

Kaludodol A very rich sweetmeat. The main ingredient being coconut milk, jaggery and rice flour. It is black in colour, firm and not hard or leathery in texture.

Kambaranga A fruit about 3-4 inches in length and about 1/2" in diameter with flap like segments protruding outwards.It is bright green in colour but when mature it takes on different hues from yellow to orange.

Kiri Hodi A white gravy made with coconut milk and spices. Onions and fenugreek are added to give the necessary thickening or binding effect. Turmeric is added to give yellow colour. Usually served with string hoppers or rice.

Koththamalli (coriander) A condiment that is used very commonly in the preparation of curries. In fact every part of the koththamalli plant is used. The leaves are used for sambols, chutneys and garnishings or may be boiled in water and used as a drink. The seeds are used in the preparion of curries or a drink that act as a prophylactic against colds or throat complaints. Koththamalli contains carminative,anthelminitic, laxative and diuretic properties.

Lemmonine A hybrid of the citrus plant. The fruits are usually round shaped with a little point. The trees bear within 1 1/2 years time and fruits are plenty right through the year. They have an advantage over the other varieties of citrus in the sense that they can be grown in pots even in a flat. The acid content is not as strong as in the lime but it is definitely stronger than in the lemon. The fruits are yellow in colour when ripe and usually found in clusters.

Lunu Miris A very pungent or piquant preparation with dry chillies, red onions and maldive fish. Highly seasoned with salt and lime juice.

Mallums A preparation in which a fruit, edible root, leaf, vegetable or coconut may be finely shredded or grated and cooked until done with coconut. In the case of leafty mallums the coconut is usually cooked first with a little turmeric and onion and the shredded leaves only partially cooked to retain most of the vitamin C content. In the case of carrots and papaw the vegetables are first cooked until done and the coconut added last which is partially cooked to retain the flavour of the fresh coconut.

Manioc (Tapioca) A root found in plenty and grown extensively in Sri Lanka. The prussic acid which is present in manioc and is also volatile, must always be allowed to evaporate by cooking the manioc in plenty of water with the lid open and draining the water after the manioc is boiled. Manioc makes excellent chips, good starch for laundry and an excellent binding agent in place of potatoes for meat, fish or vegetable croquettes or cutlets.

Measure of rice A measure equals 2 lb.

Moju A type of preserved fish or meat preparation in which some type of acid is used as a preservative.

Murukku mould Like a string-hopper mould with different discs to pipe patterns. The plates resemble biscuit press plates. See picture, breakfast preparations.

Nambiliya A concave grooved vessel used for washing rice. The sand gets lodged in the grooves thus getting seperated from the rice. It is usually made out of earthenware but now aluminium and cast iron vessels are available.

Num num This is a type of brown fruit, very tart in flavour with a heart shaped flat seed in the centre, found grown on the trunk of the num num tree.

Paddy A grain similar to wheat. All paddy, except highland paddy is grown in muddy fields in the early stages. It takes about 3-4 months to bear depending on the variety. Sri Lanka usually has 2 harvest seasons, the Maha and Yala. There are many varieties of paddy but some varieties give a better yield. The straw after the paddy is threshed is used as fodder for cattle, thatching roofs and in the manufacture of paper.

Parboiled rice Rice obtained from paddy boiled with the husk for 45-60 minutes, sun dried and milled or pounded to remove the husk. This type of rice when cooked, is never starchy and is fairly rich in vitamin B.

Pillau This is also a rice preparation with meat but the meat is only boiled with a few spices, cloves cardamoms and cinnamon. The stock, after the meat is boiled is utilized for the preparation of rice. Spanish saffron is added in the same manner as for Buriyani. Fried onions, peas and hard boiled eggs are generally used as a garnish.

Pittu Pittu is a breakfast preparation usually made out of freshly pounded raw rice flour mixed with coconut. Other varieties of pittu may be made with kurakkan, tapioca (see section on breakfast preparation).

Pulses Pulses and Dhals are referred to here as the dried seeds of beans and other leguminous plants.They supply vegetable protein necessary in a vegetarian diet or in a low cost non-vegetarian diet.

Pungent Pungency and piquancy or hotness or the sting that is caused on the tongue as a result of certain ingredient found in chillies, capsicum, pepper, mustard and other pungent fruits.

Rampe (Pandanus) A buttress root plant with dark green spear-shaped leaves. The leaf has a high aromatic flavour and is used as a condiment.

Roti A breakfast preparation made out of flour and coconut and cooked on a griddle. There are other forms of roti, made of the white wheat flour or whole wheat flour with or without the addition of coconut.

Sambol	Any type of uncooked mixture containing vegetable, coconut or fruits with seasoning added. Other condiments may be used. Usually onions, chillies and some form of acid is used.
Samba	This is a small grain of rice. The grains may be long or small like muthu samba that is pearl shaped.
Stomachic	A substance that increases the digestive powers in the stomach.
Sududuru	Cummin, small cummin or black cummin. It has a carminative effect and is said to have medicinal value. It is used lightly roasted, boiled with water in case of indigestion or diarrhoea, and used as a drink. It has anthelmitics properties.
Thalanabatu and Thibbatu	These belong to the brinjal family. In the case of Thalanabatu the seeds are generally removed and the fruit is washed. Unless this is done, it tends to be bitter. In the case of Thibbatu the fruit should be washed and the seeds also usd in the curry as it gives a milky pleasant flavour when cooked.
Thosai	This is a breakfast preparation of the Tamil community. It is made out of Bengal gram or black gram, rice or wheat flour and is fermented. Resembles the American pancake with the perforation.
Thumba	A variety of karawila (bitter ground) which is considered as a delicacy Karawila and grows in the jungles.
Toddy	The fermented sap of the coconut flower with a characteristic flavour of its own. Used as a raising agent instead of yeast.

Watalappan A swetmeat. Very similar to a custard preparation but coconut milk, jaggery and eggs are used instead of cow milk and sugar.

White curries The only pungent ingredient that is used in white curries is green chillies. This is cooked with the second extract of coconut milk with turmeric to give it yellow colour. The first extract of coconut milk is usually added towards the end of the cooking procedure. Coconut and raw rice ground fine are added to certain white curries to give the necessary thickening body to the curry.

Yams All varieties of tuberous roots that grow beneath the soil with the exception of the king yam, a purple variety of yam that grows and has its tuberous root above the soil.

BIBLIOGRAPHY

Administrative Report of the Commissioner for Development of Marketing for 1966/67 by K.B. Dissanayake.

Dietetics by Dr. Ananda Nimalsooriya, M.B.B.S.(Lon), M.R.C.P.(Lon).

Herbs for Health by Claire Loewenfeld and Philippa Black.

Journals of Food Science and Technology.

Materia Medica by John Attygalle.

Market Intelligence issued by the Government Marketing Department.

Proposed Ceylon Standards of Aluminiun Utensils by Bureau of Standards.

The Chemistry and Pharmacology of Ceylon and Indian Medicinal Plants by Chandrasena.

Tropical Planting and Gardening by H.F. Macmillan F.L.S. and A.R.H.S.

INDEX

D

E

Q

R

W

Y